Helping People Overcome Suicidal Thoughts, Urges and Behaviour

Helping People Overcome Suicidal Thoughts, Urges and Behaviour draws together practical and effective approaches to help individuals at risk of suicide.

The book provides a framework and outlines skills for anyone working with adults who present with suicidal thoughts or intent. Part 1 introduces a basic understanding of our knowledge about suicide and UK policy; Part 2 outlines the research into the treatment of suicidality and the general principles for working in the safest possible way. Part 3 outlines ten key psychological skills in the context of evidence-based best practice. The book also discusses the role of health and social care professionals in the prevention of suicide in the context of Covid-19.

The book will be a valuable addition to the resources of professionals including psychotherapists, nurses, social workers, occupational therapists, prison and probation officers, drug and alcohol workers, general practitioners and support staff in any health or social care context.

Lorraine Bell is a Consultant Clinical Psychologist with Solent NHS Trust, fellow of the British Psychological Society and leads the Psychological Therapies Service in secondary mental health for Portsmouth. She is also the Suicide Prevention and Dialectical Behavior Therapy lead for the Trust.

Helping People Overcome Suicidal Thoughts, Urges and Behaviour

Suicide-focused Intervention Skills for Health and Social Care Professionals

Lorraine Bell

LONDON AND NEW YORK

First published 2021
by Routledge
2 Park Square, Milton Park, Abingdon, Oxon OX14 4RN

and by Routledge
52 Vanderbilt Avenue, New York, NY 10017

Routledge is an imprint of the Taylor & Francis Group, an informa business

British Library Cataloguing-in-Publication Data
A catalogue record for this book is available from the British Library

Library of Congress Cataloging-in-Publication Data
Names: Bell, Lorraine, 1956– author.
Title: Helping people overcome suicidal thoughts, urges and behaviour: suicide-focused intervention skills for health and social care professionals / Lorraine Bell.
Description: Abingdon, Oxon; New York, NY: Routledge, 2021. | Includes bibliographical references and index.
Identifiers: LCCN 2020044765 (print) | LCCN 2020044766 (ebook) | ISBN 9780367566531 (hbk) | ISBN 9780367566456 (pbk) | ISBN 9781003098805 (ebk)
Subjects: LCSH: Suicide—Great Britain—Psychological aspects. | Suicidal behavior—Great Britain—Prevention. | Suicidal behavior—Great Britain—Treatment.
Classification: LCC HV6548.G7 B45 2021 (print) | LCC HV6548.G7 (ebook) | DDC 616.85/844505—dc23
LC record available at https://lccn.loc.gov/2020044765
LC ebook record available at https://lccn.loc.gov/2020044766

ISBN: 9780367566531 (hbk)
ISBN: 9780367566456 (pbk)
ISBN: 9781003098805 (ebk)

Typeset in Adobe Caslon Pro
by codeMantra

The book is dedicated to all those whose lives have ended prematurely and traumatically by suicide, and in memory of Sarah and Cass.

CONTENTS

List of figures

List of Tables

Acknowledgements

Thank you to Libby Peppiatt, Sarah Taylor and Kate Whitfield for their help with preparing the manuscript and to everyone who has supported me in my professional journey, especially all the service users I have had the pleasure to work with.

Key sources include
Suicide Prevention Resource Center & Rodgers (2011)
StayingSafe.net
http//www.connectingwithpeople.org

PART 1

UNDERSTANDING SUICIDE AND RISK

1.1 Suicide statistics and UK policy

Suicide accounts for an estimated 1.4% of all deaths worldwide (World Health Organisation, WHO 2014). On average, someone dies by suicide every 40 seconds somewhere in the world (Preventing Suicide: A Global Imperative 2014). Many more people die by suicide each year than in road traffic accidents, yet the funding for suicide prevention has been significantly lower in comparison to road accident prevention (Aleman & Denys 2014). Recent findings indicate that over 100 people are affected by every single suicide (Cerel et al 2019), with an increased likelihood of suicidal ideation, depression and anxiety for those closest to the individual (Cerel et al 2016).

In the United Kingdom, approximately 6,000 people die by suicide per year (Office for National Statistics, ONS 2018, 2019). According to the latest ONS statistics, the 2019 suicide rate for England and Wales was 11.0 deaths per 100,000 people (ONS 2020), the highest seen since 2000. Suicide and injury or poisoning of undetermined intent was the leading cause of death for both males and females aged 20–34 years in the United Kingdom between 2001 and 2018. Males had over three times the number of deaths from suicide compared with females for each year observed in this age group. Over the past decade, middle-aged men in their 40s and 50s have had the highest suicide rates of any age group or gender (ONS 2020). Despite significant efforts in public health initiatives to prevent suicide and the roll-out of crisis teams across the United Kingdom, there has been little variation in the rate of suicide since 2008 (Brown et al 2020).

Less than one third of people who end their life by suicide (28%) have accessed mental health services in the 12 months prior to death (Brown et al 2020). About one third of people who think about ending their life go on to attempt suicide, and 60% of these transitions occur within the first year after onset of suicidal thoughts (Nock et al 2008). It is estimated that for each adult who dies by suicide, there are likely to be 20–30 suicide attempts, though this varies widely according to age and gender. Suicide and suicide-related behaviours also cause considerable distress to those who lose a friend or family member through suicide. For all these reasons it is a major public health problem which requires an informed and compassionate response from anyone who can help.

Over the last decade important progress has been made to reduce suicide. In 2012, the UK government published its national suicide prevention strategy, which set out groups at higher risk and priority areas for action. In 2014, the WHO set the goal of a 10% reduction in suicide by 2020 through raising awareness, systematically mapping occurrences and developing nationally tailored suicide prevention strategies within the general population, and health services in particular (WHO 2014). The Five Year Forward View for Mental Health (Mental Health Task Force 2016) set a national ambition to reduce suicides by 10% by 2020/21. The National Strategy committed to tackling suicide in six key areas for action, with the scope of the strategy subsequently expanded (HMG 2017) to include addressing self-harm as a new key area:

- reducing the risk of suicide in high-risk groups;
- tailoring approaches to improve mental health in specific groups;
- reducing access to means of suicide;
- providing better information and support to those bereaved or affected by suicide;
- supporting the media in delivering sensitive approaches to suicide and suicidal behaviour;
- supporting research, data collection and monitoring; and
- reducing rates of self-harm as a key indicator of suicide risk.

In 2018, the National Institute for Health and Care Excellence (NICE 2018) published guidelines on how to prevent suicides in community and custodial settings. The National Suicide Prevention Alliance (NSPA) is the leading England-wide, cross-sector coalition of public, private and voluntary organisations for suicide prevention and is continuing to grow in its reach and membership. The responsibility for the strategic suicide prevention planning in England lies with the Local Authority Public Health Teams, working in partnership https://www.local.gov.uk/sites/default/files/documents/1.37_Suicide%20prevention%20WEB.pdf.

Nearly every local area in England now has a multi-agency suicide prevention plan in place. As we move towards Integrated Care Systems, all local health systems are expected to develop cross-organisational five-year plans to be implemented from August 2019 detailing how they will deliver the Long-Term Plan. This includes a continued focus on multi-agency work to prevent and reduce suicide (DOH 2012; NICE 2018). Priorities are:

- delivering our ambition for zero suicide amongst mental health inpatients and improving safety across mental health wards and extending this to whole community approaches;
- addressing the highest risk groups including middle-aged men and other vulnerable groups such as people with autism and learning disabilities, and people who have experienced trauma by sexual assault and abuse;
- tackling the societal drivers of suicide such as debt, gambling addiction and substance misuse and the impact of harmful suicide and self-harm content online;
- addressing increasing suicides and self-harming in young people; and
- improving support for those bereaved by suicide.

One aim of suicide prevention is to improve detection of suicide risk in general practice. Luoma et al (2002) found 77% on average had had contact with a general practitioner (GP) in the previous 12 months, and 45% in the month prior to their death by suicide. In England, Pearson et al (2009) found that 91% of people who ended their life had consulted their GP at least once in the year before death, with an average of seven consultations, almost double the general population rate (Galway et al 2007). A case-control study of suicides in England over a ten-year period concluded that suicide risk is associated with increasing frequency of GP consultations, particularly in the three months prior to suicide. These patients had consulted their GP more than 24 times in the year before ending their life (National Confidential Inquiry into Suicide and Safety in Mental Health, NCISH 2014). Despite widespread and frequent contact, many suicidal patients are missed by GPs (Leavey and Hawkins 2017).

1.2 Definitions of suicide and related terms

ASSISTED SUICIDE, also known as **assisted dying**, is suicide undertaken with the help of another person (often a physician) by providing the individual with the means to end their life or by providing advice on how to do it.

ATTEMPTED SUICIDE OR SUICIDE ATTEMPT is an attempt to take one's life that does not end in death but may result in self-injury or the non-fatal attempt to inflict self-harm with the intent to die.

PARASUICIDE refers to any suicidal behaviour or self-harm where there is no result in death. It is a non-fatal act in which a person deliberately causes injury to him- or herself or ingests excess prescribed medication.

POSITIVE RISK-TAKING OR POSITIVE RISK MANAGEMENT is identifying the potential risks involved and developing plans and actions that reflect the positive potentials and stated priorities of the service user. It involves using available resources and support to achieve desired outcomes and minimise potentially harmful outcomes. It requires an agreement of goals, or a clear explanation of any differences of opinion regarding the goals or courses (Southern Health NHS Trust 2012). Its purpose is for individuals to take control of their lives and make choices – either positive or negative – and learning from the consequences of those choices – again positive or negative. In practice this requires a balance between the interests of the individual and societal pressures to control risk (Felton et al 2017).

POSTVENTION is a term that was first coined by Shneidman (1972), which he used to describe "appropriate and helpful acts that come after a dire event". A **postvention** is an intervention conducted after a suicide, to support those bereaved (family, friends, professionals and peers) who may be at increased risk of suicide themselves and may develop complicated grief reactions.

REASONS FOR LIVING (RFL) and **REASONS FOR DYING** (RFD) are important individual reasons for staying alive (e.g. family) or wanting to die (e.g. hopelessness) and reflect the internal motivational conflict of the suicidal mind (Jobes & Mann 1999).

RISK is the likelihood, imminence and severity of a negative event occurring such as violence, self-harm or self-neglect (Department of Health, DOH 2007). It is the *likelihood* of an event happening with potentially harmful or beneficial outcomes for self and others. Risk behaviours include suicide, self-harm, neglect, aggression and violence (Southern Health NHS Trust 2012).

RISK ASSESSMENT: A risk assessment is a detailed clinical assessment that includes the evaluation of a wide range of biological, social and psychological factors that are relevant to the individual and future risks, including suicide and self-harm (NICE 2011). A good risk assessment will combine consideration of psychological (e.g. current mental health) and social factors (e.g. relationship problems, employment status) as part of a comprehensive client review to capture care needs and assess the client's risk of harm to themselves or other people (NCISH 2018).

RISK FACTORS AND PROTECTIVE FACTORS: Risk factors are characteristics that make it more likely that individuals will consider, attempt or die by suicide. **Protective factors** are characteristics that make it less likely that individuals will consider, attempt or die by suicide.

RISK FORMULATION informs risk management and involves organising and summarising risk data and the identification of risk factors.

RISK MANAGEMENT aims to minimise the likelihood of adverse events within the context of the overall management of an individual's care plan. It is the activity of exercising a duty of care where risks (positive and negative) are identified. It may involve preventative, responsive and supportive measures to diminish the potential negative consequences of risk and to promote potential benefits of taking appropriate risks. It will occasionally involve more restrictive measures and crisis responses where the identified risks have an increased potential for harmful outcomes (Southern Health NHS Trust 2012).

SELF-HARM is an intentional act of self-poisoning or self-injury, irrespective of the motivation or apparent purpose of the act (NICE 2004). It includes suicidal acts but usually refers to non-fatal self-injury.

SUICIDAL ACT: a self-inflicted, potentially injurious behaviour with any intent to die as a result of the behaviour. It may or may not end in death, i.e. suicide (O'Connor et al 2011).

SUICIDE ATTEMPT: self-injurious behaviour that is intended to kill oneself but is not fatal.

SUICIDAL IDEATION: thinking about, considering or planning suicide. The range of suicidal ideation varies from fleeting thoughts, to extensive thoughts, to detailed planning (Klonsky et al 2016).

ACTIVE SUICIDAL IDEATION: thinking of taking action to kill oneself, e.g. "I want to kill myself" or "I want to end my life and die".

PASSIVE SUICIDAL IDEATION: thinking about death or wanting to be dead without any plan or intent, e.g. "I would be better off dead", "My family would be better off if I was dead", or "I hope I go to sleep and never wake up".

SUICIDAL INTENT: the seriousness or intensity of the person's wish to end his or her life. Intent refers to the aim, purpose, or goal of the behaviour rather than the behaviour itself (Silverman et al 2007).

SUICIDALITY *is used broadly to include suicidal ideation (serious thoughts about taking one's own life), suicide plans and "completed" or attempted suicide or the tendency of a person to die by suicide.* Meyer et al (2010) argue the term "suicidality" is not as clinically useful as more specific terminology (ideation, behaviour, attempts and suicide).

SUICIDE (OR COMPLETED SUICIDE*) is the act of deliberately killing oneself or intentionally causing one's own death. Many definitions require there to be evidence that a self-inflicted act led to the person's death (from injury poisoning or suffocation). HQIP (2018) defines suicide as deaths that receive a conclusion of suicide or are "undetermined" (open) at coroner's inquest, as is conventional in suicide research (HQIP 2018). The Office for National Statistics' definition of suicide includes all deaths from intentional self-harm for persons aged 10 and over, and deaths where the intent was undetermined for those aged 15 and over (ONS 2019).

SUICIDE ATTEMPT: a non-fatal, self-inflicted, potentially injurious behaviour with any intent to die as a result of that behaviour (O'Connor et al 2011).

SUICIDE MITIGATION involves encouraging help-seeking behaviour, removing or restricting access to means, and ensuring an appropriate and early response to suicidal behaviour. Increasing hopefulness, emotional resilience and helping someone to identify their reasons for living have all been proven to lead to a reduction in suicide rates (Cole-King & Lepping 2010; Cole-King et al 2013; Zalsman et al 2016).

SUICIDE PACT: an agreement between two or more people to die by suicide together.

SUICIDE PREVENTION: a strategy or approach that reduces the likelihood of suicide. Effective suicide prevention should combine population strategies aimed at high-risk groups (Lewis et al 1997) and suicide-focused interventions for individuals at risk. This includes restricting the availability of means of suicide and targeted social programmes.

SUICIDE THREAT: thoughts of engaging in self-injurious behaviour that are verbalised and intended to lead others to think that one wants to die.

SUICIDOLOGY is the scientific study of suicidal behaviour, the causes of suicidality and suicide prevention.

*It is valuable to consider the connotation of the language used about suicide. The term "complete" is usually used for a positive achievement such as completing a course or task. It implies that attempted suicide is incomplete.

1.3 Stigma and common myths about suicide

Stigma and perceived stigma are barriers to people seeking help for mental health problems in general (Corrigan 2004; Vogel et al 2009) and suicidal thoughts and urges in particular (Niederkrotenthaler et al 2014). Batterham et al (2013) found more than 25% of 676 staff and students at the Australian National University agreed in an online survey that people who ended their life by suicide were "weak", "reckless" or "selfish". The language used to describe suicide is often stigmatising which is unsurprising given that suicide was illegal for centuries in the United Kingdom and is considered a sin in many religions. According to one Gallup poll, 82% of Americans find suicide to be morally unacceptable, https://www.religiousforums.com/threads/whats-so-morally-wrong-with-suicide.207488/.

Many people who attempted suicide were sent to prison for this in the United Kingdom, and it took years of campaigning to realise that care, not prosecution, was needed. Suicide was finally decriminalised in the United Kingdom in 1961. It is imperative therefore that when we communicate with clients at risk of suicide, we use non-stigmatising language and applaud any steps they have taken towards help-seeking. There are a number of terms used in both public discourse and the suicide literature which are stigmatising such as "failed suicide attempt" (implying death by suicide is some kind of success). The term "committed suicide" is outmoded and stigmatising as it is associated with committing serious crimes. It is much clearer and less stigmatising to use the term *death by suicide*. The term *failed* suicide attempt should be avoided as it suggests that death by suicide is a success. I would also avoid the term "suicide gesture" as this is judgemental language and may dismiss the potential for actual risk even if the action was not intended to be fatal.

Stigma towards mental health is associated with negative help-seeking attitudes for people who are experiencing suicidal thoughts. However, it may not be the strongest barrier to them seeking help (Czyz et al 2013). In this online US study of 157 students, the most commonly reported barriers included the perception that treatment is not needed (66%), lack of time (26.8%) and preference for self-management (18%).

Myth: If you talk about wanting to end your life you probably won't do it.

Many people who end their life have told someone, most likely significant others, about their suicidal feelings in the weeks prior to their death. People may also deny having suicidal thoughts when last asked prior to their death or communicate their risk in more *behavioural* ways (Appleby et al 1999).

Myth: People who repeatedly harm themselves aren't a suicide risk.

A history of self-harm is an important risk factor for future suicide. It elevates the risk of suicide 50- to 100-fold within the year following self-harm (Chan et al 2016).

Myth: Talking about suicidal thoughts and feelings could make you more likely to act on them./Never ask a person if they are suicidal as this could put the idea in their head.

Evidence suggests that asking people about suicide does not increase their risk and may be beneficial (Gould et al 2005; Dazzi et al 2014; Blades et al 2018).

Myth: Media stories about suicide do not affect suicide rates.

When a famous person dies by suicide the rate increases at a statistically significant level (Cheng et al 2007).

Myth: Only people with a mental illness think about or attempt suicide.

Recent statistics indicate that more than half of deaths by suicide do not merit a psychiatric diagnosis (Stone et al 2018). Suicidal behaviour is not an illness but an expression of intense personal distress.

Myth: Suicide is selfish.

In fact, many people who end their life believe they are releasing others from a burden. The interpersonal-psychological theory of suicide (Joiner et al 2005) identifies perceived burdensomeness as a primary component of suicidal desire and a possible point of intervention for suicide prevention (see review by Hill & Pettit 2014). Joiner and colleagues (2002) analysed 20 suicide notes written by people who attempted suicide alongside 20 notes written by people who completed suicide. They found that, of five variables, the only statistical difference was that the notes of those who died by suicide included more detail about how they were a burden to others and society at large compared to those who attempted suicide.

1.4 From thought to contemplation to preparation to action

A survey of Mental health and well-being in England (2014) found one in five adults in England report experiencing suicidal thoughts at some point in their lifetime. Kessler et al (1999) found 13.5% of participants in a national survey of 5,877 people reported lifetime ideation, 3.9% a plan and 4.6% an attempt. Cumulative probabilities were 34% for the transition from ideation to a plan, 72% from a plan to an attempt and 26% from ideation to an unplanned attempt. About 90% of unplanned and 60% of planned first attempts occurred within one year of the onset of ideation. All significant risk factors were more strongly related to ideation than to progression from ideation to a plan or an attempt. Suicidal ideation substantially increases the odds of future suicide attempts (Harris & Barraclough 1997) but suicide is far from inevitable, thus providing an important window for intervention and suicide prevention. The majority of those who attempt suicide do not die by suicide; less than 10% of people who attempt suicide die by suicide (Owens et al 2002). However, rates of death by suicide increase in those who make repeated and life-threatening attempts (Paris 2006). Individuals are at the highest risk of repeating a suicide attempt during the first three months following their first suicide attempt (Monti et al 2003).

The World Health Organization's World Mental Health Survey Initiative studied 84,850 people from the general population in 28 countries to identify any association between suicidal thoughts and plans and suicidal behaviour (Nock et al 2008). It found that 29% of people with suicidal thoughts went on to make a suicide attempt, 60% within a year of onset of suicidal thoughts. If those people who were experiencing suicidal thoughts also had a well-formed plan, they were far more likely to engage in suicidal behaviour. Individuals with a suicide plan had a 56% probability of making a "suicide attempt" whilst those without a plan had a 15.4% probability of a "suicide attempt". The strongest risk factor for acting on suicidal thoughts in high-income countries was a mood disorder, particularly if accompanied by substance misuse or stressful life events. Impulsivity alone did not predict suicide but may have increased the risk of a patient acting on suicidal thoughts. This cross-national study also found among individuals with a lifetime history of suicidal ideation, the probability of ever making a plan was approximately 33%, and the probability of ever making a suicide attempt was approximately 30%.

Nock et al (2009) found episodes of suicidal ideation tend to be brief, with participants reporting most episodes are shorter than an hour. They also found that thoughts of suicide were distinct from thoughts of non-suicidal self-injury (NSSI), and co-occur less than half the time, even among those who frequently engage in NSSI. Kleiman et al (2017) confirmed that suicidal ideation is typically episodic, with a quick onset. However, some people do experience persistent, low-level suicidal ideation. In my experience this can be the case for people with enduring mental health problems. The severity of suicidal ideation varies considerably over a short period of time and between individuals (Kleiman & Knock 2018).

Cummings and Cummings (2012) see suicide as a three-stage process and argue for the relevance of timely psychological interventions. They propose that stage 1 is the "ideation" stage, during which a person finds him- or herself thinking about suicide more and more. However, the fear of suicide still outweighs its attraction. The person may be thinking dark thoughts ("my family would be better off without me") but has not yet begun to formulate a specific plan. People in stage 1 are not at acute risk; psychological therapy will be helpful and may be sufficient. This stage may last indefinitely or may escalate to stage 2. Stage 2 is the "planning" stage, during which the person begins to formulate a specific plan for suicide. Friends and family may notice the person's mood lowering or them withdrawing. People in stage 2 are in critical need of effective psychological care. Stage 3 begins when the suicidal person makes the decision to end their life. People in stage 3 are at imminent high risk, but may appear low risk as they experience relief and potentially a lift in mood as they see an end to their suffering and feel some sense of control. Cummings and Cummings suggest that instead of relaxing, we should become more vigilant and watch closely for any indication that the individual has decided to end their life and caution us to be alert when a depressed patient has a lift in mood. Because biological or "vegetative" features of depression may respond sooner to medication than cognitive features, they strongly recommend that *antidepressant medication should never be used as a stand-alone treatment for suicidal depression*. Bryan et al (2015) concluded that individuals move along the continuum of risk from suicidal ideation to plan (34%) and from ideation to attempt (29%), with most suicide attempts occurring during the first year after the onset of suicidal ideation.

> ***Good practice point***
>
> Evaluating the pattern of suicidal ideation in each individual is critical to understanding, formulating and helping them reduce their risk.

Suicide rehearsals (mental or behavioural) may precede suicide or attempted suicide. A suicide rehearsal is a mental or behavioural enactment of a suicide method, usually as part of a suicide plan. Rehearsing suicidal behaviour can lower the barrier to a suicide plan, thereby increasing a patient's resolve and risk. Joiner (2005) argues that engaging in behavioural or mental suicide rehearsals increases the risk of suicide.

Rehearsing suicide (Simon 2012) is likely to:

- diminish the prohibition against suicidal behaviour and the fear of pain and dying;
- reduce ambivalence about dying;
- desensitise anxiety about performing the suicide act;
- test or "perfect" the method of a planned suicide;
- firm one's resolve to carry through suicide.

Studies suggest mental rehearsal of suicide is associated with suicide attempts and death by suicide (Buchman 2015).

1.5 Help-seeking and barriers to help-seeking

An early study found that in a sample of 134 people who had ended their life, over two-thirds (69%) had communicated suicidal thoughts and 41% had specifically stated they intended to end their lives (Robins et al 1959). Sixty per cent had communicated suicidal thoughts to a spouse and 50% to a relative. In a study of 60 deaths by suicide in Wisconsin, half had informed their spouses or another close relative of their suicide intent, but only 18% had relayed their suicidal intent to health care providers (Mays 2004). A review of 468 suicides over four years in a US metropolitan area found that 38% had either written a suicide note or had informed others of their intent (Shen et al 2006).

Importantly, most people who end their life have had contact with a health care provider within days or weeks of their suicide. Around half of people who have died by suicide speak to a GP in the previous month, though not necessarily disclosing their suicidal thoughts (Harwitz & Ravizza 2000; Luoma et al 2002; Stene-Larsen & Reneflot 2019). Of those appointments, where the cause of the appointment was known, 50% were for psychological or psychosocial reasons (Isometsä et al 1995). On average, 45% of suicide victims have had contact with primary care providers within one month of suicide. Older adults had higher rates of contact with primary care providers within one month of suicide than younger adults. A systematic review of 44 studies from 2000 to 2017 (Stene-Larsen & Reneflot 2019) found *less than one in three people who end their life by suicide had contact with a mental health service in the previous month.* So the majority of people who die by suicide do not approach mental health services for support. However, many do visit their GP in the preceding months before their death, although they may present with physical, rather than mental health, problems.

Good practice point

Primary care has a crucial role to play in identifying people at risk of suicide and ensuring they receive appropriate treatment and care (Centre for Mental Health 2019; Stene-Larsen & Reneflot 2019). Ideally GPs should be alert to the possibility of depression and suicide risk in high-risk groups, even if the patient does not present with this as their main problem (Booth et al 2000).

See https://elearning.rcgp.org.uk/course/info.php?popup=0&id=166 for suicide awareness training for GPs.

Not all patients at risk communicate suicidal ideation to clinicians (Hall et al 1999). Of those people who are referred to mental health services and assessed, there is a small but important minority of patients who do not inform their providers of their plans or intent. A prospective study of patients who killed themselves within six months of a thorough mental health assessment found that more than half denied any suicidal ideation or reported, at most, vague suicidal ideation (Fawcett et al 1993). For those individuals who do have contact with health care services, only 3–22% had reported suicidal intent at their final appointment with a health care professional before ending their life (Matthews et al 1994; Isometsä et al 1995; Pearson et al 2009).

There are a number of barriers people may have to approaching mental health services or even their GP, including the stigma of having a mental health problem and using mental health services.

Czyz et al (2013) found the most commonly reported barriers to help-seeking included perception that treatment is not needed (66%), lack of time (26.8%) and preference for self-management (18%). Stigma was mentioned by only 12% of students. There were notable differences based on gender, race and severity of depression and alcohol abuse. Online surveys indicate that men in particular are less likely to seek professional help for suicidal thoughts and urges. A Samaritans survey published in March 2019 found two in five (41%) men in England, Scotland and Wales aged 20–59 do not seek support when they need to, because they prefer to solve their own problems. The survey also showed that men often do not want to feel a burden and don't feel their problems will be understood.

See https://www.samaritans.org/news/real-people-awareness-campaign-encourage-men-seek-help/.

An online survey conducted by Atomik Research among 501 adult men aged 18 and over in the Republic of Ireland found one in four men (25%) who had suicidal thoughts in the previous 12 months did not reach out for help due to feeling they had no one to trust, with 37% feeling like a burden. The survey also found that some of the main reasons why these men find life so challenging include job loss or employment issues (38%), relationship or family problems (38%) and debt or financial worries (37%).

See https://www.samaritans.org/news/samaritans-to-encourage-men-to-seek-help-talk-to-us/.

Patients who are intent on attempting suicide may not reveal their plans. Those who truly want to die and see no hope of relief have little reason to disclose their risk and may even actively deny it. Even if their ambivalence about attempting suicide leads them to voluntarily call a crisis line or go to an Emergency Department (ED), they may be quite cautious about revealing the full truth. They may share only some of their suicidal ideation, plan or actions taken toward that plan, whilst hiding their real intent. The more intensely someone wants to proceed with suicide, the more likely they are to withhold their true intent. Shea (2016) gives a number of reasons why people may be hesitant to openly share. They may:

- lack extensive suicidal ideation before attempting suicide but act with impulsivity;
- have had marked suicidal ideation and be serious about dying by suicide but purposely not relaying suicidal ideation or withholding the method of choice because they do not want the attempt to be thwarted;
- feel that suicide is a sign of weakness, immoral or a sin and be ashamed to acknowledge it;
- fear the consequences – they may be detained or hospitalised; others will find out or be at risk of losing their children;
- not believe that anyone can help;
- have alexithymia or difficulty describing emotional pain or material.

They may also have had negative previous experiences of health care when they have previously disclosed suicidal thoughts or urges. For all these reasons, Shea argues that determining the credibility of the person's self-report is vital. Other sources of information such as family members, therapists and police can also have an important role in a comprehensive risk assessment.

1.6 Suicide and mental health

Mental health problems are a significant risk factor for suicide. Most diagnosed mental illnesses are associated with an increased suicide risk. Suicide prevention is often only seen as an issue for mental health services. However, the Report of the National Confidential Inquiry into Suicide and Homicide with Mental Illness (Appleby et al 1999) suggest only one in four people who took their own lives (about 1,000 each year) had been in contact with specialist mental health services in the year before their death. More recent data suggests this is approximately one-third (NCISH 2018; NICE 2019). Arsenault-Lapierre et al (2004) carried out a systematic review of a sample of people who died by suicide and found 87.3% had a history of psychiatric disorders. They also found that men and women who end their life by suicide have a different psychiatric profile and that the relative proportion of psychiatric disorders in people who die by suicide tends to vary according to geographical region.

Clinical depression is a strong predictor of suicide and attempted suicide (Cheng et al 2000; Harwitz & Ravizza 2000). Although considerable research has been carried out into the relationship between depression and suicide, depression is too general a category to have clinically meaningful predictive value (Westermeyer et al 1991). Other mental health conditions also have a high risk of suicide such as Emotionally Unstable Personality Disorder (EUPD) (Soloff et al 2000), psychosis (Westermeyer et al 1991) and gender identity disorder (di Ceglie 2000), irrespective of co-existing rates of depression (Soloff et al 2000). Patients most at risk are those with a combination of risk factors, such as people with high-risk mental health problems (major depression, EUPD and/or substance misuse) who then experience loss (Cheng et al 2000). Self-harm and substance misuse have both been identified as significant risk factors for suicide (see below). EUPD is the diagnosis with the highest risk of suicide, followed by depression, bipolar disorder, opioid use and schizophrenia (Chesney et al 2014). One study found that 73% of patients with borderline personality disorder (EUPD) have attempted suicide, with the average patient having 3.4 attempts (Soloff et al 2000). Anorexia nervosa has the highest standardised mortality rate of any psychiatric disorder and approximately one in five patients dies from suicide, not starvation (Arcelus et al 2011).

Although suicidal behaviour is strongly associated with mental disorders, there is no simple linear relationship between the two. Leboyer and colleagues (2005) noted that suicidal thoughts and behaviour may constitute an isolated psychological phenomenon, partially independent from other expressions of psychopathology (Ahrens & Linden 1996; Ahrens et al 2000). The vast majority of people with mental disorders do not attempt suicide (O'Connor & Nock 2014). Thus, psychiatric disorders as risk factors for suicidal behaviour have only limited predictive power (Nock et al 2010). Further, there is minimal evidence that treating mental illness reduces suicidality. Whilst medication has undoubtedly helped many people who suffer with mental health problems, there is extensive evidence that targeting and treating mental disorders has little or mixed impact on suicidal risk (Cuijpers et al 2013; Braun et al 2016; Jakobsen et al 2017). Despite the widespread use of medication, there is fairly limited data (based on randomised controlled trials [RCTs]) about the efficacy of medicine in reducing suicidality (Zalsman et al 2016).

Given that suicidality does not exclusively arise in the context of pre-existing mental health problems, an additional challenge for suicide prevention is appropriate provision for those with non-mental-health-related needs (Windfuhr & Kapur 2011). Individuals with suicidality present with a variety of needs that are not exclusively mental-health-based, including societal, community, relationship and individual risk factors (Turecki & Brent 2016).

Self-harm and suicide

Self-harm is the single biggest indicator of suicide risk, with around half of people dying by suicide having a history of self-harm at some point in their life (Foster et al 1997). Following an act of self-harm, the rate of suicide increases to between 50 and 100 times the rate of suicide in the general population (Owens et al 2002; Hawton et al 2003) within the year following self-harm (Chan et al 2016). Different studies find differing rates for this association for men and women (Hawton et al 2003; Cooper et al 2005). Hawton et al found the risk increases greatly with age for both men and women. A large study by Klonsky et al (2013) also found NSSI (and suicidal ideation) was a very robust predictor of suicide attempts. They suggest NSSI may be a uniquely important risk factor for suicide because it is associated with both increased desire and capability for suicide.

The relationship between self-harm and suicide is complex. Mental health staff often under-rate suicide risk in patients who self-harm repeatedly. People may indeed self-harm repeatedly but not attempt suicide. Only a small percentage of people who self-harm attempt suicide (Carroll et al 2014). A person who self-harms does not typically intend to die by suicide but does so for a variety of reasons and with a variety of intentions, not always with suicidal intent. Self-harm may be viewed as lying on a continuum of suicidal behaviour, with death by suicide at the extreme end of the continuum (Stanley et al 1992; Kapur et al 2013). There is growing evidence of a distinction between NSSI, suicidal ideation and suicide attempts (Mars et al 2019). In 2018 in the United Kingdom, as in previous years, the most common method of suicide for both males and females was hanging, suffocation or strangulation (all grouped together), and, second, poisoning – usually drug overdose (ONS 2019). These differ from the most common forms of non-fatal self-harm (cutting or burning). However, many individuals engage in both behaviours (Jacobson et al 2008; Klonsky et al 2013). Repeatedly injuring oneself intentionally, causing pain, bleeding or scars, is clearly likely to erode the natural aversion to pain and avoidance of harm that helps prevent us acting on suicidal thoughts or urges. For this reason, any self-harm is targeted as a potentiality life-threatening behaviour in dialectical behaviour therapy (DBT) (Linehan 1993). Self-harm may result in an accidental death or escalate and result in death. A suicide mitigation approach recognises that self-harm increases the likelihood of future suicide, which is why every episode of self-harm needs to be taken seriously. Early identification and intervention can minimise distress and reduce the likelihood of such a coping mechanism becoming established and entrenched.

A thorough risk assessment is important for any individual who presents to services with self-harm (NICE 2011). It is important to identify if the self-harm ever requires medical intervention (which indicates escalated risk) or if the person could end their life incrementally, for example moving from minor cutting to cutting an artery or self-harming when under the influence of drugs and alcohol. The National Confidential Inquiry into Suicide and Safety in Mental Health (2018) highlighted that recent self-harm is increasingly common as an antecedent of suicide in people with mental health problems but may not be given sufficient weight at assessment. The enquiry concluded that protocols for managing self-harm in patients who are under mental health care should highlight the short-term risk (NICE 2019).

To conclude, self-harm (which includes intentional self-poisoning or self-injury) is common, often repeated and associated with suicide. This highlights the importance of early intervention after an episode of self-harm in suicide prevention. Cooper et al (2005) suggest treatment should include attention to physical illness, alcohol problems and living circumstances. In 2010, the Royal College of Psychiatry report on Self-harm, Suicide and Risk recommended the provision of evidence-based psychological therapies for people who self-harm, which sadly, ten years later, many services still lack. In a Cochrane review of treatment for self-harm, Hawton et al (2016) conclude that Cognitive Behaviour Therapy (CBT)-based psychological therapy can result in fewer individuals repeating self-harm. In a study by Birkbak et al (2016), psychosocial therapy after deliberate self-harm led to reduced deaths, including deaths by suicide.

Good practice point

All localities should have a treatment pathway for people who self-harm. The absence of this can unintentionally promote some individuals to escalate their self-harm to access care. A minority of people self-harm as an alternative to suicide, as if they were buying off acting on suicidal urges via a lesser action. These individuals usually have complex mental health needs and should be screened for EUPD and, if indicated, offered a more comprehensive evidence-based treatment such as DBT.

Substance use and suicide

Alcohol dependence and alcohol intoxication are important risk factors for suicidal behaviour (Padmanathan et al 2020). Harris and Barraclough (1997) found those who had abused alcohol were at six times greater risk for dying by suicide than those who had not abused alcohol. Forty-five and thirty-three per cent of those who died by suicide in England whilst in contact with services have a history of alcohol or other drug misuse respectively (Oates 2018). The National Confidential Inquiry into Suicide and Safety in Mental Health (2018) estimated the collective figure as 57%.

Although alcohol and drug misuse are implicated in a high proportion of suicides, this association is not found in every country (Sher 2006). The inconsistent results of the relationship between alcohol use and suicide in epidemiological studies indicate that multiple socio-cultural and environmental factors influence suicide.

High rates of positive blood alcohol concentrations have been found in 33–69% of people who die by suicide (Hufford 2001; May et al 2002). Alcohol intoxication increases suicide risk up to 90 times, in comparison with abstinence from alcohol if one has suicidal ideation (Hufford 2001). Hufford distinguished the time impact of substance use as a risk factor for suicide. *Distal risk factors* create a statistical potential for suicide. Alcohol dependence, as well as associated comorbid psychopathology and negative life events, act as distal risk factor for suicidal behaviour. *Proximal risk factors* determine the timing of suicidal behaviour. The acute effects of alcohol intoxication act as important proximal risk factors for suicidal behaviour among both those who are alcohol-dependent and non-alcohol-dependent.

Alcohol and substance abuse problems contribute to suicidal behaviour in several ways (Padmanathan et al 2020). People dependent on substances often have a number of other risk factors for suicide. They are likely to have social and financial problems and/or be depressed. Substance use can lead to unemployment, social isolation and marginalisation. Alcohol and drug problems disrupt someone's relationships and social support. The abuse of alcohol or drugs secondary to depression is arguably the most frequent risk factor for suicidal behaviour. The risks increase if Substance Use Disorder (SUD) co-occurs with depression (major depressive disorder) or other mental health disorders such as Post-Traumatic Stress Disorder (PTSD), anxiety disorder, bipolar disorder, schizophrenia and some personality disorders.

Substance use and abuse can be common in people prone to be impulsive or engage in many types of high-risk behaviours that result in self-harm. Substance use can induce negative affect or emotions and influence cognition and behaviour, which may result in disinhibition, impulsivity or impaired judgement and problem-solving skills. Pain, distress and psychiatric disorders increase the likelihood of both SUD and suicide (Esang & Ahmed 2018; Bohnert & Ilgen 2019). Drugs and alcohol can also be used as a means to ease the distress associated with attempting suicide (Brady 2006). Unlike other risk factors, substance use may respond to interventions (DOH 2012). In light of these specific mechanisms, Padmanathan and colleagues suggest it cannot be assumed that interventions targeting suicide and self-harm reduction in the general population can be applied to people with substance use problems who may need more specific strategies.

Good practice point

Because alcohol and drug addiction are leading risk factors for suicidal behaviour and suicide, anyone presenting for one problem should be assessed for the other. The identification of alcohol and drug use and dependence is critical to the proper assessment of suicide risk. Comorbid substance use should always be addressed in the treatment of suicidal patients regardless of severity, as it reduces the threshold for suicidal action or shortens the length of time between the final decision to make a suicide attempt and the act itself, i.e. the presence of alcohol or drug use narrows the window for intervening effectively in a crisis.

This is a helpful document 'Working with the client who is suicidal: a tool for adult mental health and addiction services (2007). Produced by the Centre for Applied Research in Mental Health and Addiction (CARMHA); and is available at: http://citeseerx.ist.psu.edu/viewdoc/download?doi=10.1.1.587.6144&rep=rep1&type=pdf.

1.7 Risk assessment

The Department of Health's Best Practice in Managing Risk (2007) defines risk as relating to the likelihood, imminence and severity of a negative event occurring (i.e. violence, self-harm, self-neglect). It is the *gathering of information* through processes of communication, investigation, observation and persistence; and *analysis* of the potential outcomes of identified behaviours. It identifies specific *risk factors* of relevance to an individual, and the circumstances in which they may occur. This process requires linking the *context* of historical information to current circumstances, to anticipate possible future change (Southern Health NHS Trust 2012).

NICE CG133 (2011) Recommendation 1.3.6 states:

When assessing the risk of repetition of self-harm or risk of suicide, identify and agree with the person who self-harms the specific risks for them, taking into account:

- methods and frequency of current and past self-harm;
- current and past suicidal intent;
- depressive symptoms and their relationship to self-harm;
- any psychiatric illness and its relationship to self-harm;
- the personal and social context and any other specific factors preceding self-harm, such as specific unpleasant affective states or emotions and changes in relationships;
- specific risk factors and protective factors (social, psychological, pharmacological and motivational) that may increase or decrease the risks associated with self-harm;
- coping strategies that the person has used to either successfully limit or avert self-harm or to contain the impact of personal, social or other factors preceding episodes of self-harm;
- significant relationships that may either be supportive or represent a threat (such as abuse or neglect) and may lead to changes in the level of risk;
- immediate and longer-term risks.

Method of self-harm can indicate different levels of suicide risk and individuals using more dangerous methods (e.g. hanging or gassing by carbon monoxide or other gas) should receive intensive follow-up (Bergen et al 2012).

> ***Good practice point***
> Assessing someone's risk of suicide should be a therapeutic intervention itself and delivered with compassion. The emphasis should be from the outset on engaging the person with the intention of reducing risk rather than estimating or recording it.

The low-risk paradox

In mental health services, risk assessment has traditionally focused on prediction. Patients may be categorised into low, medium or high risk of a particular outcome. Large et al (2011) found about 3% of patients categorised as being at high risk can be expected to die by suicide in the year after discharge. However, about 60% of the patients who die by suicide were likely to be categorised as low risk. The authors conclude that risk categorisation does not help reduce the numbers of patients who will die by suicide after discharge. National data shows that, of those who ended their life after having had contact with mental health services, many had factors associated with high risk of suicide (such as self-harm, substance misuse, economic problems) but the majority (88%) were judged to be at low or no immediate risk of suicide by clinicians at their final contact with services (NCISH 2018). Rahman et al (2013) found the overall quality of risk assessment and management was unsatisfactory in over one-third of cases. Bolton et al (2015) and Large et al (2017) conclude that categorising risk in such a way is unhelpful in guiding the treatment and management of a patient. Further research suggests that categories have poor predictive value (Quinlivan et al 2016; Steeg et al 2018). The National Confidential Inquiries into Suicide and Safety in Mental Health (NCISH 2018) found the immediate risk of suicide at the final service contact was judged by clinicians to be low or not present for the majority of patients who died by suicide (NCISH 2018) and describes this as the "low-risk paradox".

Risk scales

Checklists of characteristics or risk scales are sometimes used to estimate risk. A national survey of risk assessment in UK mental health services by HQIP (NCISH 2018) found there was little consistency in the use of risk tools and most tools sought to predict future behaviour. Scores on the tool also determined management decisions, which is contrary to national guidance for self-harm assessment. National Institute for Health and Care Excellence (NICE) guidelines on the long-term management of self-harm (2011) state that risk assessment tools and scales should not be used to predict future suicide or repetition of self-harm, or to determine who should or should not be offered treatment but could be used as prompts or measures of change.

HQIP conclude that:

1. Risk assessment tools should not be seen as a way of predicting future suicidal behaviour. This is consistent with the NICE self-harm guidelines.
2. Risk is not a number, and risk assessment is not a checklist. Treatment decisions should not be determined by a score.
3. There is a growing consensus that risk tools and scales have little place *on their own* in the prevention of suicide.

Graney et al 2020 found little had changed in the UK. 156 risk assessment tools were in use by 85 NHS mental health organisations. There was little consistency in their use; most tools aimed to predict self-harm or suicidal behaviour and scores were used to determine management decisions. The authors recommend that assessment processes need to be consistent across mental health services and include adequate training on how to assess, formulate, and manage suicide risk. They repeat the recommendations that patient and carer involvement is needed, risk assessment should not be seen as a way to predict future behaviour and should not be used as a means of allocating treatment. And that risk management plans should be personalised and collaboratively developed with patients and their families and carers.

NCISH (2018) findings also emphasise that risk fluctuates and the need for carer involvement, and clarity about what to do in a crisis. Patients' suggestions to improve risk assessment in their survey included:

- a personalised approach, not based on the completion of a checklist'
- a focus on suicidal thoughts, i.e. encourage staff to confidently tackle difficult questions;
- involvement of carers/families, including sharing crisis/safety plans with them.

Psychosocial assessment

The provision of psychosocial assessment following an attendance for self-harm at an ED (previously known as Accident and Emergency, or A&E) reduces future risk of self-harm and premature death by 40–51% in the ensuing 12 months (Bergen et al 2010; Kapur et al 2015). NICE (2011) and the National Collaborating Centre for Mental Health (NCCMH) (2018) recommend risk assessment should take place as part of a psychosocial assessment, i.e. a comprehensive assessment of the patient's needs, taking into account previous suicidal behaviour, psychological and social factors and other problems such as substance misuse. A psychosocial assessment should be collaborative, patient-centred and needs-based (Hawgood & De Leo 2016). It identifies a person's risks and resources with a view to deciding practical next steps towards keeping the patient safe. In one of the few studies of service user perspectives, Hunter et al (2013) analysed 13 interviews with service users following hospital attendance, and seven follow-up interviews conducted three months later. Few participants had a clear understanding of assessment's purpose. Assessment had the potential to promote or challenge hope, dependent on whether it was experienced as accepting or critical. If follow-up care did not materialise, this reinforced hopelessness and promoted disengagement from services. The authors suggest re-conceptualising psychosocial assessment as primarily an opportunity to engage service users therapeutically. In order to maintain the benefits established during an assessment in hospital following self-harm or attempted suicide, follow-up needs to be timely and integrated with assessment.

In summary, the assessment of clinical risk in mental health care is challenging but provides an opportunity to engage with patients and their carers and families to promote the patients' safety, recovery and well-being (Worthington et al 2013). A good risk assessment will combine consideration of psychological (e.g. current mental health) and social factors (e.g. relationship problems, employment status) as part of a comprehensive review of the patient to capture their care needs and assess their risk of harm to themselves or other people. The primary benefits of an assessment derive from (i) identifying steps towards further support and (ii) the patient-centred nature of the interaction. However, if further support is not forthcoming or if the assessment is conducted as a "tick box" exercise, its value is likely to be diminished.

What should a risk assessment cover?

- past and current suicidal behaviour and self-harm;
- specific details about suicidal thought, plans; identify if the person has a concrete plan;
- current psychosocial situation/crisis;
- identify psychological strengths as well as vulnerabilities.

> *Good practice point*
>
> Once a patient has indicated that they are feeling suicidal and you have assessed their risk, rather than trying to quantify and categorise their risk in a standardised format, it is more helpful to assume the risk is serious and think about how best to support that individual (Hawgood & De Leo 2016; Cole-King & Platt 2017).

Follow-up and treatment planning

Fazel and Runeson (2020) concluded that when assessing and treating suicide risk, a person who presents with suicidal thoughts may be at risk for suicide even if there are few overt symptoms of a psychiatric disorder. They recommend suicide risk should be assessed by considering predisposing factors (those which make us vulnerable to suicide including genetics, life events or temperament) and precipitating factors (specific events or triggers to suicidality) and that the risk of suicide should be managed through regular follow-up and brief psychological therapy.

> *Good practice point*
>
> As we are poor at predicting risk, we should take any risk seriously; reviewing each person's risk regularly and providing focused interventions directly aimed at reducing suicide risk.

HQIP research has shown that despite common risk factors, risk is often individual and suggests risk management should be personalised (Chan et al 2016; Quinlivan et al 2016). They suggest clinical risk assessment processes might be improved in the following ways:

- The emphasis should be on clinical judgement and building relationships, and by gathering good information on (i) the current situation, (ii) history of risk and (iii) social factors to inform a collaboratively developed management plan.
- Families and carers should have as much involvement as possible in the assessment process, including the opportunity to express their views on potential risk.
- The management plan should be **collaboratively developed** where possible. Communication with primary care may also be may also be helpful.
- **The management of risk should be personal and individualised,** but it is one part of a whole system approach that should aim to strengthen the standards of care for everyone, ensuring that supervision, delegation and referral pathways are all managed safely.

NICE CG123 (2019) Recommendation 1.3.3.2: If a person with a common mental health disorder presents considerable and immediate risk to themselves or others, refer them urgently to the emergency services or specialist mental health services.

1.8 Risk and protective factors

Risk and protective factors play a critical role in suicide prevention (Suicide Prevention Resource Center, SPRC 2011). For clinicians, identifying risk and protective factors provides critical information to assess and manage suicide risk in individuals. Risk factors are characteristics that make it more likely that individuals will consider, attempt or die by suicide. Protective factors are characteristics that make it less likely that individuals will consider, attempt or die by suicide. Risk and protective factors are found at various levels:

- individual (e.g. genetic predispositions, mental health problems, personality traits);
- family (e.g. cohesion, dysfunction);
- community (e.g. availability of mental health services).

They may be *fixed* (those things that cannot be changed, such as a family history of suicide) or *modifiable* (those things that can be changed, such as depression). Researchers identify risk and protective factors by comparing groups of individuals who have died by (or attempted or contemplated) suicide with a group of similar individuals who have not died by (or attempted or contemplated) suicide.

Suicide rates differ by sex, age, ethnic origin and death registration system, as well as by region and over time. Suicide results from many complex socio-cultural factors and is likely to occur particularly during periods of socioeconomic, family and personal crisis situations (e.g. loss of a loved one, employment). In a review of suicidal behaviour in patients with bipolar disorder, Hawton et al (2005) found the main risk factors for suicide were a previous suicide attempt and hopelessness, which differed from risk factors for non-fatal suicidal behaviour. Chan et al (2016) found that of seven risk factors evaluated, four had robust evidence to support their association with suicide following the index episode of self-harm:

- previous episodes of self-harm (prior to the index episode);
- male gender;
- suicidal intent;
- poor physical health.

An extensive meta-analysis of the previous 50 years' research into risk factors for suicide (Franklin et al 2016) found that:

- predictive ability has not improved across 50 years of research;
- no risk factor category or subcategory is substantially stronger than any other;
- studies rarely examined the combined effect of multiple risk factors or protective factors.

Consistent with other research and many hypotheses and theories about suicide, the authors conclude that accurate prediction of suicidal thoughts and behaviours requires a complex combination of a large number of factors, many of which vary over time.

In the United Kingdom at-risk groups include:

- men (men are three times more likely to die by suicide than women are);
- people in the age group 40–44 years;
- people in the care of the mental health services;
- people with a history of self-harm;
- people in contact with the criminal justice system;
- people who have been bereaved or affected by suicide;
- people living in areas of higher socioeconomic deprivation; *
- people who are unemployed;
- people working in the least skilled occupations (e.g. construction workers);
- people with a low level of educational attainment;
- people who do not own their home (Samaritans 2017; Centre for Mental Health Report 2019).

*this may reflect other indices of inequality, in particular unemployment

NICE (2019) identified high-risk groups as people:

- with long-term physical health problems, in particular those with chronic pain;
- who self-harm;
- with drug and alcohol problems;

- who have attempted suicide;
- who have a family history of suicide;
- with mental health problems, in particular those with a diagnosis of a personality disorder and/or receiving inpatient treatment;

and

- middle-aged men;
- older people who have an unrecognised mental health problem.

Many chronic risk factors are static or unchangeable (e.g. a history of a suicide attempt or a history of violence), but others may be modifiable or dynamic such as employment status.

Types of suicide risk factors

Dynamic risk factors are present at some point but may fluctuate in duration and intensity, such as hopelessness or substance misuse.

Static risk factors are fixed and historical and do not change, for example, a family history of suicide.

Stable risk factors are long term and likely to endure for many years, but are not fixed: for example, a diagnosis of personality disorder.

Future risk factors can be anticipated and may result from changing circumstances, such as future stress or access to means.

Static risk factors

Psychiatric admission and discharge. Discharge from a psychiatric inpatient unit confers the highest magnitude of all risk factors, with risk of suicide peaking immediately after admission as well as discharge (Qin & Nordentoft 2005; NCI 2014). The highest risk is in the first two weeks after leaving hospital (The National Confidential Inquiry 2014 and 2019). Thankfully suicides within psychiatric inpatient settings have gone down since 2016 (NCI 2019). The first three months after discharge remain the time of highest risk but especially in the first 1-2 weeks and the highest number of deaths occurred on day 3 post-discharge. This collective data shows that the immediate post-discharge period is a time of marked risk, but rates of suicide remain high for many years after discharge. Appleby et al (1999) compared the characteristics of 149 people who died by suicide within 5 years of discharge from psychiatric wards in Greater Manchester with control patients. Those who died by suicide were more likely to have had a past history of deliberate self-harm or had a decrease in the level of care agreed at their last appointment before dying. Other aspects of a patients' experience which can raise suicide risk include having a key worker on holiday or about to leave the service at the time of the incident (King et al 2001). A meta-analysis by Large et al 2011 found a moderately strong association between both a history of self-harm and depressive symptoms with post-discharge suicide, but not a diagnosis of major depression or male sex. They calculated that about 3% of patients categorized as being at high risk can be expected to commit suicide in the year after discharge. However, about 60% of the patients who commit suicide are likely to be categorized as low risk and concluded that risk categorization is of no value in attempts to decrease the numbers of patients who will commit suicide after discharge. A later meta-analysis by Chung et al 2017 found the suicide rate was highest within 3 months after discharge and among patients admitted with suicidal ideation or behaviour. Higher rates of suicide following discharge from general medical wards provide further evidence that the transition from in-patient care to home is a stressful one.

The findings of the Confidential Inquiry into Suicide and Homicide by People with Mental Illness led to the recommendation that all patients with severe mental illness or a history of deliberate self-harm within the previous 3 months should be followed up within a week of their discharge (Department of Health 2001). For many years since it has been a national target to follow up service users within 7 days of discharge from an adult mental health inpatient unit. However, in order to see patients who do not make this appointment as their disengagement may indicate high risk, this was reviewed and reduced to 72 hours (CQUIN 2019) see https://www.england.nhs.uk/wp-content/uploads/2019/03/CQUIN-Guidance-1920-080319.pdf. Crawford (2004) suggests a range of interventions to reduce the rate of post-discharge suicide. Helping patients prepare for discharge by providing them with clear information about follow-up plans and crisis services and helping them readjust to life at home through periods of leave from the ward would seem worthwhile. Crawford also suggests discharge preparation groups, meeting out-patient staff before discharge and the efforts of care coordinators can lead to increased patient attendance at follow-up appointments. These interventions aim to improve continuity of care and increase the amount of social support that patients experience following their discharge from hospital. HQIP (NCISH 2014) warned that brief admissions may not give adequate time to address the adverse events that can precede admissions and are associated with post-discharge deaths by suicide.

The latest guidance from HQIP (NCISH 2019) recommends

- safer wards, including removal of low-lying ligature points;
- comprehensive care planning for discharge and preparation for discharge;
- follow-up within 2-3 days of discharge from in-patient care;
- phased leave with trial periods out of hospital before discharge.

> ***Good practice point***
>
> 72-hour follow-up of patients discharged from mental health units should be delivered to at least 80% of patients and in particular for those with suicidal ideation or behaviour before or during their admission.

A history of previous suicide attempts is the strongest predictor for future suicidal ideation and behaviour, including suicidal ideation, suicide attempts and suicide. Harris and Barraclough (1997) found that those who had attempted suicide were at 38 times greater risk for dying by suicide than those who had not attempted suicide. A study of 100 people who had attempted suicide followed them up for 37 years and found that 13% ended their own lives. In females the rate of suicide was 8% and in men 26%. Their eventual suicide was quite often far removed in time from the index suicide attempt. Two-thirds of the suicides occurred 15 or more years after the index attempt

(Suominen et al 2004). Studies have found that up to half of people who end their life have deliberately harmed themselves prior to their suicides. That percentage rises to two-thirds in younger people (Cooper et al 2005). Most recently, Parra-Uribe et al (2017) found as many as 10–15% of individuals who have attempted suicide will ultimately end their life.

Male gender. Suicide is the leading cause of death for men under 50. The ratio of male to female suicides in this country is currently over 4 to 1 (ONS 2019, 2020). Unemployment is a key risk factor for suicidal behaviour in men alongside economic uncertainty and unmanageable debt. We know that men are less likely than women to seek help or talk about suicidal feelings and can be reluctant to engage with health and other support services (Wyllie et al 2012). Men more often use violent and highly lethal methods, which is a significant cause of higher rates of death by suicide in males in all European countries (Mergl et al 2015). In the Samaritans' Men, Suicide and Society report (2012), men talk about relationships breaking down, separation from children, job loss, addiction, lack of close friendships, loneliness and being unable to open up (NHS England 2018).

"You've failed" – unless you have gone out and secured that job, that house, that car, that woman, those children and that sunny family life...." You're divorced? Don't see your kids much now and don't live with them? Lost your job? You can't pay your debts, your rent, your mortgage, your bills? Your life is over, man!"

Family history of suicide. People affected by suicide have an increased likelihood of suicidal ideation and poor psychiatric outcomes for those closest to the individual (Cerel et al 2016). In a national UK-wide study of 3,432 young bereaved adults (Pitman et al 2016), those bereaved by suicide had a higher probability of attempting suicide (65% higher risk of attempting suicide) than those bereaved by sudden natural causes. There was no such increased risk in adults bereaved by sudden unnatural causes. Nine per cent of those bereaved make a suicide attempt. The increased risk includes parents who have lost a child by suicide, especially mothers (Qin & Mortensen 2003). Explanations for this increased risk include the particular psychological trauma of a suicide loss (which involves grief and agonising self-questioning), shared familial and environmental risk, "suicide contagion" through the process of social modelling, and the burden of stigma associated with violent losses (Pitman et al 2016).

Age. Increasing age is generally associated with increasing risk for suicide. This relationship seems to persist even when there is no accompanying mental illness. Despite this, older people are less likely to receive the mental health care they need. Morgan et al (2018) found that older people who self-harm are less likely to be referred to specialist mental health services than younger adults are, despite a higher risk of suicide in this group. Two leading figures in old age psychiatry quote similarly alarming statistics. Among the facts listed by Burns and Warner (2015) are that 85% of older people with depression receive no help from the NHS and that older people are a fifth as likely as younger age groups to have access to talking therapies but six times as likely to be on medication.

Also, other risk factors vary with age. Over the past decade, middle-aged men in their 40s and 50s have had the highest suicide rates of any age or gender, especially if they lived in deprived areas. The gap between the most and least deprived areas was not found among those aged 20 years and below, particularly in men, or in those of retirement age. For these ages, it's likely that risk factors other than deprivation are more important. For young people, risk factors include adverse childhood experiences (ACEs), stressors such as academic pressures and relationship difficulties, and recent events such as bereavement. For older people, psychiatric illness and deterioration of physical health and functioning are known risk factors (ONS 2020).

History of childhood trauma. ACEs including childhood sexual abuse are significantly associated with lifetime suicide attempts, even when mental and substance use disorders are controlled (Choi et al 2017; Hughes et al 2017). This is especially so for people in prison (Ford et al 2020). Thompson et al (2019) found that physical, sexual and emotional abuse, parental incarceration and family history of suicidality each increased the risk for suicidal ideation and suicide attempts in adulthood by 1.4–2.7 times. The accumulation of ACEs increased the odds of suicidal ideation and attempts. Compared to those with no ACEs, the odds of seriously considering suicide or attempting suicide in adulthood increased more than threefold among those with three or more ACEs.

Stable risk factors

Being single. This includes individuals who are widowed, divorced and those who have never been married. In 2015, divorced men were almost three times more likely to end their lives than men who were married or in a civil partnership (ONS 2017). Although the individual themselves may change their relationship status, it is unlikely to be achieved by a professional intervention.

Dynamic risk factors

Mental illness or emotional distress. These should be identified and treated with psychopharmacologic or psychological interventions. HQIP Annual Report 2017 recommended that services should be aware of the potential suicide risk in patients with a diagnosis of an eating disorder, ASD or dementia, and this should be part of a comprehensive assessment. Mental health staff should have access to specialist support in these conditions. The latest mortality surveillance report by MBRRACE-UK (Knight et al 2018) shows that suicide continues to be the leading cause of maternal death in the first year after giving birth and highlights the important role of specialist perinatal mental health services, particularly in forward planning for the care of women with known pre-existing mental health problems.

> ***Good practice point***
>
> Whilst the use of risk categories to decide treatment and referral is strongly discouraged, the clinician should nevertheless be familiar with established risk factors and risk groups for suicide at a population level (Chan et al 2016).

Physical health. A government "think tank" Demos et al (2011) produced a report showing one in ten suicides are linked to chronic physical illness. UK records showed those who died by suicide were 3.1 times more frequently last discharged from general, than from psychiatric, hospitals; and only 14% of those discharged from a general hospital had a recorded psychiatric diagnosis at their last visit (Dougall et al 2014).

Being in prison. The risk of suicide in the UK prison population is considerably higher than among the general population (NICE 2019). A report on preventing prison suicide highlighted that staff felt the initial reception assessment on arrival at prison consistently failed to detect and address vulnerability due to time constraints, staff skills and a lack of information from the court. Given the high proportion of suicides that happen during the first month of prison, staff stressed the importance of improving the initial assessment process (Centre for Mental Health 2017). People on probation are also at high risk of suicide (Sirdifield et al 2020).

Social deprivation and unemployment. Over the past decade, middle-aged men in their 40s and 50s have had the highest suicide rates of any age or gender. The latest UK statistics (ONS 2020) indicate that middle-aged men living in the most deprived areas face almost triple rates of suicide; up to 36.6 per 100,000 compared to 13.5 per 100,000 in the least deprived areas (figures for men aged 43 years). In the least deprived areas, rates among middle-aged men are like those of other ages. In 2016, the Samaritans commissioned eight leading social scientists to review the connection between socioeconomic disadvantage and suicidal behaviour. Their report, "Dying from Inequality", was launched in March 2017 and included key findings on the link between suicide and deprivation and recommendations for mitigating this connection. They confirmed that financial instability and poverty increase suicide risk and that low income and unmanageable debt, unemployment, poor housing conditions and other socioeconomic factors all contribute to high suicide rates. The report concludes that tackling inequality should be central to suicide prevention and support should be targeted to the poorest groups who are likely to need it most.

See https://www.nspa.org.uk/wp-content/uploads/2017/10/NSPA_InfoSheet_SocioeconomicDeprivationSuicidalBehaviour_v1.pdf.

Lewis and Sloggett (1998) studied UK suicide data between 1983 and 1992. They found a strong independent association between suicide and individuals who were unemployed and permanently sick. Those without access to a car had an increased risk, but other measures of socioeconomic status were not associated with suicide. The authors conclude that the association between suicide and unemployment is more important than the association with other socioeconomic measures. The findings support the idea that social and economic policies which reduce unemployment will also reduce the rate of suicide. A Canadian study by Burrows et al (2011) found that *individual disadvantage* was associated with suicide mortality, particularly for males and also recommend prevention strategies should primarily focus on individuals who are unemployed or out of the labour force and have low education or income and individuals with low income or who are living alone in deprived areas should also be targeted. Nordt et al (2015) investigated the specific effect of unemployment on suicide by analysing global public data. The relative risk of suicide associated with unemployment was elevated by about 20–30% during the study period

2000–2011. The authors recommend that prevention strategies focused on the unemployed and on employment are necessary not only in difficult times but also in times of stable economy.

Protective factors include the following:

- effective mental health care;
- connectedness to individuals, family, community and social institutions;
- problem-solving skills;
- contacts with caregivers. Contacts, even those as simple as letters or postcards from health care providers to patients, have demonstrated reductions in suicide risk (Motto & Bostrom 2001; Fleischmann et al 2008);
- mental health care and treatment, including Cognitive Behavioural Therapy and dialectical behaviour therapy, can reduce suicide risk (Brown et al 2005; Méndez-Bustos et al 2019).

Social support

Observational studies suggest that those with established social relationships are less likely to engage in self-harm and suicide than those who are socially isolated (Miller et al 2015). For example, a study of people hospitalised following a suicide attempt reported that those with greater family and peer connectedness were less likely to have re-attempted suicide after 12 months than those with less connectedness (Czyz et al 2012). Evidence from two national samples (in the United States and the United Kingdom) suggested that perceived support from friends and family was associated with decreased likelihood of a lifetime suicide attempt, controlling for a variety of related predictors (Kleiman & Liu 2013). Frey et al (2019) found disclosing a suicide attempt to one's family, regardless of whether one receives supportive responses as well as social support from family and friends, can promote post-traumatic growth.

> Good practice point: Clinicians and practitioners working with people who have attempted suicide should discuss with the person disclosure to family and friends and consider the potential reactions of recipients. It will be helpful to develop a plan for how to cope with unhelpful or hurtful responses to mitigate possible negative responses (Frey et al 2019).

There are a number of ways in which social support may be protective against suicide. First, social support may have a stabilising effect to buffer against stress (Motto & Bostrom 2001). Hence, those with greater social support may perceive less need for mental health services, which suggests that supportive relationships might be a substitute for or a complement to formal treatment (Thoits 2011). Other researchers suggest that those with more frequent social support contact are more likely to access mental health services following a stressful life event than those with infrequent contact (i.e. social support expedites access to services), and are less likely to require specialist psychiatric services, i.e. confirming social support plays a stress reduction role (Maulik et al 2011).

Risk factors are not warning signs

Risk factors are often confused with warning signs of suicide, and frequently suicide prevention materials mix the two into lists of "what to watch out for". *Warning signs* indicate an *immediate* risk of suicide, whereas risk factors indicate someone is at heightened risk for suicide, but little or nothing about immediate risk (Rudd et al 2006) (Table 1.1).

Table 1.1 Risk factors and warning signs

Risk factors	*Warning signs*
Risk factors indicate someone is at heightened risk for suicide, but indicate little or nothing about immediate risk (Rudd et al 2006)	Warning signs indicate an immediate risk of suicide.
Risk and protective factors are found in individuals and communities.	Warning signs are applicable only to individuals.
Talking about risk factors helps people understand *what might need to change within an individual or a community* in order to decrease suicide risk over time.	Talking about warning signs helps people know what actions they can take *right now* to help someone at immediate risk for suicide.
Risk factors for suicide (such as prior attempts, mood disorders and substance abuse) indicate that someone is at heightened risk for suicide.	Warning signs (such as threatening suicide, seeking means for suicide and dramatic mood changes) indicate that someone may be at immediate risk for suicide.

Suicide Prevention Resource Center and Rodgers (2011).

Why are risk and protective factors important?

Risk and protective factors provide areas of emphasis for interventions that help prevent suicide. Decreasing risk factors and/or increasing protective factors should reduce suicide risk. For example, depression is a significant risk factor for suicide; therefore, decreasing the number of individuals with depression should result in reduced suicide. A Swedish study found that when primary care physicians were trained to identify and treat depression in their patients, the suicide rate went down (Rihmer et al 1995). Similarly, the restriction of lethal means – creating barriers to jumping from bridges as well as reducing access to poisons, drugs and firearms – has demonstrated reductions in suicide risk (Daigle 2005; Mann et al 2005). Risk factors can also be used to identify and target prevention efforts for members of groups that are at higher risk for suicide, for example, those who have attempted suicide in the past (Harris & Barraclough 1997), those with mood disorders (Cavanagh et al 2003; Arsenault-Lapierre et al 2004), gay and lesbian individuals who have been rejected by their families (Ryan et al 2009), individuals in substance abuse treatment (Britton & Conner 2010), and older males (Conwell et al 2011). By identifying groups at higher risk, suicide prevention teams can create and target interventions to the needs of members of those groups.

When considering risk and protective factors, keep these points in mind (SPRC 2011):

- Not all risk and protective factors are equal. Some risk factors have been shown to significantly increase risk, whereas other risk factors do not have as strong or well-demonstrated relationships to risk. Lists mask the fact that some risk factors are much more powerful than others.
- High risk for suicide, whether for individuals or communities, is usually found in a combination or “constellation” of multiple risk factors.
- The significance of particular risk and protective factors varies among individuals and communities, so the degree of risk or protection conveyed by any one factor will differ among individuals and communities.

- Although risk factors generally contribute to long-term risk, immediate stressors or tipping point may create the final impetus for the suicidal act. Tipping points may include relationship problems or break-ups, financial hardships, legal difficulties, public humiliation or shame, worsening medical prognosis and other stressful events.

Identifying risk and protective factors plays a critical role at several stages in strategic planning. The Suicide Prevention Resource Centre's strategic planning process gives further details about this: http://www.sprc.org/effective-prevention/strategic-planning.

In summary

- Risk and protective factors play a critical role in the prevention of suicide for both individuals and communities.
- Risk factors are not warning signs.
- Major risk factors include prior suicide attempt(s), mood disorders, substance abuse and access to lethal means.
- Major protective factors include effective mental health care, connectedness, problem-solving skills and contacts with caregivers.
- Risk and protective factors provide targets for intervention in both individuals and communities.
- Risk and protective factors vary between individuals and across settings.
- Suicide prevention efforts should begin with a strategic planning process that, among other goals, identifies and targets specific risk and protective factors for intervention.

1.9 Models of suicide

Suicidal behaviour had been traditionally understood within the biomedical-illness model. However, this model is limited as the focus is on the identification of underlying pathology despite the fact that pathology alone is not a sufficient explanation for suicidal behaviour (Sheehy & O'Connor 2002).

Shneidman's cubic model (1972, 1987, 1993)

Shneidman was an early pioneer of the psychological understanding and treatment of suicidality. In 1968, he founded the American Association of Suicidology and the principal US journal for suicide studies, *Suicide and Life Threatening Behavior*. Until Shneidman, suicide was seen as the consequence of mental illness or derangement. In Shneidman's "cubic model" of suicidal behaviour, "psychache" is the primary dimension when individuals are considering suicide. (The two other dimensions are stress and perturbation.) Psychache is defined as general psychological pain reaching intolerable intensity. It encompasses shame, guilt, humiliation, loneliness, fear, angst and dread. For Shneidman, suicide is best understood as the complete stopping of one's consciousness and unendurable pain. It is seen by the suffering person as the solution to life's painful and pressing problems. A suicide-focused intervention then attempts to help the suicidal person find other ways to reduce or manage their pain (Figure 1.1).

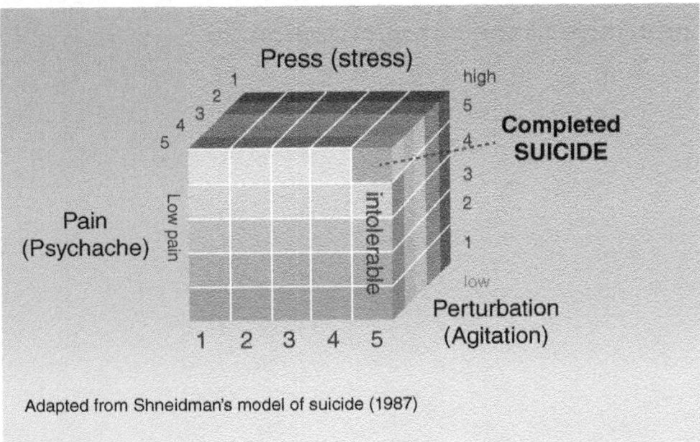

Figure 1.1 Shneidman's cubic model of suicide (1987).

CBT

CBT posits that most suicide attempts function as an escape or an avoidance of intense psychological emotional pain. This involves a process known as *negative reinforcement* via the reduction of aversive, internal emotional states (Linehan 1993; Joiner 2005). Positive reinforcement of suicidal behaviour, for example from being rescued and concern from others, can apply but in a minority of cases. Beck (1996) introduced the concept of the suicide mode which Rudd (2000) elaborated on. CBT addresses four elements to the suicide mode:

1. Cognition (suicidal belief system), e.g. perceived burdensomeness;
2. Emotion (depression, guilt, anxiety, shame);
3. Physiology (e.g. insomnia, chronic physical pain);
4. Behaviour (maladaptive coping strategies including substance use, social withdrawal and self-harm).

Cry of pain or entrapment model

Mark Williams is Professor of Clinical Psychology at the University of Oxford, Director of the Oxford Mindfulness Centre and works with the Oxford Centre of Suicide Research investigating psychological mechanisms in suicidal behaviour in recurrent depression. Williams (Williams 1997; Williams & Pollock 2000, 2001) broadened Baumeister's (1990) theory of Suicide as Escape from Self. The cry of pain (CoP) model conceptualises suicidal behaviour as the response (or cry) to a situation that has three components: defeat, no escape and no rescue. It is founded on an evolutionary approach to understanding suicidal behaviour in depression.

The CoP model has introduced a number of important concepts. "Arrested flight" (Gilbert & Allan 1998) is a phenomenon which describes a situation where an animal, such as a bird, is defeated but flight is blocked and cannot escape. It has been suggested that suicidal ideation arises from the feeling of entrapment, but it is when the individual fails to find alternative ways to solve their problems that this can be exacerbated into suicidal behaviour (Williams et al 2005). The CoP model has a strong empirical basis demonstrating the importance of defeat and entrapment affecting mood and behaviour. It has incorporated psychobiological and evolutionary factors and has established the importance for the perceptions of defeat and entrapment in mediating stress and depression. Recognising that not all depressed patients are suicidal, it implicates the role of entrapment and hopelessness in exacerbating feelings of defeat and depression in the development of suicidality. In some studies, hopelessness has been a better predictor of suicide than depression itself (Wetzel 1976; Beck et al 1989). The model has led to the development of treatment interventions. For example, based on the observation that hopelessness is related to an inability to generate possible positive future events (MacLeod et al 1993), Williams and Pollock (2001) suggest that the therapy could encourage clients to practise generating positive events with a focus on the near future, which may engender a sense of possible change.

However, this model has been widely criticised for lack of clarity. Johnson et al 2008 argue the concepts are unclear in their theoretical basis because:

- They are not clear in their usage, definition and measurement.
- The concepts are unclear in that being derived from animal behaviour they do not map clearly on to human cognition. This is not to say they are not useful, but they are not coterminous.
- Most tellingly, the one study that tested the CoP model did not find that the concepts were significant and independent predictors of suicide behaviour.
- The translation of concepts from the model into treatment strategies has not been particularly forthcoming or productive

Joiner's interpersonal-psychological theory

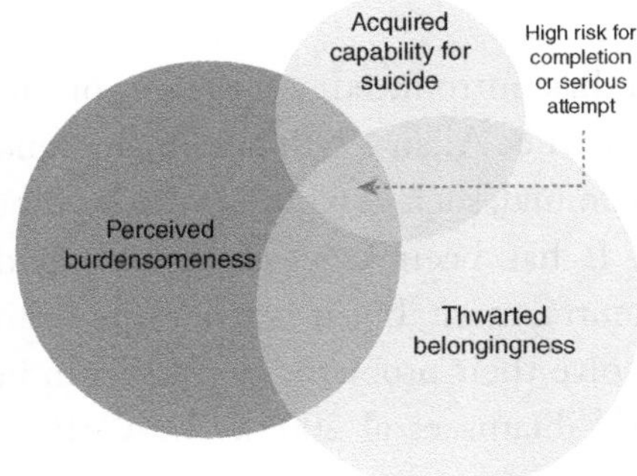

Figure 1.2 The interpersonal psychological theory of suicidal behaviour (Adapted from Joiner (2005)).

According to Joiner's model (Joiner, 2005), the simultaneous presence of thwarted belongingness and perceived burdensomeness produces the desire for suicide. Whilst the desire for suicide is necessary, it alone will not result in suicide. Rather, Joiner asserts that one must also have acquired the capability to overcome one's natural fear of death. The desire to end one's life from hopelessness, perceived burdensomeness, or low belongingness plus the ability to do so leads to suicidal intent. The model predicts that suicidality is reduced by these protective factors which act as buffers:

- connectedness;
- perceived social support;
- engagement with children; family and services.

Joiner's is widely recognised as probably the most comprehensive model for understanding and predicting suicide in an individual, but it has limited utility in terms of treatment.

The fluid vulnerability theory (FVT)

Rudd (2006) proposes the fluid vulnerability theory (FVT) in which suicide risk is conceptualised as an interaction of baseline risk (e.g. genetic predisposition and trauma history) with acute risk (e.g. recent loss of a job or end of a relationship). Upon resolution of an acute suicidal episode, individuals return to their baseline level. This can remain high in chronically suicidal individuals and clinicians need to be alert to that. The baseline risk for patients with a history of multiple suicide attempts is higher and endures for a longer period of time than those with a minimal history or no history of previous suicide attempts.

The integrated motivational-volitional model (IMV)

O'Connor and Kirtley (2018) propose that defeat and entrapment drive the emergence of suicidal ideation and that a group of factors, entitled volitional moderators (VMs), govern the transition from suicidal ideation to suicidal behaviour. According to the integrated motivational-volitional model, VMs include:

- access to the means of suicide;
- exposure to suicidal behaviour;
- capability for suicide (fearlessness about death and increased physical pain tolerance);
- planning;
- impulsivity;
- mental imagery;
- past suicidal behaviour.

1.10 Intervening to help people at risk of suicide – who, where and when

Clearly specialist mental health services have a duty of care to provide effective interventions for those individuals who presents or are referred at risk of suicide. The treatments with the most evidence for effectiveness in reducing suicidality are psychosocial interventions that specifically focus on treating suicide independently of mental disorder diagnosis (Comtois et al 2011, Rudd et al 2015).

> ***Good practice point***
>
> All mental health services should provide specific psychosocial interventions for people who are at risk of suicide.

Helping people to reduce suicidal thoughts, urges and behaviours is not the exclusive domain of mental health professionals. Only one in four people who died by suicide has been in contact with specialist mental health services in the year before their death (Appleby et al 1999). Suicidal ideation and behaviour are not the same as mental illness. Whilst mental illness, particularly depression, can be an underlying factor in most suicides (Rihmer 2011), recent statistics indicate that more than half of suicides do not merit a psychiatric diagnosis (Stone et al 2018). Clinicians are often inclined to consider suicidal ideation a symptom of major depression. Whilst improving the diagnosis and treatment of depression can help to lower suicide rates (Zalsman et al 2016), only a minority of depressed patients die by suicide, and a large percentage of severely depressed patients never think about suicide (Bostwick & Pankratz 2000; Pompili 2019). There is an over-reliance on prescribing medication for people at risk of suicide. While medication has undoubtedly helped many people who suffer with mental health problems, there is extensive evidence that targeting and treating mental disorders has little or mixed impact on suicidal risk (Cuijpers et al 2013; Braun et al 2016; Jakobsen et al 2017). Despite the widespread use of medication, there is fairly limited data (based on RCTs) about the efficacy of medicine in reducing suicidality (Zalsman et al 2016).

People with suicidal risk present in a range of settings and may not engage in mental health services or get treated by them when they do present. Engagement and retention in services is a significant challenge in managing suicidal behaviour. At times of suicide risk, people may not seek help for their mental health but present at EDs with suicidal crises. The ED is therefore a key site for intervention.

> ***Good practice point***
> EDs (or A&E) should provide personalised safety planning and a brief suicide-focused intervention such as or teachable moment brief intervention (TMBI) (O'Connor et al 2015, 2018) for anyone presenting after a suicide attempt. Any mental health liaison team in a general hospital setting should be commissioned to treat as well as assess individuals at risk of suicide. Interventions at this juncture are evidence-based and best practice (Miller et al 2017; Stanley et al 2018).

The Samaritans (a charity providing free 24-hour support by telephone) have an invaluable role in suicide prevention in the United Kingdom. They respond to more than 5 million calls for help each year, offering emotional support by phone, email, text and face to face.

The fragmentation of services and increasing restriction to access (due in the main to demand exceeding capacity in underfunded public services) often result in clients having to tell their story over and over again because they have been "signposted" to another service. This can lead clients to feel demoralised and give up. Reducing suicide requires us to manage pathways between services more sensitively with the individual not being asked to start again with a new service and repeated assessment.

Due to the COVID-19 pandemic in 2020, there have been unprecedented increases in unemployment and social isolation nationally and globally. The impact of the pandemic, both economically and emotionally, is a major concern for suicide prevention. The latest ONS figures show that there were over 700,000 fewer people on payroll during lockdown, and the most deprived local areas have been affected the most, in terms of mortality.

See https://www.ons.gov.uk/employmentandlabourmarket/peopleinwork/employmentandemployeetypes/bulletins/uklabourmarket/august2020.

Further, almost one in five adults (19.2%) was likely to be experiencing some form of depression during the COVID-19 pandemic in June 2020, almost double the number before the pandemic (July 2019 to March 2020). See https://www.ons.gov.uk/peoplepopulationandcommunity/wellbeing/articles/coronavirusanddepressioninadultsgreatbritain/june2020.

Weems et al (2020) identified available evidence and from this predicted the increased rate of suicide worldwide was approximately 50,000. It is therefore imperative that services supporting people at risk respond sensitively and effectively. Individuals at risk after the pandemic may approach debt advisory services rather than a mental health service. It may have taken the individual a lot of courage to ask for help and signposting to mental health services is not likely to be heard positively by someone overwhelmed with stress and possibly suicidal. If the response they receive is signposting to another service, this may well feel too overwhelming and they may simply give up. Where signposting is necessary (because a service cannot help the individual address their suicide risk), it is important to establish if the person is willing and able to go to another service and provide them with the support to do so or, if need be, take more assertive action to keep them safe (Figure 1.3).

See https://oxfordhealthbrc.nihr.ac.uk/our-work/oxppl/prevention-of-suicide-self-harm-in-the-context-of-covid-19/.

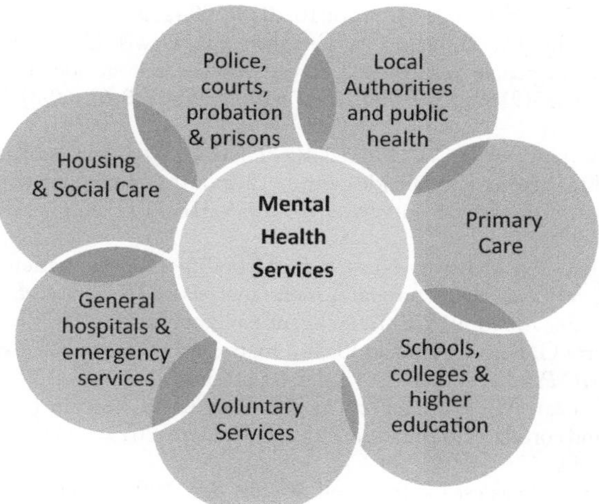

Figure 1.3 We can all play our part.

In summary, many professionals can play a role in helping someone who is suicidal. You may have a unique opportunity to help someone because you already have a relationship with them, and they have disclosed suicidal thoughts or urges to you. You may also have many relevant skills to help someone, especially if you have counselling or motivational interviewing skills. The caveat to this is that you will need to practise in line with safeguarding policies and procedures within your organisation and receive training and supervision. There are a number of excellent organisations which can provide training; see 2.12 page (115).

> ***Good practice point***
>
> People at risk of suicide should not be signposted to another service without establishing first that they feel able to contact that service, and subsequently do access that service. If necessary, support should be provided to help them to do so.

References

Ahrens B, Linden M. Is there a suicidality syndrome independent of specific major psychiatric disorder? Results of a split half multiple regression analysis. *Acta Psychiatr Scand.* 1996;94(2):79–86. doi:10.1111/j.1600-0447.1996.tb09829.x

Ahrens B, Linden M, Zäske H, Berzewski H. Suicidal behavior—Symptom or disorder? *Compr Psychiatry.* 2000;41(2 Suppl 1):116–121. doi:10.1016/s0010-440x(00)80017-6

Aleman A, Denys D. Mental health: A road map for suicide research and prevention. *Nature.* 2014;509(7501):421–423. doi:10.1038/509421a

Appleby L, Dennehy JA, Thomas CS, Faragher EB, Lewis G. Aftercare and clinical characteristics of people with mental illness who commit suicide: a case-control study. *Lancet.* 1999;353(9162):1397-400. doi: 10.1016/S0140-6736(98)10014-4. PMID: 10227220.

Appleby L, Shaw J, Amos T, McDonnell R, Harris C, McCann K, Kiernan K, Davies S, Bickley H, Parsons R. Suicide within 12 months of contact with mental health services: National clinical survey. *BMJ.* 1999;318(7193):1235–1239. doi:10.1136/bmj.318.7193.1235

Arcelus J, Mitchell AJ, Wales J, Nielsen S. Mortality rates in patients with anorexia nervosa and other eating disorders. A meta-analysis of 36 studies. *Arch Gen Psychiatry.* 2011;68(7):724–731. doi:10.1001/archgenpsychiatry.2011.74

Arsenault-Lapierre G, Kim C, Turecki G. Psychiatric diagnoses in 3275 suicides: A meta-analysis. *BMC Psychiatry.* 2004;4:37. doi:10.1186/1471-244X-4-37

Batterham PJ, Calear AL, Christensen H. The Stigma of Suicide Scale. Psychometric properties and correlates of the stigma of suicide. *Crisis.* 2013;34(1):13–21. doi:10.1027/0227-5910/a000156

Baumeister RF. Suicide as escape from self. *Psychol Rev.* 1990;97(1):90–113. doi:10.1037/0033-295x.97.1.90

Bazalgette L, Bradley W, Ousbey J. *The Truth about suicide.* 2011. https://demosuk.wpengine.com/files/Suicide_-_web.pdf?1314370102

Beck AT. Beyond belief: A theory of modes, personality, and psychopathology. In: Salkovskis P, editor. *Frontiers of cognitive therapy*. New York: Guilford; 1996. pp. 1–25.

Beck AT, Brown G, Steer RA. Prediction of eventual suicide in psychiatric inpatients by clinical ratings of hopelessness. *J Consult Clin Psychol.* 1989;57(2):309–310. doi:10.1037//0022-006x.57.2.309

Bergen H, Hawton K, Waters K, Cooper J, Kapur N. Epidemiology and trends in non-fatal self-harm in three centres in England: 2000–2007. *Br J Psychiatry*. 2010;197(6): 493–498. doi:10.1192/bjp.bp.110.077651

Bergen H, Hawton K, Waters K, Ness J, Cooper J, Steeg S, Kapur N. How do methods of non-fatal self-harm relate to eventual suicide? *J Affect Disord.* 2012;136(3):526–533. doi:10.1016/j.jad.2011.10.036

Birkbak J, Stuart EA, Lind BD, Qin P, Stenager E, Larsen KJ, Wang AG, Nielsen AC, Pedersen CM, Winsløv JH, Langhoff C, Mühlmann C, Nordentoft M, Erlangsen A. Psychosocial therapy and causes of death after deliberate self-harm: A register-based, nationwide multicentre study using propensity score matching. *Psychol Med.* 2016:1–9. doi:10. 1017/S0033291716001872

Blades CA, Stritzke WGK, Page AC, Brown JD. The benefits and risks of asking research participants about suicide: A meta-analysis of the impact of exposure to suicide-related content. *Clin Psychol Rev*. 2018;64:1–12. doi:10.1016/j.cpr.2018.07.001

Bohnert ASB, Ilgen MA. Understanding links among opioid use, overdose, and suicide. *N Engl J Med*. 2019;380(1):71–79. doi:10.1056/NEJMra1802148

Bolton JM, Gunnell D, Turecki G. Suicide risk assessment and intervention in people with mental illness. *BMJ*. 2015;351:h4978. doi:10.1136/bmj.h4978

Booth N, Briscoe M, Powell R. Suicide in the farming community: Methods used and contact with health services. *Occup Environ Med.* 2000;57(9):642–644. doi:10.1136/oem.57.9.642

Bostwick JM, Pankratz VS. Affective disorders and suicide risk: A re-examination. *Am J Psychiatry*. 2000;157(12):1925–1932. doi:10.1176/appi.ajp.157.12.1925

Brady J. The association between alcohol misuse and suicidal behaviour. *Alcohol Alcohol.* 2006;41(5):473–478. doi:10.1093/alcalc/agl060

Braun C, Bschor T, Franklin J, Baethge C. Suicides and suicide attempts during long-term treatment with antidepressants: A meta-analysis of 29 placebo-controlled studies including 6,934 patients with major depressive disorder. *Psychother Psychosom.* 2016;85(3):171–179. doi:10.1159/000442293

Britton PC, Conner KR. Suicide attempts within 12 months of treatment for substance use disorders. *Suicide Life Threat Behav*. 2010;40(1):14–21. doi:10.1521/suli.2010.40.1.14

Brown GK, Ten Have T, Henriques GR, Xie SX, Hollander JE, Beck AT. Cognitive therapy for the prevention of suicide attempts: A randomized controlled trial. *JAMA.* 2005;294(5):563–570. doi:10.1001/jama.294.5.563

Brown S, Iqbal Z, Burbidge F, Sajjad A, Reeve M, Ayres V, Melling R, Jobes D. Embedding an evidence-based model for suicide prevention in the national health service: A service improvement initiative. *Int J Environ Res Public Health.* 2020;17:4920.

Bryan CJ, Bryan AO, May AM, Klonsky ED. Trajectories of suicide ideation, non-suicidal self-injury, and suicide attempts in a nonclinical sample of military personnel and veterans. *Suicide Life Threat Behav*. 2015;45(3):315–325. doi:10.1111/sltb.12127

Buchman JM. *Rehearsing pain: Mental rehearsal and the ability to enact lethal self-harm* (dissertation). Florida: Florida State University; 2015.

Burns A, Warner J. *Better access to mental health services for older people*. 2015. www.england.nhs.uk/blog/mh-better-access

Burrows S, Auger N, Gamache P, St-Laurent D, Hamel D. Influence of social and material individual and area deprivation on suicide mortality among 2.7 million Canadians: A prospective study. *BMC Public Health*. 2011;11:577. doi:10.1186/1471-2458-11-577

Carroll R, Metcalfe C, Gunnell D. Hospital presenting self-harm and risk of fatal and non-fatal repetition: Systematic review and meta-analysis. *PLoS One*. 2014 Feb 28;9(2):e89944. doi:10.1371/journal.pone.0089944

Carter G, Milner A, McGill K, Pirkis J, Kapur N, Spittal M. Predicting suicidal behaviours using clinical instruments: Systematic review and meta-analysis of positive predictive values for risk scales. *Br J Psychiatry*. 2017;210:387–395.

Cavanagh JT, Carson AJ, Sharpe M, Lawrie SM. Psychological autopsy studies of suicide: A systematic review. *Psychol Med*. 2003;33(3):395–405. doi:10.1017/s0033291702006943

Centre for Mental Health. *Preventing prison suicide: Staff perspectives*. 2017. ISBN: 978-1-911114-14-7

Centre for Mental Health. *Strengthening the front line*. Investing in primary care for effective suicide prevention April 2019.

Cerel J, Brown MM, Maple M, Singleton M, van de Venne J, Moore M, Flaherty C. How many people are exposed to suicide? not six. *Suicide Life Threat Behav*. 2019;49(2): 529–534. doi:10.1111/sltb.12450

Cerel J, Maple M, van de Venne J, Moore M, Flaherty C, Brown M. Exposure to suicide in the community: Prevalence and correlates in one U.S. state. *Public Health Rep*. 2016;131(1):100–107. doi:10.1177/003335491613100116

Chan MK, Bhatti H, Meader N, Stockton S, Evans J, O'Connor RC, Kapur N, Kendall T. Predicting suicide following self-harm: Systematic review of risk factors and risk scales. *Br J Psychiatry*. 2016;209(4):277–283. doi:10.1192/bjp.bp.115.170050

Cheng AT, Chen TH, Chen CC, Jenkins R. Psychosocial and psychiatric risk factors for suicide. Case-control psychological autopsy study. *Br J Psychiatry*. 2000;177:360–365. doi:10.1192/bjp.177.4.360

Cheng AT, Hawton K, Lee CT, Chen TH. The influence of media reporting of the suicide of a celebrity on suicide rates: A population-based study. *Int J Epidemiol*. 2007;36(6):1229–1234. doi:10.1093/ije/dym196

Chesney E, Goodwin GM, Fazel S. Risks of all-cause and suicide mortality in mental disorders: A meta-review. *World Psychiatry*. 2014;13(2):153–160. doi:10.1002/wps.20128

Choi NG, DiNitto DM, Marti CN, Segal SP. Adverse childhood experiences and suicide attempts among those with mental and substance use disorders. *Child Abuse Negl*. 2017;69:252–262. doi:10.1016/j.chiabu.2017.04.024

Chung DT, Ryan CJ, Hadzi-Pavlovic D, Singh SP, Stanton C, Large MM. Suicide Rates After Discharge From Psychiatric Facilities: A Systematic Review and Meta-analysis. *JAMA Psychiatry*. 2017;74(7):694-702. doi:10.1001/jamapsychiatry.2017.1044

Cole-King A, Green G, Gas, L, Hines K, Platt S. Suicide mitigation: A compassionate approach to suicide prevention. *Advances in Psychiatric Treatment*. 2013;19:276–283. doi:10.1192/apt.bp.110.008763

Cole-King A, Lepping P. Suicide mitigation: Time for a more realistic approach. *Br J Gen Pract*. 2010;60(570):e1–e3. doi:10.3399/bjgp10X482022

Cole-King A, Platt S. Suicide prevention for physicians: Identification, intervention and mitigation of risk. *Medicine*. 2017;45(3):131–134.

Comtois KA, Jobes DA, S O'Connor S, Atkins DC, Janis K, E Chessen C, Landes SJ, Holen A, Yuodelis-Flores C. Collaborative assessment and management of suicidality (CAMS): Feasibility trial for next-day appointment services. *Depress Anxiety*. 2011;28(11):963–972. doi:10.1002/da.20895

Conwell Y, Van Orden K, Caine ED. Suicide in older adults. *Psychiatr Clin North Am*. 2011;34(2):451–468. doi:10.1016/j.psc.2011.02.00

Cooper J, Kapur N, Webb R, Lawlor M, Guthrie E, Mackway-Jones K, Appleby L. Suicide after deliberate self-harm: A 4-year cohort study. *Am J Psychiatry*. 2005;162(2): 297–303. doi:10.1176/appi.ajp.162.2.297

Corrigan P. How stigma interferes with mental health care. *Am Psychol*. 2004;59(7): 614–625. doi:10.1037/0003-066X.59.7.614

Crawford M. Suicide following discharge from in-patient psychiatric care. *Advances in Psychiatric Treatment*. 2004;10(6), 434–438. doi:10.1192/apt.10.6.434
Cuijpers P, Berking M, Andersson G, Quigley L, Kleiboer A, Dobson KS. A meta-analysis of cognitive-behavioural therapy for adult depression, alone and in comparison with other treatments. *Can J Psychiatry*. 2013;58(7):376–385. doi:10.1177/070674371305800702
Cummings NA, Cummings JL. *Refocused psychotherapy as the first line intervention in behavioral health*. New York: Routledge; 2012.
Czyz EK, Horwitz AG, Eisenberg D, Kramer A, King CA. Self-reported barriers to professional help seeking among college students at elevated risk for suicide. *J Am Coll Health*. 2013;61(7):398–406. doi:10.1080/07448481.2013.820731
Czyz EK, Liu Z, King CA. Social connectedness and one-year trajectories among suicidal adolescents following psychiatric hospitalization. *J Clin Child Adolesc Psychol*. 2012;41(2):214–226. doi:10.1080/15374416.2012.651998
Daigle MS. Suicide prevention through means restriction: Assessing the risk of substitution. A critical review and synthesis. *Accid Anal Prev*. 2005;37(4):625–632. doi:10.1016/j.aap.2005.03.004
Dazzi T, Gribble R, Wessely S, Fear NT. Does asking about suicide and related behaviours induce suicidal ideation? What is the evidence? *Psychol Med*. 2014;44(16):3361–3363. doi:10.1017/S0033291714001299
Department of Health. *Safety First: Five Year Report of The Confidential Inquiry into Suicide and Homicide by People with Mental Illness*. London: Department of Health; 2001.
Department of Health. *Best practice in managing risk*. London: Department of Health; 2007.
Department of Health. *Preventing suicide in England: A cross-government outcomes strategy to save lives*. London: Department of Health; 2012.
Di Ceglie D. Gender identity disorder in young people. *Advances in Psychiatric Treatment*. 2000;6:458–466.
Dougall N, Lambert P, Maxwell M, Dawson A, Sinnott R, McCafferty S, Morris C, Clark D, Springbett A. Deaths by suicide and their relationship with general and psychiatric hospital discharge: 30-year record linkage study. *Br J Psychiatry*. 2014;204:267–273. doi:10.1192/bjp.bp.112.122374
Esang M, Ahmed S. A closer look at substance use and suicide. *Am J Psychiatry Resid*. 2018;13:6–8. doi:10.1176/appi.ajp-rj.2018.130603
Fawcett J, Clark DC, Busch KA. Assessing and treating the patient at risk for suicide. *Psychiatr Ann*. 1993;23:244–255.
Fazel S, Runeson B. Suicide. *N Engl J Med*. 2020;382(3):266–274. doi:10.1056/NEJMra1902944
Felton A, Wright N, Stacey G. Therapeutic risk-taking: A justifiable choice. *B J Psych Advances*. 2017;23:81–88. doi:10.1192/apt.bp.115.015701
Fleischmann A, Bertolote JM, Wasserman D, De Leo D, Bolhari J, Botega NJ, De Silva D, Phillips M, Vijayakumar L, Värnik A, Schlebusch L, Thanh HT. Effectiveness of brief intervention and contact for suicide attempters: A randomized controlled trial in five countries. *Bull World Health Organ*. 2008;86(9):703–709. doi:10.2471/blt.07.046995
Ford K, Bellis MA, Hughes K, Barton ER, Newbury A. Adverse childhood experiences: A retrospective study to understand their associations with lifetime mental health diagnosis, self-harm or suicide attempt, and current low mental wellbeing in a male Welsh prison population. *Health Justice*. 2020;8(1):13. doi:10.1186/s40352-020-00115-5
Foster T, Gillespie K, McClelland R. Mental disorders and suicide in Northern Ireland. *Br J Psychiatry*. 1997;170:447–452. doi:10.1192/bjp.170.5.447
Franklin JC, Ribeiro JD, Fox KR, Bentley KH, Kleiman EM, Huang X, Musacchio KM, Jaroszewski AC, Chang BP, Nock MK. Risk factors for suicidal thoughts and behaviors: A meta-analysis of 50 years of research. Psychol Bull. 2017 Feb;143(2):187-232. doi: 10.1037/bul0000084. Epub 2016 Nov 14. PMID: 27841450.

Frey LM, Drapeau CW, Fulginiti A, Oexle N, Stage DL, Sheehan L, Cerel J, Moore M. Recipients of suicide-related disclosure: The link between disclosure and posttraumatic growth for suicide attempt survivors. *Int J Environ Res Public Health*. 2019;16(20):3815. doi:10.3390/ijerph16203815

Galway KJ, Murphy AW, O'Reilly D, O'Dowd T, O'Neill C, Shryane E, Steele K, Bury G, Gilliland A, Kelly A. Perceived and reported access to the general practitioner: An international comparison of universal access and mixed private/public systems. *Ir Med J*. 2007;100(6):494–497.

Gilbert P, Allan S. The role of defeat and entrapment (arrested flight) in depression: An exploration of an evolutionary view. *Psychol Med*. 1998;28(3):585–598. doi:10.1017/s0033291798006710

Gould MS, Marrocco FA, Kleinman M, Thomas JG, Mostkoff K, Cote J, Davies M. Evaluating iatrogenic risk of youth suicide screening programs: A randomized controlled trial. *JAMA*. 2005;293(13):1635–1643. doi:10.1001/jama.293.13.163

Graney J, Hunt IM, Quinlivan L, Rodway C, Turnbull P, Gianatsi M, Appleby L, Kapur N. Suicide risk assessment in UK mental health services: a national mixed-methods study. *Lancet Psychiatry*. 2020 Nov 10:S2215-0366(20)30381-3. doi: 10.1016/S2215-0366(20)30381-3. Epub ahead of print. PMID: 33189221.

Hall RC, Platt DE, Hall RC. Suicide risk assessment: A review of risk factors for suicide in 100 patients who made severe suicide attempts. Evaluation of suicide risk in a time of managed care. *Psychosomatics*. 1999;40(1):18–27. doi:10.1016/S0033-3182(99)71267-3

Harris EC, Barraclough B. Suicide as an outcome for mental disorders. A meta-analysis. *Br J Psychiatry*. 1997;170:205–228. doi:10.1192/bjp.170.3.205

Harwitz D, Ravizza L. Suicide and depression. *Emerg Med Clin North Am*. 2000;18(2): 263–271. doi:10.1016/s0733-8627(05)70123-1

Hawgood J, De Leo D. Suicide prediction–A shift in paradigm is needed. *Crisis*. 2016;37(4):251–255. doi:10.1027/0227-5910/a000440

Hawton K, Harriss L, Hall S, Simkin S, Bale E, Bond A. Deliberate self-harm in Oxford, 1990–2000: A time of change in patient characteristics. *Psychol Med*. 2003;33(6): 987–995. doi:10.1017/s0033291703007943

Hawton K, Sutton L, Haw C, Sinclair J, Deeks JJ. Schizophrenia and suicide: Systematic review of risk factors. *Br J Psychiatry*. 2005;187:9–20. doi:10.1192/bjp.187.1.9

Hawton K, Witt KG, Taylor Salisbury TL, Arensman E, Gunnell D, Hazell P, Townsend E, van Heeringen K. Psychosocial interventions for self-harm in adults. *Cochrane Database Syst Rev*. 2016;(5):CD012189. doi:10.1002/14651858.CD012189

Hawton K, Zahl D, Weatherall R. Suicide following deliberate self-harm: Long-term follow-up of patients who presented to a general hospital. *Br J Psychiatry*. 2003;182: 537–542. doi:10.1192/bjp.182.6.537

Hill RM, Pettit JW. Perceived burdensomeness and suicide-related behaviors in clinical samples: Current evidence and future directions. *J Clin Psychol*. 2014;70(7):631–643. doi:10.1002/jclp.22071

HM Government. *Preventing suicide in England: Third progress report of the cross-government outcomes strategy to save lives*. January 2017.

Hufford MR. Alcohol and suicidal behavior. *Clin Psychol Rev*. 2001;21(5):797–811. doi:10.1016/s0272-7358(00)00070-2

Hughes K, Bellis MA, Hardcastle KA, Sethi D, Butchart A, Mikton C, Jones L, Dunne MP The effect of multiple adverse childhood experiences on health: A systematic review and meta-analysis. *Lancet Public Health*. 2017;2(8):e356–e366. doi:10.1016/S2468-2667(17)30118-4

Hunter C, Chantler K, Kapur N, Cooper J. Service user perspectives on psychosocial assessment following self-harm and its impact on further help-seeking: A qualitative study. *J Affect Disord*. 2013;145(3):315–323. doi:10.1016/j.jad.2012.08.009

Isometsä ET, Heikkinen ME, Marttunen MJ, Henriksson MM, Aro HM, Lönnqvist JK. The last appointment before suicide: Is suicide intent communicated? *Am J Psychiatry*. 1995;152(6):919–922. doi:10.1176/ajp.152.6.919

Jacobson CM, Muehlenkamp JJ, Miller AL, Turner JB. Psychiatric impairment among adolescents engaging in different types of deliberate self-harm. *J Clin Child Adolesc Psychol*. 2008;37(2):363–375. doi:10.1080/15374410801955771

Jakobsen JC, Katakam KK, Schou A, Hellmuth SG, Stallknecht SE, Leth-Møller K, Iversen M, Banke MB, Petersen IJ, Klingenberg SL, Krogh J, Ebert SE, Timm A, Lindschou J, Gluud C. Selective serotonin reuptake inhibitors versus placebo in patients with major depressive disorder. A systematic review with meta-analysis and Trial Sequential Analysis. *BMC Psychiatry*. 2017;17(1):58. doi:10.1186/s12888-016-1173-2

Jobes DA, Mann RE. Reasons for living versus reasons for dying: Examining the internal debate of suicide. *Suicide Life Threat Behav*. 1999;29(2):97–104.

Johnson J, Tarrier N, Gooding P. An investigation of aspects of the cry of pain model of suicide risk: The role of defeat in impairing memory. *Behav Res Ther*. 2008;46(8):968–975. doi:10.1016/j.brat.2008.04.007

Joiner TE. *Why people die by suicide*. Cambridge, MA: Harvard University Press; 2005.

Joiner TE Jr, Pettit JW, Walker RL, Voelz ZR, Cruz J, Rudd MD, Lester D. Perceived burdensomeness and suicidality: Two studies on the suicide notes of those attempting and those completing suicide. *J Soc Clin Psychol*. 2002;21(5):531–545. doi:10.1521/jscp.21.5.531.22624

Kapur N, Cooper J, O'Connor RC, Hawton K. Non-suicidal self-injury v. attempted suicide: New diagnosis or false dichotomy? *Br J Psychiatry*. 2013;202(5):326–328. doi:10.1192/bjp.bp.112.116111

Kapur N, Steeg S, Turnbull P, Webb R, Bergen H, Hawton K, Geulayov G Townsend E, Ness J, Waters K, Cooper J. Hospital management of suicidal behaviour and subsequent mortality: A prospective cohort study. *Lancet Psychiatry*. 2015;2(9):809–816. doi:10.1016/S2215-0366(15)00169-8

Kessler RC, Borges G, Walters EE. Prevalence of and risk factors for lifetime suicide attempts in the national comorbidity survey. *Arch Gen Psychiatry*. 1999;56(7):617–626. doi:10.1001/archpsyc.56.7.617

King EA, Baldwin DS, Sinclair JM, Baker NG, Campbell MJ, Thompson C. The Wessex Recent In-Patient Suicide Study, 1. Case-control study of 234 recently discharged psychiatric patient suicides. *Br J Psychiatry*. 2001;178:531-6. doi: 10.1192/bjp.178.6.531. PMID: 11388969.

Kleiman EM, Liu RT. Social support as a protective factor in suicide: Findings from two nationally representative samples. *J Affect Disord*. 2013;150(2):540–545. doi:10.1016/j.jad.2013.01.033

Kleiman EM, Nock MK. Real-time assessment of suicidal thoughts and behaviors. *Curr Opin Psychol*. 2018;22:33–37. doi:10.1016/j.copsyc.2017.07.026

Kleiman EM, Turner BJ, Fedor S, Beale EE, Huffman JC, Nock MK. Examination of real-time fluctuations in suicidal ideation and its risk factors: Results from two ecological momentary assessment studies. *J Abnorm Psychol*. 2017;126(6):726–738. doi:10.1037/abn0000273

Klonsky ED, May AM, Glenn CR. The relationship between non-suicidal self-injury and attempted suicide: Converging evidence from four samples. *J Abnorm Psychol*. 2013;122(1):231–237. doi:10.1037/a0030278

Klonsky ED, May AM, Saffer BY. Suicide, suicide attempts, and suicidal ideation. *Annu Rev Clin Psychol*. 2016;12:307–330. doi:10.1146/annurev-clinpsy-021815-093204

Knight M, Bunch K, Tuffnell D, Jayakody H, Shakespeare J, Kotnis R, Kenyon S, Kurinczuk JJ (Eds.) on behalf of MBRRACE-UK. Saving Lives, Improving Mothers' Care - Lessons learned to inform maternity care from the UK and Ireland Confidential Enquiries into Maternal Deaths and Morbidity 2014-16. Oxford: National Perinatal Epidemiology Unit, University of Oxford 2018

Large M, Sharma S, Cannon E, Ryan C, Nielssen O. Risk factors for suicide within a year of discharge from psychiatric hospital: A systematic meta-analysis. *Aust N Z J Psychiatry*. 2011;45(8):619–628. doi:10.3109/00048674.2011.590465

Large MM, Ryan CJ, Carter G, Kapur N. Can we usefully stratify patients according to suicide risk? *BMJ*. 2017;359:j4627. doi:10.1136/bmj.j4627

Leavey K, Hawkins R. Is cognitive behavioural therapy effective in reducing suicidal ideation and behaviour when delivered face-to-face or via e-health? A systematic review and meta-analysis. *Cogn Behav Ther*. 2017;46(5):353–374. doi:10.1080/16506073.2017.1332095

Leboyer M, Slama F, Siever L, Bellivier F. Suicidal disorders: A nosological entity per se?. *Am J Med Genet C Semin Med Genet*. 2005;133C(1):3–7. doi:10.1002/ajmg.c.30040

Lewis G, Hawton K, Jones P. Strategies for preventing suicide. *Br J Psychiatry*. 1997;171:351–354.

Lewis G, Sloggett A. Suicide, deprivation, and unemployment: Record linkage study. *BMJ*. 1998;317(7168):1283–1286. doi:10.1136/bmj.317.7168.1283

Linehan MM. *Cognitive-behavioral treatment of borderline personality disorder. Diagnosis and treatment of mental disorders*. New York: Guilford Press; 1993.

Luoma JB, Martin CE, Pearson JL. Contact with mental health and primary care providers before suicide: A review of the evidence. *Am J Psychiatry*. 2002;159(6):909–916. doi:10.1176/appi.ajp.159.6.909

MacLeod AK, Rose GS, Williams JMG. Components of hopelessness about the future in parasuicide. *Cogn Ther Res*. 1993;(17):441–455. doi:10.1007/BF01173056

Mann JJ, Apter A, Bertolote J, Beautrais A, Currier D, Haas A, Hegerl U, Lonnqvist J, Malone K, Marusic A, Mehlum L, Patton G, Phillips M, Rutz W, Rihmer Z, Schmidtke A, Shaffer D, Silverman M, Takahashi Y, Varnik A, Wasserman D, Yip P, Hendin H. Suicide prevention strategies: A systematic review. *JAMA*. 2005;294(16): 2064–2074. doi:10.1001/jama.294.16.2064

Mars B, Heron J, Klonsky ED, Moran P, O'Connor RC, Tilling K, Wilkinson P, Gunnell D. Predictors of future suicide attempt among adolescents with suicidal thoughts or non-suicidal self-harm: A population-based birth cohort study. *Lancet Psychiatry*. 2019;6(4):327–337. doi:10.1016/S2215-0366(19)30030-6

Matthews K, Milne S, Ashcroft GW. Role of doctors in the prevention of suicide: The final consultation. *Br J Gen Pract*. 1994;44(385):345–348.

Maulik PK, Eaton WW, Bradshaw CP. The effect of social networks and social support on mental health services use, following a life event, among the Baltimore Epidemiologic Catchment Area cohort. *J Behav Health Serv Res*. 2011;38(1):29–50. doi:10.1007/s11414-009-9205-z

May PA, Van Winkle NW, Williams MB, McFeeley PJ, DeBruyn LM, Serna P. Alcohol and suicide death among American Indians of New Mexico: 1980–1998. *Suicide Life Threat Behav*. 2002;32(3):240–255. doi:10.1521/suli.32.3.240.22172

Mays D. Structured assessment methods may improve suicide prediction. *Psychiatr Ann*. 2004;34:367–372.

Méndez-Bustos P, Calati R, Rubio-Ramírez F, Olié E, Courtet P, Lopez-Castroman J. Effectiveness of psychotherapy on suicidal risk: A systematic review of observational studies. *Front Psychol*. 2019;10:277. doi:10.3389/fpsyg.2019.00277

Mental Health and wellbeing in England: Adult Psychiatric Morbidity Survey 2014. https://files.digital.nhs.uk/pdf/q/3/mental_health_and_wellbeing_in_england_full_report.pdf (accessed on 25 January 2020).

Mergl R, Koburger N, Heinrichs K, Székely A, Tóth MD, Coyne J, Quintão S, Arensman E, Coffey C, Maxwell M, Värnik A, van Audenhove C, McDaid D, Sarchiapone M, Schmidtke A, Genz A, Gusmão R, Hegerl U. What are reasons for the large gender differences in the lethality of suicidal acts? An epidemiological analysis in four European countries. *PLoS One*. 2015;10(7): e0129062. doi:10.1371/journal.pone.0129062

Meyer RE, Salzman C, Youngstrom EA, Clayton PJ, Goodwin FK, Mann JJ, Alphs LD, Broich K, Goodman WK, Greden JF, Meltzer HY, Normand SL, Posner K, Shaffer D,

Oquendo MA, Stanley B, Trivedi MH, Turecki G, Beasley CM Jr, Beautrais AL, Bridge JA, Brown GK, Revicki DA, Ryan ND, Sheehan DV. Suicidality and risk of suicide-definition, drug safety concerns, and a necessary target for drug development: A consensus statement. *J Clin Psychiatry*. 2010;71(8):e1–e21. doi:10.4088/JCP.10cs06070blu

Miller AB, Esposito-Smythers C, Leichtweis RN. Role of social support in adolescent suicidal ideation and suicide attempts. *J Adolesc Health*. 2015;56(3):286–292. doi:10.1016/j.jadohealth.2014.10.265

Miller IW, Camargo CA Jr, Arias SA, et al; ED-SAFE Investigators. Suicide prevention in an emergency department population: The ED-SAFE study. *JAMA Psychiatry*. 2017;74:563–570.

Monti K, Cedereke M, Ojehagen A. Treatment attendance and suicidal behavior 1 month and 3 months after a suicide attempt: A comparison between two samples. *Archiv Suicide Res*. 2003;7(2):167–174.

Morgan C, Webb RT, Carr MJ, Kontopantelis E, Chew-Graham CA, Kapur N, Ashcroft DM. Self-harm in a primary care cohort of older people: Incidence, clinical management, and risk of suicide and other causes of death. *Lancet Psychiatry*. 2018;5(11): 905–912. doi:10.1016/S2215-0366(18)30348-1

Motto JA, Bostrom AG. A randomized controlled trial of post-crisis suicide prevention. *Psychiatr Serv*. 2001;52(6):828–833. doi:10.1176/appi.ps.52.6.828

National Collaborating Centre for Mental Health (NCCMH). *Self-harm and suicide prevention competence framework: Community and public health*. London: October 2018.

National Confidential Inquiry into Suicide and Safety in Mental Health (NCISH). *National confidential inquiry into suicide and homicide by people with mental illness: Suicide in primary care in England: 2002–2011*. Manchester: University of Manchester; 2014.

National Institute for Health and Care Excellence (NICE). *Preventing suicide in community and custodial settings NICE guideline* [NG105]. London: September 2018.

National Institute for Health and Care Excellence (NICE). *Self-Harm. The short-term physical management and secondary prevention of self-harm in primary and secondary care*. London: NICE; 2004.

National Institute for Health and Care Excellence (NICE). *Self-harm in over 8s: Long-term management. Clinical guideline*. London: NICE, 2011. https://www.nice.org.uk/guidance/cg133/resources/selfharm-in-over-8s-longtermmanagement-pdf-35109508689349

National Institute for Health and Care Excellence (NICE). *Suicide prevention Quality standard [QS189]*. September 2019. NICE CG28. https://www.nice.org.uk/guidance/qs189/documents/briefing-paper

NCISH. *The assessment of clinical risk in mental health services*. Manchester: University of Manchester; 2018.

NCISH. *Annual report 2019: England, Northern Ireland, Scotland and Wales*. Manchester: University of Manchester; 2019.

Mental Health Task Force. *The five year forward view for mental health: A report from the independent Mental Health Taskforce to the NHS in England*. London: NHS England; 2016. https://www.england.nhs.uk/wp-content/uploads/2016/02/Mental-Health-Taskforce-FYFVfinal.pdf

NHS England. 2018. https://www.england.nhs.uk/blog/tackling-the-root-causes-of-suicide/

Niederkrotenthaler T, Reidenberg DJ, Till B, Gould MS. Increasing help-seeking and referrals for individuals at risk for suicide by decreasing stigma: The role of mass media. *Am J Prev Med*. 2014;47(3 Suppl 2):S235–S243. doi:10.1016/j.amepre.2014.06.010

Nock MK, Borges G, Bromet EJ, Alonso J, Angermeyer M, Beautrais A, Bruffaerts R, Chiu WT, de Girolamo G, Gluzman S, de Graaf R, Gureje O, Haro JM, Huang Y, Karam E, Kessler RC, Lepine JP, Levinson D, Medina-Mora ME, Ono Y, Posada-Villa J, Williams D. Cross-national prevalence and risk factors for suicidal ideation, plans and attempts. *Br J Psychiatry*. 2008;192(2):98–105. doi:10.1192/bjp.bp.107.040113

Nock MK, Hwang I, Sampson NA, Kessler RC. Mental disorders, comorbidity and suicidal behavior: Results from the National Comorbidity Survey Replication. *Mol Psychiatry.* 2010;15(8):868–876. doi:10.1038/mp.2009.29

Nock MK, Prinstein MJ, Sterba SK. Revealing the form and function of self-injurious thoughts and behaviors: A real-time ecological assessment study among adolescents and young adults. *J Abnorm Psychol.* 2009;118(4):816–827. doi:10.1037/a0016948

Nordt C, Warnke I, Seifritz E, Kawohl W. Modelling suicide and unemployment: A longitudinal analysis covering 63 countries, 2000–2011. *Lancet Psychiatry.* 2015;2(3): 239–245. doi:10.1016/S2215-0366(14)00118-7

Oates A. *Learning from suicide-related claims: A thematic review of NHS resolution data.* London: NHS Resolution; 2018.

O'Connor RC, Kirtley OJ. The integrated motivational-volitional model of suicidal behaviour. *Philos Trans R Soc Lond B Biol Sci.* 2018;373(1754):20170268. doi:10.1098/rstb.2017.0268

O'Connor RC, Nock MK. The psychology of suicidal behaviour. *Lancet Psychiatry.* 2014;1(1):73–85. doi:10.1016/S2215-0366(14)70222-6

O'Connor RC, Platt S, Gordon J. Eds. *International handbook of suicide prevention: Research, policy and practice.* Oxford: Wiley-Blackwell; 2011. doi:10.1002/9781119998556

O'Connor SS, Comtois KA, Wang J, Russo J, Peterson R, Lapping-Carr L, Zatzick D. The development and implementation of a brief intervention for medically admitted suicide attempt survivors. *Gen Hosp Psychiatry.* 2015;37(5):427–433. doi:10.1016/j.genhosppsych.2015.05.001

O'Connor SS, Mcclay MM, Choudhry S, et al. Pilot randomized clinical trial of the teachable moment brief intervention for hospitalized suicide attempt survivors. *Gen Hosp Psychiatry.* 2020;63:111–118. doi:10.1016/j.genhosppsych.2018.08.001

Office for National Statistics. Suicides by age, sex, and IMD quintile, England and Wales, 2010 to 2019 registrations combined. September 2020.

Office for National Statistics. Suicides in the UK: 2017 registrations. Updated 2018.

Office for National Statistics. *Leading causes of death, UK: 2001 to 2018.* March 2020. https://www.ons.gov.uk/releases/leadingcausesofdeathuk

Office for National Statistics. *Who is most at risk of suicide? Analysis and explanation of the contributory risks of suicide.* September 2017.

Owens D, Horrocks J, House A. Fatal and non-fatal repetition of self-harm. Systematic review. *Br J Psychiatry.* 2002;181:193–199. doi:10.1192/bjp.181.3.193

Padmanathan P, Hall K, Moran P, Jones HE, Gunnell D, Carlisle V, Lingford-Hughes A, Hickman M. Prevention of suicide and reduction of self-harm among people with substance use disorder: A systematic review and meta-analysis of randomised controlled trials. *Compr Psychiatry.* 2020;96:152135. doi:10.1016/j.comppsych.2019.152135

Paris J. Predicting and preventing suicide: Do we know enough to do either? *Harv Rev Psychiatry.* 2006;14(5):233–240. doi:10.1080/10673220600968662

Parra-Uribe I, Blasco-Fontecilla H, Garcia-Parés G, Martínez-Naval L, Valero-Coppin O, Cebrià-Meca A, Oquendo MA, Palao-Vidal D. Risk of re-attempts and suicide death after a suicide attempt: A survival analysis. BMC Psychiatry. 2017 May 4;17(1):163. doi: 10.1186/s12888-017-1317-z. PMID: 28472923; PMCID: PMC5415954.

Pearson A, Saini P, Da Cruz D, Miles C, While D, Swinson N, Williams A, Shaw J, Appleby L, Kapur N. Primary care contact prior to suicide in individuals with mental illness. *Br J Gen Pract.* 2009;59(568):825–832. doi:10.3399/bjgp09X472881

Pitman AL, Osborn DP, Rantell K, King MB. Bereavement by suicide as a risk factor for suicide attempt: A cross-sectional national UK-wide study of 3432 young bereaved adults. *BMJ Open.* 2016;6(1):e009948. doi:10.1136/bmjopen-2015-009948

Pompili M. Critical appraisal of major depression with suicidal ideation. *Ann Gen Psychiatry.* 2019;18:7. doi:10.1186/s12991-019-0232-8

Preventing suicide: A global imperative. 2014. https://www.who.int/mental_health/suicideprevention/world_report_2014/en/

Qin P, Mortensen PB. The impact of parental status on the risk of completed suicide. *Arch Gen Psychiatry*. 2003;60(8):797–802. doi:10.1001/archpsyc.60.8.797

Qin P, Nordentoft M. Suicide risk in relation to psychiatric hospitalization: evidence based on longitudinal registers. *Arch Gen Psychiatry*. 2005;62(4):427-32. doi: 10.1001/archpsyc.62.4.427. PMID: 15809410.

Quinlivan L, Cooper J, Davies L, Hawton K, Gunnell D, Kapur N. Which are the most useful scales for predicting repeat self-harm? A systematic review evaluating risk scales using measures of diagnostic accuracy. *BMJ Open*. 2016;6(2):e009297. doi:10.1136/bmjopen-2015-009297

Rahman MS, Gupta S, While D, Windfuhr K, Shaw J, Kapur N, Appleby L. *Quality of risk assessment prior to suicide and homicide: A pilot study*. Manchester: University of Manchester; 2013. http://documents.manchester.ac.uk/display.aspx?DocID=37580

Rihmer Z. Depression and suicidal behaviour. In: O'Connor RC, Platt S, Gordon J, editors. *International handbook of suicide prevention: Research, policy and practice*. Chichester: John Wiley & Sons, Ltd.; 2011. pp. 181–198.

Rihmer Z, Rutz W, Pihlgren H. Depression and suicide on Gotland. An intensive study of all suicides before and after a depression-training programme for general practitioners. *J Affect Disord*. 1995;35(4):147–152. doi:10.1016/0165-0327(95)00055-0

Robins E, Gassner S, Kayes J, Wilkinson RH Jr, Murphy GE. The communication of suicidal intent: A study of 134 consecutive cases of successful (completed) suicide. *Am J Psychiatry*. 1959;115:724–733.

Royal College of Psychiatry. *Self-harm, suicide and risk*. Report CR158. London: RCP; June 2010.

Rudd MD. Fluid vulnerability theory: A cognitive approach to understanding the process of acute and chronic suicide risk. In: Ellis TE, editor. *Cognition and suicide: Theory, research, and therapy*. Vol. 2006. Washington, DC: American Psychological Association; 2006. pp. 355–360.

Rudd MD. The suicidal mode: A cognitive-behavioral model of suicidality. *Suicide Life Threat Behav*. 2000;30(1):18–33.

Rudd MD, Berman AL, Joiner TE Jr, Nock MK, Silverman MM, Mandrusiak M, Van Orden K, Witte T. Warning signs for suicide: Theory, research, and clinical applications. *Suicide Life Threat Behav*. 2006;36(3):255–262. doi:10.1521/suli.2006.36.3.255

Rudd MD, Bryan CJ, Wertenberger EG, et al. Brief cognitive-behavioral therapy effects on post-treatment suicide attempts in a military sample: Results of a randomized clinical trial with 2-year follow-up. *Am J Psychiatry*. 2015;172(5):441–449. doi:10.1176/appi.ajp.2014.14070843

Ryan C, Huebner D, Diaz RM, Sanchez J. Family rejection as a predictor of negative health outcomes in white and Latino lesbian, gay, and bisexual young adults. *Pediatrics*. 2009;123(1):346–352. doi:10.1542/peds.2007-3524

Samaritans. *Dying from inequality. Socioeconomic disadvantage and suicidal behaviour*. UK: Summary Report; London: 2017.

Samaritans. *Men, suicide and society. Why disadvantaged men in mid-life die by suicide*. UK: Research Report; London: 2012.

Shea S. *Psychiatric interviewing. The art of understanding: A practical guide for psychiatrists, psychologists, counselors, social workers, nurses, and other mental health professionals, with online video modules*. 3rd ed. Elsevier; Edinburgh: 2016.

Sheehy N, O'Connor RC. Cognitive style and suicidal behaviour: Implications for therapeutic intervention, research lacunae and priorities. *British Journal of Guidance & Counselling*. 2002;30(4), 353–362.

Shen X, Hackworth J, McCabe H, Lovett L, Aumage J, O'Neil J, Bull M. Characteristics of suicide from 1998–2001 in metropolitan area. *Death Stud*. 2006;30(9):859–871. doi:10.1080/07481180600853074

Sher L. Alcohol consumption and suicide. *QJM*. 2006;99(1):57–61. doi:10.1093/qjmed/hci146

Shneidman ES. *Deaths of man*. New York: Quadrangle Books; 1972.

Shneidman ES. A psychological approach to suicide. In: VandenBos GR, Bryants BK, editors. *Cataclysms, crises, and catastrophes: Psychology in action*. Washington, DC: American Psychological Association; 1987. pp. 147–183.

Shneidman ES. Suicide as psychache. *J Nerv Ment Dis.* 1993;181(3):145–147. doi:10.1097/00005053-199303000-00001

Silverman MM, Berman AL, Sanddal ND, O'Carroll PW, Joiner TE. Rebuilding the tower of Babel: A revised nomenclature for the study of suicide and suicidal behaviors. Part 1: Background, rationale, and methodology. *Suicide Life Threat Behav.* 2007;37(3): 248–263. doi:10.1521/suli.2007.37.3.248

Simon RI. Suicide rehearsals: A high-risk psychiatric emergency; patients who rehearse a suicide provide opportunities for clinical interventions. *Curr Psychiatr.* 2012;11(7):28.

Sirdifield C, Brooker C, Marples R. Suicide and probation: A systematic review of the literature. *Forensic Sci Int: Mind and Law.* 2020;1:100012.

Soloff PH, Lynch KG, Kelly TM, Malone KM, Mann JJ. Characteristics of suicide attempts of patients with major depressive episode and borderline personality disorder: A comparative study. *Am J Psychiatry.* 2000;157(4):601–608. doi:10.1176/appi.ajp.157.4.601

Southern Health NHS Trust. *Positive risk-taking practical ways of working with risk "Whose risk is it anyway?"* March 2012. http://staff.southernhealth.nhs.uk/_resources/assets/inline/full/0/90051.pdf

Stanley B, Winchel R, Molcho A, Simeon D, Stanley M. Suicide and the self-harm continuum: Phenomenological and biochemical evidence. *Int Rev Psychiatry.* 1992;4:149–155.

Steeg S, Quinlivan L, Nowland R, Carroll R, Casey D, Clements C, Cooper J, Davies L, Knipe D, Ness J, O'Connor RC, Hawton K, Gunnell D, Kapur N. Accuracy of risk scales for predicting repeat self-harm and suicide: A multicentre, population-level cohort study using routine clinical data. *BMC Psychiatry.* 2018;18(1):113. doi:10.1186/s12888-018-1693-z

Stene-Larsen K, Reneflot A. Contact with primary and mental health care prior to suicide: A systematic review of the literature from 2000 to 2017. *Scand J Public Health.* 2019;47(1):9–17. doi:10.1177/1403494817746274

Stone DM, Simon TR, Fowler KA, Kegler SR, Yuan K, Holland KM, Ivey-Stephenson AZ, Crosby AE. Vital signs: Trends in state suicide rates - United States, 1999–2016 and circumstances contributing to suicide -27 states, 2015. *MMWR Morb Mortal Wkly Rep.* 2018;67(22):617–624. doi:10.15585/mmwr.mm6722a1

Suicide Prevention Resource Center, Rodgers, P. *Understanding risk and protective factors for suicide: A primer for preventing suicide.* Newton, MA: Education Development Center Inc; 2011.

Suominen K, Isometsä E, Suokas J, Haukka J, Achte K, Lönnqvist J. Completed suicide after a suicide attempt: A 37-year follow-up study. *Am J Psychiatry.* 2004;161(3): 562–563. doi:10.1176/appi.ajp.161.3.562

Thoits PA. Perceived social support and the voluntary, mixed, or pressured use of mental health services. *Soc Ment Health.* 2011;1(1):4–19.

Thompson MP, Kingree JB, Lamis D. Associations of adverse childhood experiences and suicidal behaviors in adulthood in a U.S. nationally representative sample. *Child Care Health Dev.* 2019;45(1):121–128. doi:10.1111/cch.12617

Turecki G, Brent DA. Suicide and suicidal behaviour. *Lancet.* 2016;387(10024):1227–1239. doi:10.1016/S0140-6736(15)00234-2

Vogel DL, Wade NG, Ascheman PL. Measuring perceptions of stigmatization by others for seeking psychological help: Reliability and validity of a new stigma scale with college students. *J Counsel Psychol.* 2009;56:301–308. doi: 10.1037/a0014903

Weems C, Victor C, McCurdy B, Scozzafava M. *Increased risk of suicide due to economic and social impacts of social distancing measures to address the covid-19 pandemic: A forecast.* 2020. doi:10.13140/RG.2.2.21601.45926

Westermeyer JF, Harrow M, Marengo JT. Risk for suicide in schizophrenia and other psychotic and nonpsychotic disorders. *J Nerv Ment Dis.* 1991;179(5):259–266. doi:10.1097/00005053-199105000-00003

Wetzel RD. Hopelessness, depression, and suicide intent. *Arch Gen Psychiatry.* 1976;33(9):1069–1073. doi:10.1001/archpsyc.1976.01770090059005

Williams JM. *The cry of pain.* London: Penguin; 1997.

Williams JM, Barnhofer T, Crane C, Beck AT. Problem solving deteriorates following mood challenge in formerly depressed patients with a history of suicidal ideation. *J Abnorm Psychol.* 2005;114(3):421–431. doi:10.1037/0021-843X.114.3.421

Williams JMG, Pollock LR. Psychological aspects of the suicidal process. In: van Heeringen K, editor. *Understanding suicidal behaviour.* Chichester: John Wiley and Sons; 2001. pp. 76–93.

Williams JMG, Pollock LR. The psychology of suicidal behaviour. In: Hawton K, van Heeringen K, editors. *The international handbook of suicide and attempted suicide.* Chichester: John Wiley and Sons Ltd; 2000. pp. 79–93. doi:10.1002/9780470698976.ch5

Windfuhr K, Kapur N. Suicide and mental illness: A clinical review of 15 years findings from the UK National Confidential Inquiry into Suicide. *Br Med Bull.* 2011;100: 101–121. doi:10.1093/bmb/ldr042

World Health Organisation (WHO). *Preventing suicide: A global imperative.* Geneva: World Health Organisation; 2014.

Worthington A, Rooney P, Hannan R. *The triangle of care, carers included: A guide to best practice in mental health care in England.* London: Carers Trust; 2013. https://professionals.carers.org/sites/default/files/thetriangleofcare_guidetobestpracticeinmentalhealthcare_engla nd.pdf

Wyllie C, Platt S, Brownlie J, Chandler A, Connolly S, Evans R, Kennelly B, Kirtley O, Moore G, O'Connor R and Scourfield J. *Men, suicide and society. Why disadvantaged men in mid-life die by suicide.* Surrey: Samaritans; 2012.

Zalsman G, Hawton K, Wasserman D, van Heeringen K, Arensman E, Sarchiapone M, Carli V, Höschl C, Barzilay R, Balazs J, Purebl G, Kahn JP, Sáiz PA, Lipsicas CB, Bobes J, Cozman D, Hegerl U, Zohar J. Suicide prevention strategies revisited: 10-year systematic review. *Lancet Psychiatry.* 2016;3(7):646–659. doi:10.1016/S2215-0366(16)30030-X

Websites

https://www.stayingsafe.net/
http://www.sprc.org/collegesanduniversities/strategic-planning
https://sites.manchester.ac.uk/ncish/
https://www.ons.gov.uk/peoplepopulationandcommunity/birthsdeathsandmarriages/deaths/bulletins/suicidesintheunitedkingdom/previousReleases

Part 2

Safety and Treatment Planning Principles

2.1 Suicide-focused interventions (SFIs) and protocols

Introduction

Conventional mental health approaches aim to reduce suicide risk by the effective treatment of the person's psychiatric disorder. However, there is little evidence to support this approach which leads to insufficient risk reduction. There is increasing evidence of psychological interventions reducing suicide risk (Institute of Medicine 2002). After a suicide attempt, psychotherapy may prevent subsequent attempts. One large study identified patients who attempted suicide and subsequently received either psychotherapy or standard care (Erlangsen et al 2015). Psychotherapy consisted of eight to ten individual sessions focused upon suicide prevention but was otherwise not standardised; different approaches were used, including cognitive behavioural therapy (CBT), problem-solving therapy (PST), dialectical behaviour therapy (DBT) or psychodynamic psychotherapy. During 20 years of follow-up, suicide deaths occurred in fewer patients who received psychotherapy rather than standard care (1.6% versus 2.2%). All-cause mortality was also lower in patients who received psychotherapy than standard care (6.9% versus 9.6%).

Most suicide-focused intervention (SFI) studies have assessed CBT interventions. A systematic review by Tarrier et al (2008) found CBT reduced suicide-related behaviour (i.e. death by suicide, suicide attempts, suicide intent and/or plans and ideation) in the three months following treatment. A significant treatment effect was found for adults (but not adolescents) and for individual CBT treatments when compared with minimal or no treatment controls. Even one-week internet-based CBT for depression reduces suicidal ideation (Watts et al 2012; Mewton & Andrews 2015). Mewton and Andrews (2016) reviewed 15 studies of CBT and concluded.

"This review identified evidence for the use of CBT in the reduction of both suicidal cognitions and behaviours. CBT is therefore a useful strategy in the prevention of suicidal cognitions and suicidal behaviours." Leavey and Hawkins (2017) concluded from their meta-analysis that

> There was a statistically significant small to medium effect for face-to-face delivered CBT in reducing suicidal ideation and behaviour, although there was significant heterogeneity between the included studies.

Multiple studies indicate that CBT can specifically reduce suicide attempts. A systematic review of ten randomised trials examined the use of CBT for people at risk for suicide and compared CBT with usual care (n > 1,200) in patients who attempted suicide. CBT reduced the risk of subsequent suicide attempts within six months of study entry by 50%, compared with various levels of treatment as usual, or TAU (Gøtzsche & Gøtzsche 2017). Group CBT for the prevention of repeated suicide attempts is currently being compared to individual supportive therapy in a multicentre randomised clinical trial (clinicaltrials.gov registration: NCT02664701).

Méndez-Bustos et al (2019) carried out a systematic review of observational studies for the effectiveness of psychotherapeutic interventions on suicidal risk. They found interventions lead to a 55% reduction in suicidal ideation and 37.5% reduction in attempts. The authors conclude helpful interventions are "not limited to CBT and DBT. Mindfulness-based strategies, integrative programs, CAMS, STEPPS or PS-CCI, just to mention some, are promising possibilities ... but it is not yet possible to identify the most effective/efficacious psychotherapeutic approach". Winter et al (2013) published a meta-review of 15 previous systematic reviews and meta-analyses of studies of counselling and psychotherapy with people at risk of suicide, including a meta-analysis of 67 outcome studies. They found evidence for the effectiveness of DBT, CBT and PST, but also for other forms of therapy. They concluded people at risk of suicide should have access to psychological interventions, including, but not necessarily limited to, those within the cognitive behavioural spectrum. A meta-analysis by Calati and Courtet (2016) found various psychotherapies had a significant reduction in suicide attempts during follow-up. A systematic review and meta-analysis of psychosocial and behavioural interventions aimed at preventing suicide and suicide attempts (Meerwijk et al 2016) found direct psychosocial and behavioural interventions that address suicidal thoughts and behaviour were more effective than indirect interventions that address symptoms associated with suicidal behaviour only (such as hopelessness, depression, anxiety, quality of life), especially at the post-treatment assessment point. The authors concluded clinicians working with patients at risk of suicide should address suicidal thoughts and behaviours with the patient directly. D'Anci et al (2019) analysed eight systematic reviews and 15 RCTs and concluded that CBT reduces suicide attempts, suicidal ideation and hopelessness compared with TAU. There was some evidence of benefits from DBT and certain medication, in particular for bipolar disorder. Other meta-analyses found that suicidal ideation and hopelessness improved more with CBT than usual care. Subsequent rates of death by suicide were comparable with CBT and usual care, but it is harder to demonstrate that an intervention can reduce suicides because they occur less frequently than suicide attempts. One recent study (Brown et al 2020) *showed that CAMS can reduce suicide rates.*

In summary, there is significant evidence that psychological interventions which address suicide risk specifically can reduce suicidal ideation and attempts.

Bryan (2015) identified that effective suicide-focused CBT interventions share the following features:

1. A primary emphasis on reducing suicidal ideation and risk. First and foremost, effective treatments directly target suicidal and the problems proximally related to risk for suicide attempts.
2. A clear theoretical framework.
3. A skills-building focus.
4. Access to crisis services and written crisis/safety plan.
5. Means restriction, i.e. reduced access to potentially lethal means. Research shows that this can significantly reduce suicide as there are fluctuating levels of suicidality. Involve family and relatives as appropriate.
6. Emphasis on personal responsibility by the patient. Wherever possible, emphasise choice and autonomy.
7. Extensive training and supervision.

Brodsky et al (2018) recommend ten steps within an SFI (Table 2.1)

Step 1: Inquire explicitly about suicidal ideation and behaviour, past and present.

Step 2: Identify risk factors in addition to suicidal ideation and behaviour.

Step 3: Implement and maintain continued focus on safety.

Step 4: Introduce and develop a collaborative Safety Plan Intervention for managing suicidality, including lethal means reduction.

Step 5: Initiate coping strategies and supports.
Step 6: Integrate suicide-specific treatment targets.
Step 7: Increase flexibility and contact availability.
Step 8: Initiate increased monitoring during periods of highest risk.
Step 9: Involve family and other social supports.
Step 10: Invoke clinician peer support and consultation.

Table 2.1 SFI models and studies

SFI models	*Intervention*	*Studies*
Brief interpersonal psychodynamic therapy	Four sessions delivered in the patients' home	Guthrie et al (2001)
Brief contact interventions (BCIs)	Brief non-face-to-face contact inc. cards, telephone contact or a volitional help-sheet (VHS)	Motto and Bostrom (2001), Carter et al (2005), Vaiva et al (2006), Wang et al (2015), O'Connor et al (2017), Vaiva et al (2018)
Cognitive therapy for suicide prevention (CT-SP)	Ten sessions	Power et al (2003), Wenzel et al (2009), Wenzel and Jager-Hyman (2012)
CBT for suicide prevention (CBT-SP)	Ten sessions	Brown et al (2005), Stanley et al (2009), Stanley et al (2010), Ghahramanlou et al (2012)
Post-admission cognitive therapy (PACT)	Six to eight sessions adapted for inpatients	Brown et al (2005), Ghahramanlou-Holloway et al (2012, 2014, 2015), LaCroix (2018)
Collaborative assessment and management of suicidality (CAMS)	1–12 (modal 6–8)	Jobes et al (2005), Comtois et al (2011), Ellis et al (2015), Jobes et al (2017), Ryberg et al (2019), Brown (2020)
Motivational interviewing to address suicidal ideation (MISI)	One or two sessions	Britton et al (2008, 2011, 2012)
Brief intervention and contact (BIC)	Ten sessions	Fleishmann (2008), Vijayakumar et al (2011), Riblet et al (2019)
Safety planning intervention (SPI)	One session	Stanley and Brown (2012), Miller et al (2017), Stanley et al (2018)

(*Continued*)

SFI models	*Intervention*	*Studies*
CBT-based intervention to reduce suicide risk in primary care	Two months, no limit	King et al (2013)
Apps and text messages, e.g. Reconnecting After a Suicide Attempt (RAFT); Suicide Intervention Assisted by Messages (SIAM), MYPLAN	Safety plan app Hope Box app An ACT-based app	Andreasson et al (2017) Bush et al (2017) Tighe (2017)
Acceptance and commitment therapy (ACT)	Seven sessions	Ducasse et al (2014)
Brief CBT for suicide (BCBT)	Minimum of 12 sessions weekly or biweekly, S1 – 90 minutes, further sessions 60 minutes.	Rudd et al (2015)
Attempted suicide short intervention program (ASSIP)	Three therapy sessions followed by personalised letters over 24 months	Michel and Gysin-Maillart (2015), Gysin-Maillart et al (2016), Krysinska (2016)
Teachable moment brief intervention (TMBI)	1 × 90-minute session drawn from CAMS, plus functional analysis of self-harm from DBT	O'Connor et al (2015), O'Connor et al (2018)
Problem-solving and comprehensive contact intervention (PS-CCI) to mood-disordered patients in ED	One interview about problem-solving, plus a personalised postcard and a telephone call three months later	Alonzo (2016)
Website, e.g. NowMattersNow.org	Use of website	Whiteside et al (2019)

For discussion, models have been divided into three categories – novel use of mobile phones (including some interventions in development) and two categories of interventions according to length and the service area intended for their delivery – interventions suitable for mental health services and outpatient services in particular or brief interventions provided in general hospitals for people who have self-harmed or attempted suicide. Within each category, interventions are clustered and then outlined in chronological order.

Ecological momentary assessment (EMA) and EM interventions for suicide prevention

When working with outpatients, suicidal thoughts are usually assessed at intervals and cannot be observed and monitored as they arise in real-time settings (Kleiman et al 2017). Suicidal ideation can vary within a few hours (Bagge et al 2014, 2017; Kleiman et al 2017). Furthermore, suicide attempts can occur in response to a rapid increase in suicidal thoughts within a very short time (Kleiman et al 2017; Millner et al 2017; Kleiman et al 2018). Often, suicidal risk is exacerbated when patients are in their natural environment and far from health services (Kleiman et al 2018). Arguably, therefore, intermittent assessments of suicidal ideation for clinical decision-making such as hospital discharge are unreliable (Kleiman et al 2017; Hallensleben et al 2019). Ecological Momentary Assessment (EMA) allows the collection of longitudinal detailed data as they occur in the real world. It gives a more accurate picture of someone's symptoms and reduces the impact of self-report response bias (Selby et al 2013). EMA could therefore improve the identification of high-risk individuals who require immediate help and appears particularly well suited to the study of a number of variables associated with depression, suicide and self-injury (Armey et al 2015).

Ten studies have used real-time monitoring to assess suicidal thoughts (Kleiman & Nock 2018). Broadly, they found compliance with repeated assessments in daily life is high across populations with differing levels of suicidal ideation and risk (Husky et al 2014). There appeared to be no iatrogenic effect related to repeated assessments of suicidal ideation (Gould et al 2005; Smith et al 2010; Husky et al 2014; Law et al 2015), and several studies suggested potential benefits. Smith et al (2010) found participants reported reduced suicidal ideation with EMA, and Davidson et al (2017) suggest patients may feel less hopeless by following their suicidal ideation changes over time.

Smart phone applications (apps) are affordable and widely used and may be more accessible than a written safety plan in a crisis (Bakker et al 2016). They offer new opportunities to overcome some of the barriers to help-seeking (Pauwels et al 2017; de la Torre et al 2017; Kreuze et al 2017, Jaroszewki al 2019). Nuij et al (2018) argue:

- Mobile applications provide opportunities to enhance suicide prevention methods.

- Patients can augment personalised safety plans by monitoring their own mental state.
- Real-time monitoring data of psychological processes can be analysed to improve our understanding of suicidality and develop new technology for suicide prevention.

Shand et al (2013) describe a suicide prevention ACT-based app and study for indigenous Australian youths. Results were reported by Tighe (2017), but although the treatment group had greater reduction in suicidal ideation compared to the control group, this did not reach statistical significance. MYPLAN is a mobile phone application designed to support people at risk of suicide by letting them create a safety plan (Skovgaard Larsen et al 2016). This app allows the user to create an individualised safety plan by filling in templates with strategies, actions and direct links to contact persons. It was developed in 2013 and is freely available in Denmark and Norway. Andreasson et al (2017) describe a protocol they are currently using to evaluate the effectiveness of a safety plan app (MYPLAN) compared to a safety plan on paper on reducing suicidal ideation. It is encouraging that service users have been involved in its development (Buus et al 2019). An RCT by Bush et al (2017) of 118 veterans who had recently expressed suicidal ideation assigned patients to use a virtual hope box (VHB) or to a control group that received printed materials about coping with suicidality, to supplement TAU over a 12-week period. The VHB users reported significantly greater ability to cope with unpleasant emotions and thoughts, though no significant advantage was found on other outcome measures.

In a broad review of mental health apps (Donker et at 2013), the majority of apps available lacked scientific evidence about their efficacy. The authors concluded that the public needs to be educated on how to identify the few evidence-based mental health apps available in the public domain to date. Larsen et al (2016) reviewed 123 apps referring to suicide, 49 of which were found to contain at least one interactive suicide prevention feature. Most apps focused on obtaining support from friends and family (27) and safety planning (14). Of the different suicide prevention strategies contained within the apps, the strongest evidence in the literature was found for facilitating access to crisis support (13). All apps reviewed contained at least one strategy that was broadly consistent with the evidence base or best-practice guidelines. They tended to focus on a single suicide prevention strategy, although safety plan apps provided the opportunity to provide a greater number of techniques. The authors concluded that of the many suicide prevention apps available, some provide elements of best practice, but none provide comprehensive evidence-based support. Apps with potentially harmful content were also identified. They warn that clinicians should be wary in recommending apps, especially as potentially harmful content can be presented as helpful. They thought that safety plan apps were the most comprehensive and evidence-informed, for example, "Safety Net" and "Mood-Tools--Depression Aid".

The most recent review by Martinengo et al (2019) assessed apps' adherence to six evidence-based clinical guideline recommendations:

- mood and suicidal thought tracking;
- safety plan development;
- recommendation of activities to deter suicidal thoughts;
- information and education;
- access to support networks; and
- access to emergency counselling.

Sixty-nine apps met inclusion criteria and were systematically assessed. There were three depression management and suicide prevention apps, and 46 suicide prevention apps. Only five out of 69 apps (7%) incorporated all six suicide prevention strategies. Six apps (9%), including two available in both app stores and downloaded more than 1 million times each, provided an erroneous crisis helpline number. Most apps included emergency contact information (65, 94%) and direct access to a crisis helpline through the app (46, 67%). Worryingly, non-existent or inaccurate suicide crisis helpline phone numbers were provided by mental health apps downloaded more than 2 million times. The authors thought this demonstrated a failure of app stores and the health app industry in self-governance, and quality and safety assurance.

In summary, apps clearly have a lot of potential but need to be checked for content before recommendation by clinicians or practitioners, and regulation needs to be improved. The safety planning and Hope Box apps are definitely worth using, especially in the absence of longer interventions or with service users who may prefer this to a face intervention.

Websites

Whiteside et al (2019) survey respondents reported measurable reductions in intensity of suicidal thoughts and emotions, including those rating their suicidal thoughts as completely or almost completely overwhelming and among middle-aged men. Although results from this user-experience survey administered at one point in time to a convenience sample of users must be interpreted with caution, results provide preliminary support for the potential effectiveness of the NowMattersNow.org website as a tool for short-term management of suicidal thoughts and negative emotion.

Therapies or outpatient interventions

Brief psychodynamic therapy

An early study (Guthrie et al 2001) randomised 119 adults who had deliberately tried to poison themselves to four sessions of psychodynamic interpersonal therapy or a TAU control group. Those who received therapy had a significantly greater reduction in suicidal ideation at six month follow-up compared with those in the control group. They were also more satisfied with their treatment and were less likely to report repeated attempts to harm themselves at follow-up.

CBT

Cognitive behavioural therapy for suicide prevention

Brown et al (2002) put together the first manualised therapy specifically to address suicidal ideation and behaviour. Cognitive behavioural therapy for suicide prevention (CBT-SP) consists of acute and continuation phases, each lasting about 12 sessions, and includes a chain analysis of the suicidal event, safety plan development, skill building, psychoeducation, family intervention and relapse prevention. The goal of CBT-SP is to de-activate the "suicide mode". Suicidal thoughts and/or behaviours are targeted directly. CBT-SP can be provided alongside other treatments – for instance, trauma-focused care, Alcoholics Anonymous (AA) support groups, marital therapy and psychiatric medication management. It is guided by a cognitive behavioural case formulation and emphasises skill-building and relapse prevention. CBT-SP was adapted for adolescents by Stanley et al (2009) to include family sessions. The US Substance Abuse and Mental Health Services Administration has recognised CBT-SP as a "Program with Evidence of Effectiveness" in its National Registry of Evidence-based Programs and Practices.

A small trial by Rudd et al (2015) found soldiers who received brief CBT were 60% less likely to make a suicide attempt during follow-up than soldiers in TAU. The intervention consisted of a minimum of 12 outpatient individual sessions on a weekly or biweekly basis, with the first session lasting 90 minutes and subsequent sessions 60 minutes. Participants were provided with a small pocket-sized notebook (called a "smart book") in which they were directed to record a "lesson learned" at the conclusion of each session. The intervention was delivered in three phases. In phase I (five sessions), the therapist conducted a detailed assessment of the patient's most recent suicidal episode or suicide attempt, identified patient-specific factors that contribute to and maintain suicidal behaviours, provided a cognitive behavioural conceptualisation, collaboratively developed a crisis response plan and taught basic emotion-regulation skills such as relaxation and mindfulness. The crisis response plan was reviewed and updated in each session by adding new skills and/or removing skills determined to be ineffective, impractical or too challenging. In phase II (five sessions), the therapist applied cognitive strategies to reduce beliefs and assumptions that serve as vulnerabilities to suicidal behaviour (e.g. hopelessness, perceived burdensomeness, guilt and shame). In phase III (two sessions), a relapse prevention task was conducted, in which patients imagined the circumstances of a previous suicidal episode and the internal experiences associated with this event (i.e. thoughts, emotions and physiological responses) and then imagined themselves using one or more skills taught to successfully resolve the crises. Because progress was based on demonstrated competency and skill mastery, participants had to demonstrate the ability to successfully complete this task in order to terminate the treatment. Additional sessions were conducted until participants demonstrated the ability to successfully complete this task.

Cognitive therapy

Cognitive therapy for suicide prevention (CT-SP) is based on Aaron Beck's cognitive behavioural model in which an individual's biopsychosocial vulnerabilities interact with suicidal thoughts and behaviours to produce a "suicide mode". Suicide is distinct from any mental health conditions and can occur in the context of many diagnoses. Hence CT-SP directly targets suicide-related thoughts and behaviours and is considered transdiagnostic in nature. CT-SP is structured and time-limited. The CT-SP treatment protocol was first described by Berk et al (2004) and subsequently presented as a full-length treatment manual by Wenzel et al (2009). It was originally developed for people who recently attempted suicide but can be used with anyone who has experienced a recent *suicidal* crisis; either a suicide attempt or acute suicidal ideation. CT-SP (Brown et al 2005; Wenzel et al 2009) consists of 10 × 50-minute sessions for anyone who has experienced a recent *suicidal* crisis (either a suicide attempt or acute suicidal ideation). Brown et al found CT-SP led to a 50% reduction in repeat suicide attempts compared to enhanced usual care. CBT protocols have been adapted for adolescents and older adults as well as acute care (Wenzel & Jager-Hyman 2012). CT-SP is conducted over three phases. Phase 1 develops an individualised, cognitive case conceptualisation and identifies specific treatment goals. In phase 2, specific cognitive and behavioural goals are agreed and implemented. In phase 3, skills are reviewed and guided imagery carried out for relapse prevention. CT-SP and CBT-SP clearly overlap (Ghahramanlou-Holloway et al 2015), but CT-SP is a briefer protocol.

In a trial of a cognitive therapy called LifeSPAN therapy for young adults with early onset psychosis deemed at risk of suicide, hopelessness and suicidal ideation were reduced in the treatment group, though the latter did not reach significance (Power et al 2003). Post-admission cognitive therapy (PACT, Ghahramanlou-Holloway et al 2012, LaCroix 2018) provides six to eight individual sessions of 60–90 minutes plus four telephone booster sessions up to 60 minutes within three months following discharge. Therapy sessions are preferably delivered two per day for three to five days. PACT is currently being evaluated in a multi-site randomised controlled trial (RCT).

Collaborative Assessment and Management of Suicidality

CAMS (Jobes 2006, 2016) is a therapeutic framework which uses a thorough suicide assessment and problem-focused intervention to target and treat patient-defined suicidal "drivers".

It has the following key features:

- empathy for suicidal states – no shame, no blame;
- collaboration with the suicidal person in all aspects of the intervention;
- focus on suicide throughout;
- outpatient orientation – the goal being to keep the suicidal person in outpatient care;
- flexible and "non-denominational" using a range of therapeutic approaches;
- assessment and documentation of risk at every contact.

CAMS uses a simple and powerful formulation, asking from the first session what is driving the person's suicide risk. CAMS identifies both indirect and direct drivers. "Indirect Drivers" are like risk factors – such as negative life events, psychosocial stressors and psychiatric disorders. Indirect drivers may not necessarily result in suicidality but can increase vulnerability to the direct drivers of suicide. They may be profoundly painful, but do not necessarily trigger acute crises. "Direct Drivers" are the way the person thinks or feels about indirect drivers. They serve as a bridge between a risk factor and why that person sees suicide as the solution. Research investigating suicide attempts and deaths by suicide has yielded many specific risk factors for future suicidal behaviours. However, they have limited applicability in clinical practice (Tucker et al 2015). *Direct drivers* bridge the gap between risk factors that increase the risk of suicide and the personal decision to consider suicide as an option. One question which can help elicit an individual's direct drivers is

> A lot of people struggle with …, but not everyone who does, wants to kill themselves. How are you seeing X that makes you feel like suicide is an option or the only option for dealing with it?

The SSF core assessment in CAMS, a quantitative section completed by the patient, includes five psychological constructs (psychological pain, stress, agitation, hopelessness and self-hate) and has established reliability and validity (Jobes 2006). The CAMS intervention ends after three consecutive sessions of the client successfully managing suicidal thoughts, feelings and behaviours. It therefore lasts a minimum of four sessions, with an average number of 12 sessions (Comtois et al 2011). RCT results highlight the positive impacts of CAMS in reducing suicidal ideation, overall symptom distress and instilling increased hope for individuals presenting with suicidality across a variety of settings (Comtois et al 2011; Jobes et al 2017; Ryberg et al 2019; Brown 2020). Ellis et al (2015) found people who received CAMS as inpatients showed significantly greater improvement in suicidal ideation and cognition than the TAU group. Ryberg et al found that CAMS was not superior to TAU in patients with illicit drug use or EUPD or EUPD traits. However, their findings do suggest that CAMS (with its high level of structure and focus on collaboration) may increase practitioners' ability to treat patients with initial low levels of working alliance. The authors argue, "Developing and maintaining a positive working relationship and a meaningful bond might be a fundamental therapeutic task facilitating symptom relief and decreasing suicidal lethality in these cases". There is also evidence that CAMS training can significantly decrease clinician's anxiety about working with suicidal risk and increase confidence, with results sustained at three-month follow-up (Schuberg et al 2009). Oordt et al (2009) and LoParo et al (2019) found that training which focuses specifically on the management of the suicidal drivers, factors mediating the cognitions, emotions and behaviours augmenting suicidal risk and resulting in suicidal behaviours can have a positive effect on clinicians' confidence, clinical skills and implementation of evidence-based practices.

Brief Acceptance and Commitment Therapy (Brief ACT)

In a study of 35 patients who had attempted suicide in the previous year, brief ACT (seven sessions over three months) reduced both the frequency and intensity of suicidal ideation (Ducasse et al 2014).

Follow-up or brief contact interventions following suicide attempts

Brief contact interventions (BCIs) are low-resource, non-intrusive interventions that seek to keep in contact with people after they have self-harmed. They have mostly been used with patients following presentation to an emergency department (ED) for self-harm or a suicide attempt, but also with psychiatric hospital inpatients, as a form of after-care. They include *telephone contacts; emergency or crisis cards; postcard or letter contacts; emails; text messages or a volitional help-sheet (VHS).* Most do not involve any face-to-face therapeutic contact. The content of BCI communications differ between studies, but generally involve a short sentence expressing concern for the patient and emphasising the availability of help should it be needed. The RAFT (Reconnecting AFTer a suicide attempt) text message BCI combines SMS contacts with additional Web-based brief therapeutic content targeting key risk factors. In a rare study involving service users, Larsen et al (2017) identified as priorities for an intervention:

- prompt outreach following discharge;
- initial distraction activities with low cognitive demands;
- ongoing support over an extended period.

Key content areas identified included:

- coping with distressing feelings;
- safety planning;
- emotional regulation and acceptance;
- coping with suicidal thoughts;
- connecting with others and interpersonal relationships;
- managing alcohol consumption.

There are numerous studies investigating very brief interventions following suicide attempts or self-harm, usually in general hospital ED settings (Carter et al 2005; Evans et al 2005; Vaiva et al 2006; Kapur et al 2010; Noh et al 2016; O'Connor et al 2017, Vaiva et al 2018; Inagaki et al 2019). Several of these found no statistical benefit (Carter et al 2005; Vaiva et al 2006; Noh et al 2016; O'Connor et al 2017; Vaiva et al 2018).

In an early randomised trial by Motto and Bostrom (2001), 3,005 people hospitalised for depression or suicidality were contacted 30 days after discharge about follow-up treatment. A total of 843 patients *who had refused ongoing care* were divided into two groups; one group were contacted by letter at least four times a year for five years. The control group received no further contact. Patients in the contact group had a lower suicide rate. This difference between groups was statistically significantly for the first two years but gradually diminished, and by year 14 no differences between groups were observed. However, other studies (such as Vaiva et al 2018) have failed to replicate these findings and Kapur et al (2010) concluded that a widespread introduction of these interventions cannot be justified without a better understanding of whether they work and, if so, how.

Luxton et al (2013) reviewed the evidence for follow-up interventions. Eight original studies, two follow-up studies and one secondary analysis study met inclusion criteria. Five studies showed a statistically significant reduction in suicidal behaviour. Four studies showed mixed results with trends towards a preventative effect, and two studies did not show a preventative effect. The authors concluded that repeated follow-up contacts appear to reduce suicidal behaviour but that more research is needed, especially RCTs. In a systematic review by Milner et al (2015) of RCTs using BCIs, 14 eligible studies were found, of which 12 were amenable to meta-analyses. For any subsequent episode of self-harm or suicide attempt, there was a non-significant reduction for intervention compared with control. The *number of repetitions* of self-harm or attempted suicide *per person*, however, was significantly reduced in the intervention group but no significant reduction in suicide compared with control. The authors concluded that BCIs cannot yet be recommended for widespread clinical implementation. The same team (Milner et al 2016) then conducted a systematic review of the proposed mechanisms underpinning BCIs for suicide or self-harm and identified three main areas:

- social support;
- suicide prevention literacy;
- learning alternative coping behaviours.

The authors conclude *social support and improved suicide prevention* literacy are the most likely mechanisms underpinning BCIs.

Inagaki et al (2019) systematically reviewed RCTs of suicidal patients admitted to EDs up to January 2015. Interventions were categorised into four types:

- active contact and follow-up interventions (half of the trials);
- letters or postcard;
- telephone calls;
- composite of letter/postcard and telephone).

A meta-analysis was conducted of the contact and follow-up interventions; there were not enough trials of other interventions to perform meta-analysis. Although some trials included in the meta-analysis were judged as showing risk of bias, the authors conclude brief intervention and contact (BIC) are recommended for suicidal patients admitted to an ED to prevent repeat suicide attempts during the highest-risk period of six months.

Combined face-to-face and indirect communication

The WHO Multisite Intervention Study on Suicidal Behaviours (SUPRE-MISS) was carried out in participating sites from six WHO regions. In a large-scale RCT by Fleischmann et al (2008), 1,867 people who attempted suicide were identified by medical staff in the emergency units of eight collaborating hospitals in five culturally different sites worldwide from 2002 to 2005. They participated in either TAU or TAU plus a BIC. The BIC was conducted by a person with clinical experience (e.g. doctor, nurse or psychologist) and included patient education and follow-up. This was delivered face to face with some patients. There were significantly fewer deaths from suicide in the BIC than in the TAU group. One Indian study (Vijayakumar et al 2011) randomly allocated 680 patients to a brief intervention at the time of discharge from a general hospital ED and contact for 18 months. The intervention included a standard one-hour individual information session as close to the time of discharge as possible combined with periodic follow-up contacts after discharge. The individual session provided information about:

- the psychological and social distress that often underlies suicidal behaviour;
- risk and protective factors for suicidal behaviours;
- basic community-specific epidemiology of suicide;
- repetition of suicidal behaviours;
- alternatives for constructive instead of self-destructive coping strategies;
- contacts and referral options.

Follow-up contacts involved visits at 1 week, 2, 4, 7, 11 weeks and 4, 6, 12 and 18 months after discharge. The intervention group had a significantly lower rate of suicide. Two things are worthy of note in the study. First, the follow-up of subjects proved to be a major challenge due to the complex setting and high mobility; 40% of patients were lost to the study; a challenge for other EDs that endeavour to provide follow-up interventions (Berrouiguet et al 2018). Second, unlike most studies describing their interventions as BICs, the follow-up was a substantial intervention and face-to-face. The authors also note that, given the resource limitations of low- and middle-income countries, interventions that involve highly trained staff are not feasible while BIC interventions are easily implementable.

In a meta-analysis of all suicide prevention interventions, Riblet et al (2017) identified 72 RCTs up to December 2015. BIC was associated with significantly lower likelihood of suicide (three RCTs n = 2,028). Six RCTs (n = 1,040) of CBT for suicide prevention and six RCTs of lithium (n = 619) yielded non-significant findings. The authors concluded that BIC is a promising suicide prevention strategy. No other intervention showed a statistically significant effect in reducing suicide. BIC has also been adapted for use with psychiatric inpatients (Riblet et al 2019).

Good practice point

Whilst short, non-face-to-face BCIs have potential as low-cost interventions, they are not an acceptable alternative to longer, face-to-face interventions. The best evidence currently suggests that people presenting in EDs should be given this BIC: a one-hour individual information session as close to the time of discharge as possible plus nine follow-up contacts (phone calls or visits, as appropriate) for up to 18 months (at 1, 2, 4, 7 and 11 week(s), and 4, 6, 12 and 18 months), conducted by a person with clinical experience (e.g. doctor, nurse or psychologist).

Motivational Interviewing to address Suicidal Ideation

Britton (2008, 2011) argues that MI may complement CBT as it has been shown to increase engagement and improve treatment outcomes when it is used to complement other treatments. Britton et al (2012) piloted two sessions of MI with veterans who were hospitalised with suicidal ideation. Thirteen veterans were enlisted, 9 (70%) completed both MI-SI sessions and post treatment assessment, and 11 (85%) completed the 60-day follow-up assessment. Participants reported reductions in the severity of their suicidal ideation at post-treatment and follow-up. In the two months following discharge, eight participated in mental health or substance abuse treatment. The authors concluded that MI-SI has potential to reduce risk for suicide in psychiatrically hospitalised veterans and that a more rigorous trial is needed.

Safety planning

The safety plan intervention (SPI) (Stanley & Brown 2012) is one of the recommended strategies in suicide prevention guidelines (Nuij et al 2018) and is considered a therapeutic intervention on its own (Andreasson et al 2017). An SPI consists of developing a collaborative safety plan. This takes 20–45 minutes and includes personalised warning signs, a prioritised list of coping strategies and sources of support that can be used if suicidal thoughts return or increase. It is critical for the clinician to discuss barriers to the client using the safety plan, and problem-solve this. SPIs incorporate useful CBT strategies, including identification of warning signs.

The basic components of an SPI include:

- recognising warning signs for a suicidal crisis;
- employing coping strategies;
- utilising social contacts and social settings as a means of distraction from suicidal thoughts;
- utilising family members or friends to help resolve the crisis;
- contacting mental health professionals or agencies;
- restricting access to lethal means.

The Emergency Department Safety Assessment and Follow-up Evaluation (ED-SAFE) study by Miller et al (2017) provided screening, safety plans and follow-up phone calls to at-risk patients in the ED. This combination of brief interventions administered both during and after the ED visit decreased post-ED suicidal behaviour. Compared with the TAU phase, patients in the intervention phase showed a 5% absolute reduction in suicide attempt risk (23% versus 18%). Participants in the intervention phase had 30% fewer total suicide attempts than participants in the TAU phase which was statistically significant.

A similar intervention by Stanley et al (2018) found that safety-planning interventions coupled with structured follow-up reduced the risk of suicidal behaviour by 50% and achieved a twofold increase in the odds of engaging in treatment over a six-month period. The safety-planning intervention consisted of six specific strategies:

- identifying early warning signs;
- encouraging internal coping strategies;
- reaching out to family/friends;
- identifying other individuals who can provide support during suicidal crises;
- contacting mental health professionals;
- lethal means planning.

Jobes (2016) describes a similar intervention as the first part of CAMS known as a *stabilisation plan*. Bryan et al (2017) report how a *crisis response plan* with active serving soldiers who were suicidal was associated with significantly faster reduction in suicidal ideation and shorter hospital admissions. They concluded that *crisis response planning* was more effective than a no-suicide contract.

Coping cards

A small RCT by Wang et al (2016) evaluated the effectiveness of a crisis coping cards (n = 32) compared with case management without the use of coping cards (n = 32) over a three-month intervention period. Results indicated that subsequent suicidal behaviours, severity of suicide risk, depression, anxiety and hopelessness were reduced more in the coping card intervention group compared to the case management only group. The coping card group showed a significantly longer time to reattempt suicide than the case management only group.

> ***Good practice point***
>
> Suicidal crises are often short-lived, so within every SFI, collaboratively develop and agree a safety plan that helps ensure the patient's ability to cope with current and future suicidal crises. Most people need time and coaching to "shape" their use of the safety plan which needs to be evaluated and revised for each individual. "No-suicide" contracts (asking a patient to agree not to attempt suicide) *should not* be used; they are not personalised, collaborative or supported by evidence. Instead ask the person if they are willing to explore other possible solutions to their problems with you.

Problem-solving and comprehensive contact intervention (PS-CCI)

PS-CCI (Alonzo & Stanley 2013) s a manualised problem-solving and comprehensive contact intervention. The intervention is delivered in emergency settings and includes an educative interview about problem-solving, the sending of a personalised postcard and a telephone call three months later. One study found it reduced both suicidal ideation and suicide attempts at three-month follow-up (Alonzo 2016).

Attempted Suicide Short Intervention Program (ASSIP)

ASSIP (Michel & Gysin-Maillart 2015; Krysinska 2016) is a manual-based brief therapy for patients who have recently attempted suicide, administered in addition to the usual clinical treatment. Two studies have found it efficacious in reducing suicidal behaviour in a real-world clinical setting. In a small study by Gysin-Maillart et al (2016), 120 patients in an emergency unit of a hospital in Switzerland who had recently attempted suicide were randomly assigned to receive either a structured suicide risk assessment and TAU, or the same plus ASSIP. ASSIP is a low-cost intervention comprising three or four 60- to 90-minute weekly therapy sessions plus regular, personalised follow-up letters from a clinician for 24 months. A further trial is underway in Switzerland. However, outside of research trials, retaining patients over such a long timescale would be a challenge as we know that in many patients who present in crisis, their risk presentation and motivation for care can be short-lived.

Teachable Moment Brief Intervention or TMBI

TMBI (O'Connor et al 2015) is a single 90-minute psychotherapeutic intervention for patients admitted to an acute medical setting after a serious suicide attempt. The TMBI is informed by evidence-based strategies (drawn from CAMS plus functional analysis of self-harm from DBT) to collaboratively identify:

- drivers of suicidal ideation;
- functional aspects of the recent suicide attempt;
- the patient's relationship with the concept of suicide;
- what has been lost and gained as a result of the suicide attempt;
- suicide prevention management strategies;
- documentation of factors to address in a suicide-specific treatment plan.

The TMBI emphasis on collaboration and functional analysis is designed to enhance and seize upon the elevated readiness to change that exists in a "teachable moment" window.

See https://www.ncbi.nlm.nih.gov/pmc/articles/PMC4558367/figure/F1/ for the conceptual model underlining this intervention (McBride et al 2003).

The goal of TMBI is to help the patient identify the factors underlying their suicidal ideation and actively address the problems that led to their suicide attempt; if necessary, engaging in inpatient or outpatient mental health services to resolve these issues. The patient and clinician complete a one-page worksheet documenting the factors identified as underlying their suicidal ideation and a crisis response plan to address both short-term coping strategies and long-term treatment planning. The intervention comprises rapport building, discovery of factors underlying the suicide attempt through functional assessment, short-term crisis planning and discussion of linkage to outpatient mental health services. TMBI can be delivered during the course of usual care procedures by existing care providers, with only additional costs associated with clinician training and time spent with patients. O'Connor et al (2015) found that those who received TMBI demonstrated significant positive improvement in motivation to address their problems compared to the TAU group. They also made significant improvement in Reasons for Living. Satisfaction ratings of those who received TMBI were "good" to "great". A second pilot study (O'Connor et al 2020) found similar results, including enhanced motivation in the post-hospitalisation phase. Staff from psychiatry, social work and counselling backgrounds were able to deliver the intervention with fidelity and equal adherence ratings.

In summary, over the last 20 years a number of studies have demonstrated that a range of brief interventions can reduce suicidal ideation and behaviour. Even a very brief psychological intervention may be effective in reducing subsequent deaths by suicide (Fleischmann 2008). Unfortunately, as yet there are no comparative trials between these various models, which is a major limitation in the evaluation of preventive interventions (Zaltsman et al 2016). It seems likely that different interventions are appropriate for different populations and service areas, in particular mental health services or EDs. People presenting with self-harm at EDs in general hospitals may be difficult to engage in longer interventions than patients referred to and engaged in mental health services. (See Bryan 2015 for chapters on delivering SFIs in different service contexts.) However, as patients and staff move between service areas within a mental health service, one shared model across the service has greater utility.

Based on my reading of the literature, clinical experience and training, I would say that:

- Manualised CBT can have high drop-out rates and may not be suitable for the short-term presentations of people with suicidal or para-suicidal behaviour. Senior clinicians in the suicide prevention field have also found high drop-out rates with manualised CBT, so deliver a more flexible approach (Lascelles, personal communication 2019). One study (Guthrie et al 2001) delivered the intervention in the patient's home, but this is unrealistic for many services to deliver. Some patients even decline to agree to a safety plan, so using a framework which can work flexibly using the "push it where moves" principle will engage more patients.
- CAMS has unique strengths in that patients can be oriented to the intervention in any service area within the service. This means that patients don't have to stop and start again from scratch when they move between teams (a woefully common negative feature of much mental health practice). CAMS is also unique in that it is a structured intervention that is flexible in the order, timing and length of elements of the intervention. An additional positive aspect of

CAMS is that it is not the preserved domain of psychological therapists who, in secondary care, are a scarce resource with, typically, long waiting lists. All experienced mental health professionals have relevant skills to work in a focused way with suicidal patients, and CAMS research shows that staff can learn the model in a relatively short time frame.

- Lastly, new technologies such as apps may offer promising novel interventions and may respond in a more time-sensitive manner to the natural fluctuating levels of suicidality.

2.2 Providing a suicide-focused intervention alongside other levels of intervention for people with different levels of risk

A range of care should be available for any individual according to their risk level and need. Any level of suicidality warrants the person receiving an initial assessment, safety plan and treatment plan. This is based on the fact that suicide is highly unpredictable and many who die by suicide have been deemed low risk. Delivering an SFI requires that the person is able and willing to engage with the process. This means being able to sit and have a conversation. If a person cannot do this, for example if she or he is manic or psychotic or if a person, despite repeated efforts by clinicians, refuses to engage, then alternative interventions should be considered depending on their level and immediacy of risk.

Jobes (2016) proposed a stepped care model with a range of interventions. Jobes and Chalker (2019) argue that suicidal patients are by definition seen as mentally ill and out of control, which demands hospitalisation and the treatment of the mental disorder (often using a medication-only approach). However, the evidence for inpatient care and a medication-only approach for suicidal risk is either limited or totally lacking. Thus, the "one-size-fits-all" approach to treating suicidal risk needs to be re-considered in lieu of the evolving evidence base. The authors highlight a series of evidence-based considerations for suicide-focused clinical care, culminating in a stepped care public health model for optimal clinical management of suicidal risk that is cost-effective, least-restrictive and evidence-based.

If the risk of suicide is considered to be high or uncertain, the person should be referred immediately to mental health services (Fazel & Runeson 2020). People at high risk and unable to keep themselves safe may be offered admission to a psychiatric unit and if this is refused detained involuntarily under the Mental Health Act. The Mental Health Act in England and Wales recommends that patients should generally be admitted under Section 2 (for assessment lasting 28 days) or Section 3 (for treatment lasting six months) of the Act, which requires two doctors and an approved mental health professional (e.g. a social worker) to complete. Section 4 can only be justified in emergencies when only one doctor is available, it lasts for only 72 hours, and either a Section 2 or Section 3 must be completed during this 72-hour period. Part III of the Mental Health Act applies to patients who have been alleged to have committed a crime and their detention in hospital is through the criminal justice system. Essentially detention in hospital under the Mental Health Act is considered if the patient's health or safety is at risk or the safety of others is at risk. In this context, individuals at potential risk of suicide may be involuntarily admitted. However, there is increased risk of suicide within the first seven days of involuntary hospital admission (Meehan et al 2006) (Figure 2.1).

See https://www.nhs.uk/using-the-nhs/nhs-services/mental-health-services/mental-health-act/.

most restrictive / highest cost

↕

Inpatient care
Day treatment
Crisis care
Intensive Clinical Management
Outpatient care and medication/ Evidence based therapies and SFIs
Samaritans and other help lines
Third sector support; engagement with other people with lived experience to reduce risk factors/ increase social support

Jobes 2006

Figure 2.1 Levels of care.

Least restrictive/lowest cost adapted from Jobes (2006).

2.3 Coming alongside: cultivating a trusting relationship and engaging the client

Developing an effective relationship with the person at risk of suicide is fundamental to their safe and effective care (Gilburt et al 2008). Responding effectively and engendering someone's trust requires us to be calm, compassionate, focused and non-judgemental. How we react non-verbally and the way we express things (the language we use) are as important as what we say. Guidelines for supporting individuals at risk of suicide emphasise the importance of developing a trusting working relationship from the outset, treating the person with respect, listening (Michail & Mughal 2018; NCCMH 2018) and being consistent. Research suggests the power of the therapeutic relationship to mitigate suicidal distress comes from its potential to foster feelings of hopefulness, connectedness and being cared for (Collins & Cutcliffe 2003; Cooper et al 2011). Cole-King and Lepping (2010) describe a model of care she calls *suicide mitigation* which is an active process to try to prevent suicide. It starts from the assumption that suicidal thoughts need to be taken seriously and met with compassion and understanding on every occasion in order to engage positively with the person. For the many suicidal individuals ambivalent about their wish to die, compassionate engagement can be the tipping point back to safety. A compassionate approach is also critical to facilitating patients disclosing risk.

Health care professionals who are empathetic and compassionate encourage patients to disclose their concerns, symptoms and behaviour, and are ultimately more effective at delivering care (Larson & Yao 2005). Conversely, negative reactions can cause a patient to feel that the clinician is hostile, unsympathetic and uncaring, putting the therapeutic relationship at risk (Thompson 2008). Health care staff may have negative reactions to self-harming behaviour which is detrimental to the patient's immediate safety and longer-term recovery (Royal College of Psychiatrists 2010) and can lead to frustration and/or resentment towards the patient. Suicidal patients have well-tuned "radar" which can detect a clinician's attitude. Compassionate care must also be competent care, and the establishment of a therapeutic alliance and trusting relationship between clinician and patient must be matched by a comprehensive and skilled risk assessment (Cole-King et al 2013).

Good practice point

The quality of the therapeutic relationship makes it possible for the patient to disclose suicidal thoughts. All suicidal thoughts, however "minor", require a response that needs to be compassionate, proportionate and timely.

> A positive therapeutic relationship is not only the context in which suicide prevention takes place but also a protective factor in its own right. Everyday aspects of good clinical care, such as listening to patients and treating their feelings with compassion and respect, are disproportionately important for patients who are feeling suicidal.CMH (2019)

The first aim when delivering an SFI is to engage the person who is struggling with persistent suicidal thoughts and to work alongside them as they make changes to reduce their suicide risk. If someone is especially ambivalent or hopeless, we may need to ask them to commit to *taking suicide off the table* (Jobes 2016) or *commit to a delay* (Sudak & Rajyalakshmi 2018). This is not the same as a "no self-harm contract" but is rather a "middle way". It can also be thought of as shaping the person's willingness to consider other solutions to their problem(s), a strategy in DBT known as "foot-in-the-door". Many people who are suicidal have significant psychosocial problems and experience relief when they think about dying as they see it as an escape from overwhelming stress or distress. Resolving these underlying psychosocial problems takes time. This presents what is known in DBT as a *dialectic*. The person may feel they can't give up suicide as a solution until their problems are resolved *and* we can't address their problems very effectively whilst their risk of suicide is the highest priority. Personal disclosure can be helpful here, especially if you have already established a trusting relationship, you can explain, with *radical genuineness* (Linehan 1993) that you are unlikely to be at your best in helping them address their problems if you are less worried they may die.

An SFI involves ten key elements:

- creating a therapeutic relationship with the client; being both compassionate and forthright;

- "leaning in" to address suicide risk and change and leaning back to emphasise choice;
- continuous assessment of risk;
- using validation, metaphors and similes;
- identifying and working with ambivalence;
- an individualised (personal) formulation of the key factors driving and maintaining suicidal intent;
- supporting the person whilst they start to make changes to increase safety and reduce suicidality;
- shaping and pacing behavioural change. Practising active change between sessions;
- identifying and addressing obstacles to change and regularly reviewing and adjusting safety plans;
- modelling flexibility and willingness, e.g. see family members if that could be helpful.

The "safety plan" in particular is regularly reviewed via collaborative attempts at discovering what works rather than prescribing a fixed plan. It is a collaborative rather than a formulaic, "off-the-peg" or instructional approach which, unfortunately, we can get pulled into doing when we are under time pressure to agree a risk plan.

Metaphors are especially helpful when we need to have difficult conversations and to summarise a meaning you want to convey and use again without a long explanation (see Stoddard & Afari 2014). They become a shorthand not just for conveying the issue itself but also validating and/or normalising it. They are especially helpful when we have a rift or rupture in the therapeutic alliance such as "I feel we aren't quite *on the same page* at the moment. Does it feel like that to you?" Jobes (2016) suggests a helpful metaphor of asking someone to "take suicide off the table" when they are suicidal, to enable a period when you can both work together at finding other solutions. He describes the CAMS intervention as going on a journey together and needing to *both be in the car with seat belts done up (not the car door ajar)*. Similarly, when asking someone to surf suicidal urges, rather than making it sound as if you are trivialising suicidal urges, a metaphor can convey your request compassionately such as "surfing the wave". This implies that waves go up and down without your having to spell out that suicidal urges pass and fluctuate in intensity. It is important to notice how metaphors are received and if they make sense to someone, especially if they have a different cultural or ethnic background or if you are not speaking in their first language.

Other ways to engage patients in treatment include instilling hope, demonstrating confidence that their problems can be addressed using this framework, and showing a willingness to talk about suicide and other difficult issues that patients are experiencing. Psychoeducation can also be helpful and validating. It may be appropriate at some point to explain to patients in simple ways how, for example:

- we don't problem-solve well when we are under stress or depressed as our thinking can become constricted and attention impaired.
- suicidal thinking can be reinforced as it presents the sense of an escape from our problems and pain; offering a sense of control.

See https://www.speakingofsuicide.com/2014/12/07/the-3-day-rule-and-suicide.

2.4 Assessing risk

The prediction of suicide is fraught with difficulty, and the level of accuracy is likely to be low. It is therefore advisable to take all suicidal thoughts seriously. Assessment of suicide risk requires a biopsychosocial assessment of the patient, including details of their suicidal thoughts, intent, plans, personal and demographic risk factors and a comprehensive mental state examination (Cole-King et al 2013).

Asking about suicidal feelings, thoughts, plans and behaviours

There is no evidence that asking about suicidal feelings causes harm. In fact, research indicates that it may help to reduce suicidal ideation (Dazzi et al 2014; Berman & Silverman 2017).

Asking someone about suicidal thoughts and feelings (CMH 2019) can show that you care and are taking their feelings seriously. You will also demonstrate that talking about suicide is not taboo and hopefully make it easier for them to talk about the subject. Ask simple, direct questions and encourage them to be honest about how they are feeling.

See https://www.mind.org.uk/media-a/2904/support-someone-who-feels-suicidal-2017.pdf,

https://www.rethink.org/advice-and-information/carers-hub/suicidal-thoughts-how-to-support-someone/.

> ***Good practice point***
>
> Remember that every contact with someone who could be suicidal is an opportunity to reduce their risk and engage them in process of recovery. Risk assessment should be the start of a therapeutic response or intervention, not a stand-alone process.

There is a tendency for clinicians to focus on predicting the probability of suicide despite little evidence supporting the utility of this approach (Chan et al 2016; Quinlivan et al 2017; Steeg et al 2018). The goal of risk assessment is not to predict the likelihood of suicide but to assess the person's needs and use this information to plan for safety and treatment. Hawton (2017) recommends we use a process of progressive questioning to gather relevant information to inform a **risk formulation** that leads to an **individualised intervention**.

Your first goal is to start an open and honest conversation. There isn't a single right way to ask about suicide; generally, it's worth being direct. Most people will value your honesty and may even be relieved to be able to have a conversation they or their loved ones may have felt unable to have. Open-ended questions tend to facilitate this rather than a string of closed questions (which will naturally be in your mind to ask if you are conducting a risk assessment as you want to gather important information). Any risk assessment will involve some closed questions, e.g. when discussing a person's last suicide attempt or their access to means, but try to begin with an open-ended question and then explain that you need to gather information. For example

> So you keep a rope … could you tell me a bit more about how that helps you? (After this initial exploration I may then ask 'would you be willing to tell me where the rope is? Does anyone else at home know where you keep it?' (These are all closed questions.)
>
> I would also round off such a discussion with a statement like 'Thank you. I imagine this isn't easy to talk about. I really appreciate your honesty' (if this is how you feel). 'Is there anything you haven't told me that I really should know?'

Some people find it hard to talk about their suicidal thoughts and may initially be reluctant to share them with you. Be aware of your own and the potentially suicidal person's voice and body language. If the person delays responding or if their response to a question is simply "Alright" or "OK", it might indicate that perhaps the person is not quite as "alright" as they claim (Cole-King et al 2013).

Do's

- make sure you are unlikely to be interrupted (this is especially important if you are talking on the phone and the person is at home);
- discuss limits of confidentiality;
- ask about suicide in a way that feels natural to you and that signals you are prepared to hear any answer;

- phrase the questions in a way that allows for a range of answers;
- use direct language such as "suicide", "killing yourself" or "ending your life";
- listen and be non-judgemental; listen with empathy, not sympathy;
- validate the person's feelings;
- make sure you record your assessment, concerns and actions in line with your service's policy and procedures;
- contact the local mental health crisis team if the client appears to be at high risk;
- emphasise that there is help available and agree a plan.

Don'ts

- promise absolute confidentiality;
- use indirect or infantilising language, such as "doing something silly";
- shy away from important questions;
- phrase the question negatively, e.g. "You're not thinking of killing yourself, are you?" Research has shown that when the question is phrased negatively, patients are more likely to deny suicidal feelings (McCabe et al 2017). They may see it as implying the clinician's preferred answer (Table 2.2).

Table 2.2 What to cover in a risk assessment

Twelve areas to assess	*Sample questions*
1. Suicidal intent[a] thoughts – frequency, intensity, duration and persistence	How often do you think about suicide? How long have you been having suicidal thoughts? When did you last think about suicide? Have your suicidal thoughts got worse?
2. Degree of planning (internet research; learning about method; looking for place and time). The more detailed and specific the greater the risk.[b]	Have you thought about what you might do? Do you have a plan to end your life? If so, how would you do it? Where would you do it? (if yes) Is this something you've ever rehearsed? Have you made any preparations towards this plan or any other arrangements? Do you have a timeline in mind for ending your life? Is there something (an event) that would trigger the plan?

(*Continued*)

Twelve areas to assess	*Sample questions*
3. Degree of preparation (putting affairs in order; e.g. stockpiling tablets suicide notes, changes to will). How detailed is the plan: have they thought about when, where and how?	Have you taken any steps to prepare for killing yourself, such as writing a suicide note, giving things away or going to specific locations? Have you done anything to begin to carry out the plan?
4. Access to lethal means	Do you have the… (drugs, rope) that you would use? Where is it right now? Do you have access to means of killing yourself?
5. Previous self-harm or suicide attempts.[c] If someone has a history of multiple attempts explore their most dangerous, when they most wanted to die or the most recent attempt. Any regret/remorse over current/previous attempt. How lethal were the attempts?	Have you ever made a suicide attempt? - Did you self-rescue or not? - What did you hope would happen? - Did you want to die? - How did you feel afterwards? Have you ever tried to hurt yourself (e.g. cutting self, overdosing)? What other risk-taking behaviour have you been involved in?
6. Mental state associated with their suicide mode, including features of depression and agitation, guilt and shame. Observation of appearance and behaviour, speech, mood, insight	Can you describe to me what you feel like when you are at your most suicidal? Do you have - racing thoughts, - irritability, - restlessness and - impulsivity?
7. Perception of the future and any sense of hopelessness	What are your thoughts about the future? What do you think needs to happen for you to feel better?
8. Drug and alcohol use	Do you use drugs or alcohol? Have you ever used drugs or alcohol before attempting suicide?
9. Risk factors • male • 40–44 years • under mental health services • history of self-harm ○ in criminal justice system ○ bereaved or affected by suicide ○ living in areas of higher socioeconomic deprivation ○ unemployed (Samaritans 2017; Centre for Mental Health Report 2019)	(Explore psychosocial factors in the person's life and circumstances)

Twelve areas to assess	*Sample questions*
10. Reasons for dying, e.g. to end their suffering or perceived burden on others (Joiner et al 2002)	What makes you think of suicide (e.g. worries, fears, loss)? Do you feel like you are a burden to anyone or that others would be better off without you?
11. Reasons for living and *protective factors*, including children being present at home, religious engagement, fear of death, active participation and commitment to treatment and use of effective problem-solving or coping skills.	What reasons do you have for living? Is anyone aware that you think about suicide (family, friends, professionals)? Can you talk to family and friends? Do you feel anyone cares about you?
12. How do they try to manage their suicidal thoughts? (distraction, suppression, thinking about reasons for living such as the impact on loved ones). Ability to resist acting on their thoughts of suicide or self-harm.	What helps you to not think about harming yourself or suicide? What stops you from going through with it when you have strong urges but manage not to act on them? (explore exceptions). What stops you acting on these thoughts?

a It is critical to distinguish *explicit or subjective intent* – the patient's stated intent and motivation (what they actually tell us) from *implicit or objective intent* (based on previous history, lethality of the method and inferences drawn from other knowledge of the suicidal act). It is worth revisiting this on risk assessments – gently probing later in the interview to elicit more disclosure.

b Patients who report suicide plans should be asked about the plan in detail, including the chance of rescue, preparations for and rehearsal of the suicide attempt. Interventions to reduce the risk of suicide should then be targeted towards eliminating or minimising these various factors (Welton 2007).

c Suicidal ideation at patients' worst time in their lives may better predict suicidal behaviour than current suicidal ideation (Beck et al 1999).

> ***Good practice point***
>
> Document the date, time and the key aspects of your assessment: "If you did not document it then you did not ask it".

The suicide mitigation approach

Dr Alys Cole-King is a Consultant Liaison Psychiatrist and the co-founder and Clinical Director of Connecting with People, a social enterprise which provides suicide and self-harm awareness and response training throughout the United Kingdom. Cole-King has evolved a very practical model for risk assessment which is then recorded using a continuum of risk. The key to a compassionate suicide mitigation approach is the emphasis on collaboration rather than direction (Cole-King & Lepping 2010) (Table 2.3).

Table 2.3 Evidence-based risk factors and "red flag" warning signs (Cole-King et al 2013)

Demographic and social	*Personal background*	*Clinical factors in history*	*Mental state examination and "red flag" warning signs*
Demographic factors Gender and age: male, younger men and very elderly (but recent increase in middle-aged men) Marital status: separated > divorced > widowed > single > married Unemployment: initially high risk, decreases after three months until after about one year, then higher again Profession: farmers, veterinarians, doctors (female) and dentists Economic class (high and low income) Ethnic group: minorities (e.g. Black or Asian women); refugees.	*Family history* Suicide Mental illness, particularly alcoholism and bipolar affective disorder	*Current mental illness* Repeated relapses, recent admission/discharge from psychiatric unit; recent relapse in mental illness. Self-neglect Agitation Depressive symptoms, especially anhedonia and insomnia Severe anxiety and panic Post-traumatic stress disorder	*Hopelessness* Perception of the future as persistently negative and hopeless: of particular concern if only able to see one to two hours into the future Negative thoughts, helplessness, guilt, "I'm a burden", "nothing to live for" Sense of "entrapment" Sense of shame, especially if severe and/or if in conflict with underlying religious or spiritual beliefs
Life events Significant threat or loss, e.g. health event, bereavement of partner or close family Childhood adversity No memory of being special to any adult when growing up Bullying or abuse Relationship instability Redundancy Unemployment	*Personality disorder* Personality traits of impulsivity, aggression, liability of mood Sudden unexplained changes in behaviour or uncharacteristic behaviour	*Previous self-harm* Especially high-suicide-intent attempt, superficial cutting, recent increasing intent of repeated self-harm The risk of a "completed" suicide remains raised for many years after a high-suicide-intent act	*Suicidal ideas and plans* Especially if omnipotent and compelling, recently worsened and associated with distress Suicide plans/preparations, e.g. will, goodbye note/text/email, internet search for methods; lethality of method; possible rescue/treatment Unable to distract themselves from suicidal thoughts Note: the method can easily change from low to high lethality

Social capital (lack of) Social isolation and living alone Recent loss of attachment Perception of lack of social support/confidants Institutionalisation, e.g. prison Recently leaving armed forces Major relationship instability Recently bereaved Loss of privilege Use of suicide-promoting websites.	*Substance misuse* Precipitated by loss of interpersonal relationships Especially if: high level of dependency; long history of drinking; binge drinking; depressed mood; poor physical health; poor work record in past four years (peak age 40–60 years)	*Chronic medical illness* (one in ten of "completed" suicides) Especially if accompanied by chronic pain, functional disability or incurable cancer; cardiovascular disease; dialysis; gastrointestinal disease; genitourinary disease in men; epilepsy (especially early onset); multiple sclerosis; dementia; neurological illness after cerebral trauma.	*Psychotic phenomena* Distressing phenomena; persecutory delusions; nihilistic delusions; command hallucinations perceived as omnipotent. *Cognitive functioning* Delirium Low IQ
Access to lethal means Firearms Poisons (available to, e.g., dentists, farmers, anaesthetists) Suicide hotspots	*Poor problem-solving skills* Low IQ Poor coping skills	*Medication* "Over the counter" and prescribed (consider issuing weekly prescriptions) Note the addictive effect of different medications	*Insight* High premorbid functioning and fear of deterioration Early stage of illness

There are three other forms of risk which are usually assessed alongside risk to self:

- risk to others;
- risk from others;
- risk of self-neglect.

All of these may be linked to increased risk of suicide or mortality. Domestic abuse or partner violence (especially when severe or persistent) is a strong risk factor for suicide and attempted suicide (Devries et al 2011; Munro & Aitken 2020). The distress, sense of entrapment and hopelessness arising from domestic abuse can cause victims to feel that suicide is "the only way out" (O'Connor & Knock 2014). As suggested in Part 1 with regard to substance abuse, clinicians or practitioners assessing anyone who is experiencing partner violence or suicidality should be alert for both (Salvatore 2018). Wu et al (2012) found levels of clinician-appraised risk of self-neglect, but not of suicide or violence, predicted mortality among people receiving a risk assessment in secondary mental health service. Self-neglect can occur across the lifespan but is more common in older people.

In addition to assessing what people say, we need to consider what they may not be telling us, and the potential for someone to talk risk-to-self up or down. When we are assessing risk, we may not know the person well. This can make it difficult to pitch our sense of whether someone may be talking suicide up or down. Equally when we do know someone who has survived many suicide attempts, we may under-estimate their risk. In either instance it is always important to keep an open mind.

There are many reasons why people may talk suicide "up" or "down". Reasons for talking suicide "down" include:

- shame;
- strong desire, determination or resolve to die by suicide;
- fear of involuntary detention.

Reasons for talking suicide "up" include:

- a history of invalidation leading to escalated communication of needs through self-harming behaviour or threats of self-harm;

- ambivalence and fear you will carry it out unless you are stopped;
- desperation for help;
- desire for help or hospital admission.

Management of high-risk individuals

The more serious the suicidal thoughts and planning and the greater the lack of protective factors, the more the clinician will need to "direct" rather than "co-create" support to keep the patient safe. In this situation, support is more likely to include professional intervention, with a possible admission to hospital. Once the crisis has dissipated, however, a longer-term, suicide mitigation safety plan can be created in collaboration with the patient to help address any future crisis (Cole-King et al 2013). If a high level of risk is established, ensure safety with 24-hour support through the crisis team of the local mental health service. Consider grounds for assessment and detention under the Mental Health Act if the person refuses and, if necessary, break confidentiality and contact their closest relative. It may not be advisable for the person to be alone and you may want to consider getting help with removing suicidal means (Table 2.4).

Table 2.4 When to signpost or contact a GP, ED; phone 111 (NHS) or the police (999)

Risk level of suicide	*General public/other agencies*	*Mental health professional*
Risk not imminent	GP	Address directly with patient; discussion in supervision and MDT, and review risk regularly
Urgent/out-of-hours	111 (free and open 24/7)	Crisis service[a]
Risk imminent (24–48 hours) esp. if in public place; others at risk or person non-compliant with their own safety	999 Police	999 Police
Acted on and in need of medical attention	Ensure the individual goes to ED or call 999 Ambulance	Ensure the individual goes to ED or call 999 Ambulance

a Most crisis teams will accept referrals from GPs and primary mental health services; internally from mental health teams and EDs. They would aim to see a patient face to face within four hours and ideally would be trying to contact them within an hour.

Good practice point

Risk needs to be continually reviewed as suicidality fluctuates and risk levels can change within a short time frame, so any SFI should include a regular review of risk.

Clinicians can rate the client's wish to live and their wish to die, with the idea that high wish-to-die ratings accompanied by low wish-to-live ratings are especially potent risk factors for eventual suicide (Brown et al 2005). CAMS uses a Likert scale (1–5) in which the patient is asked at every session to rate key psychological dimensions associated with suicide risk and their overall belief that they will kill themselves (Jobes 2006, 2016).

Clinicians can also gain useful and important information from third parties such as family, friends and colleagues. This can be critical supplementary information in patients who you consider may be underreporting or not fully disclosing their risk.

2.5 How many sessions?

There are broadly two approaches to SFIs. The earliest models are manualised and usually have a specified number of sessions. Highly manualised interventions are often used in clinical trials as they enable better adherence and fidelity between clinicians. It is also easier to train staff to deliver manualised models and replicate in other studies with different populations. However, they have major disadvantages. Individuals, especially if they are suicidal, may not take well to a preordained order of session topics. It is a common experience in secondary care services for these manualised approaches not to suit clients who need careful pacing and relationship building within an evidence-based format. As engagement is such a high priority, I therefore favour a more flexible approach such as CAMS or the model proposed in Part 3 of this book. This does not involve abandoning structure; CAMS, for example, has a highly structured session format, reviewing suicidal self-assessment and the person's use of their safety plan. CAMS is based on a personalised formulation built around two direct suicide drivers for each individual and has a high level of coherence. This is important as it conveys confidence for both the person delivering the intervention and the client.

Interestingly, either approach has a similar treatment length. An average of nine hours of individual CBT for the prevention of suicide has been reported to reduce the likelihood of repeat suicide attempts in approximately 50% of patients (Brown et al 2005). Studies show CAMS can reduce suicidality in 6–12 sessions; the median was 6–8 (Comtois et al 2011). This is because it takes time to assess, formulate and build the trust and the skills necessary for the person to feel some confidence that they can manage their problems differently. Interestingly, an SFI should also not be too long, as it is not intended to replace psychological therapy for any of the "other" problems which many suicidal people have (such as depression; substance misuse or EUPD) and for which there are more evidence-based interventions.

Briefer formats such as safety planning intervention (SPI) (Stanley & Brown 2012) provide one session. These studies have evaluated one element of an SFI. Safety planning could be enhanced in mental health services, for example, with the aid of audits and reflective practice. In my experience, depending on the complexity of the person's problems and duration of their suicidality, a collaborative and personalised safety plan or even a few sessions of an SFI can make a real difference.

2.6 Agreeing a treatment plan or SFI

Informed consent is important when delivering any intervention. Informed consent is a first step in engaging someone as it orients them to the treatment (Wenzel & Jager-Hyman 2012). With someone suicidal it is critical to ensure that they clearly understand the goal of treatment (to prevent future suicidal behaviour) and have realistic expectations – that participating does not guarantee that the patient will not engage in suicidal behaviour (Rudd et al 2009).

Participating in an SFI is a voluntary process which cannot be done against a person's will and requires their consent for involvement. Efforts should always be made to try to establish consent and support a person's capacity to engage. This can involve extended time working with the person or working with other staff or family members. If someone does not or cannot engage, we should also document our efforts to engage them. An SFI can take two to ten sessions, depending on the willingness, motivation risk level and complexity of the patient as well as (inevitably) the availability of time by the clinician.

Sharing one's email addresses and phone numbers – the pros and cons

Conventional practice in mental health services avoided contact with patients other than via telephone or face-to-face. This is now outmoded and it became a priority during COVID-19 and lockdown to email patients URLs for communicating via remote platform. Despite all the challenges of patients communicating with us via text messages or emails (and associated risks), the advantages are clear. Patients at risk of suicide may be able or willing to contact us this way and would not necessarily do so by phoning. I would suggest therefore that within any intervention and an SFI in particular, it is helpful to discuss the preferred methods the patient has for contacting us and agree when, how and what for. My usual practice is to ask patients never to communicate suicide risk in a text or email which may not be read and on occasion may not even arrive. If patients don't keep to the guideline, the agreement can be reviewed and more skilful communication "shaped". See 3.10 (p 176) with regard to telephone coaching.

2.7 Working with families and partners

Family involvement is of particular importance to patient safety in mental health care services, where communication with and involvement of family members may help to prevent patient deaths. Investigations of deaths in acute mental health care regularly highlight inadequate involvement of families (NCISH 2018; Manuel et al 2018; NHS Resolution 2018). Indeed, staff themselves highlight how involving families is best practice (Littlewood et al 2019). Clinicians emphasised the value of a two-way dialogue, whereby family members feel able to share their concerns about a patient's current well-being and safety, which may lead to action by the health care team. Clinicians, in turn, can involve family members by informing them when patients miss appointments or are non-adherent with medication.

However, family involvement can be challenging in mental health care settings. Clinicians also reported difficulties in negotiating confidentiality and privacy (Landeweer et al 2017) which can hinder information-sharing (NHS Resolution 2018). Whilst families can provide an effective source of support to some patients, for others, difficult family relationships may contribute to their distress or mental health problems. In a minority of cases families are part of the problem and the individual may need considerable help addressing that without their families present. These decisions are made further complex in that patients should ideally be offered the choice of whether to involve a family member or not, for example to bring them to an appointment within an SFI (as recommended by Bryan & Rudd 2018). In some cases the patient may not be able to make a judgement in their best interest or feel unable to say no. Someone very suicidal may decline permission to share information and wish to keep their family at arm's length. In such situations, best practice would be to have a number of professionals involved so that someone can work directly with the patient (ideally delivering an SFI) whilst another professional supports the family. As a rule of thumb family involvement should be the norm if the patient wishes this or if the patient is so high risk that the family can play a critical role in their safety. However, families who contribute directly to a patient's poor mental health, for example through bullying or abuse, may need to be discouraged from too much involvement. This is part of the complexities of clinical practice and the patient, their interests and autonomy should be at the heart of any decision. These complex scenarios highlight the importance of reflective practice and supervision. The key guide here is to be willing and flexible and model this for your client as willingness and flexibility are critical to getting out of the suicidal "cul-de-sac".

Ethical dilemmas may often arise with young adults where the family have significant rights and the adult may be reluctant to involve them. Best practice in some university mental health teams has changed in recent years as a result of one family's campaign who lost their son from suicide whilst he was at university. He was known to be depressed and under the care of the Bristol University mental health team, but the parents were not informed, and he died by suicide. As a result of the family's resolve to change that practice, the university introduced an "opt-in" system in which students can give consent for a parent, guardian or friend to be contacted if there are "serious concerns" about their wellbeing. In the academic year 2019–2020 94% of students at Bristol University chose to opt-in to let family or friends be contacted – and there were 36 cases in which contacts were subsequently made. See https://www.thetimes.co.uk/article/bristol-university-warns-parents-of-student-suicide-concerns-bsgvx890n.

2.8 Identifying indirect and direct drivers

Once you have done a risk assessment and agreed an SFI and safety plan (see 3.3 page 138) it is helpful to identify the indirect and direct drivers for the individual's suicide mode. Indirect drivers include any circumstances that can lead someone to believe that his or her life is not worth living – negative life events, other psychosocial stressors and mental illness. Examples of indirect drivers are homelessness, depression, substance abuse, post-traumatic stress disorder or social isolation. Indirect drivers do not necessarily relate to a specific, acute suicidal crisis (Tucker et al 2005). Direct drivers are suicide-specific thoughts, feelings and behaviours which lead to suicidality in an individual, i.e. the idiosyncratic internal experiences, behaviours and external situations that a patient associates with his or her suicidal crisis (i.e. increased suicidal ideation or a past suicide attempt). Indirect drivers may include financial instability or mental health disorders that influence an individual's ability to keep a job and hence contribute to *feelings of burdensomeness* which is the direct driver or "bridge" (Jobes 2016) to the suicidal mode for that person, i.e. the reason for his or her attempt. Direct drivers can be identified through completing a functional or chain analysis (Linehan 1993; Rizvi & Ritschel 2014) (see Part 3 p 126) or by making an individual diagrammatic formulation of the patient's suicide mode (e.g. Rudd 2000).

2.9 Planning and pacing the SFI

Most SFIs propose working in phases (Ghahramanlou-Holloway et al 2014). Wenzel and Jager-Hyman (2012) and Ghahramanlou-Holloway et al (2014) recommend three phases:

1. engagement, risk assessment and formulation; functional analysis of last suicide attempt;
2. skills-coaching;
3. relapse prevention.

It is clear there are many common elements and they are generally delivered in a similar order across SFIs. This is helpful for the clinician or practitioner and structure which aids session planning and helps contain staff anxiety is an important goal. However, people at risk of suicide present with complex needs often in a crisis and the agenda should also be driven by the patient's priorities and needs. Engagement is a high priority; see page 103 for further discussion about managing the balance between a structured intervention and one which is sensitive to the individual at that point in time (Table 2.5).

Table 2.5 Examples of pacing agenda in SFIs

	PACT Ghahramanlou-Holloway et al (2014)	*Wenzel and Jager-Hyman (2012)*
Phase 1	Developing therapeutic alliance and exploring risk Identify • ability and means • primary problem area(s) associated with the suicidal behaviour • problems with adherence to treatment • any current worries, preoccupations or outstanding problems • RFL • motivation for change • obstacles to change	Risk assessment Treatment rationale Obtaining informed consent Engaging patients in and orienting patients to treatment Developing a safety plan RFL and RFD Case conceptualisation Identification of treatment goals
Phase II	Formulation Chain analyse last or recent suicide attempt Develop and share formulation of risk Highlight key themes driving suicidality and obstacles to keeping themselves safe/seeking help Explore possibilities for change Identify any ambivalence and use motivational interviewing if indicated	Cognitive therapy strategies Activity scheduling and behavioural activation Promote treatment adherence Develop social support networks Affective self-soothing (Linehan 1993). Cognitive restructuring Coping card Development of RFL Hope Kit (Wenzel et al 2009) Problem-solving Pros and cons of acting on suicidal urges
Phase III	Intervention Shape self-care and safety behaviours Reduce access to means Increase connectedness/belongingness Collaboratively generate a safety plan Hope box, cue card, etc. How, from whom and when to seek help Imaginal rehearsal of future suicidal crisis with effective problem-solving.	Reviewing and consolidating skills Relapse prevention including guided imagery exercises Preparing for setbacks Reviewing progress with treatment goals Discharge planning and termination
Phase IV	Trouble shoot and problem-solve obstacles	
Phase V	Telephone booster Fade contact with the patient – gradual lessening of support Revise safety plan as needed before discharge	

2.10 Building skills and coping strategies and shaping effective help-seeking

Suicide is contemplated because people do not know how else to manage overwhelming or intolerable psychological pain. Developing skills to manage or address problems is therefore essential to believing there are other ways of coping or solving one's problems. In an SFI we want to enhance RFLs or a "life worth living" (Linehan 1993). This needs to be approached with sensitivity and paced so we have realistic conversations about what "a life worth living" *might* look like for that person. Don't assume how your client's life could be improved. Throughout an SFI we also want to help the person develop (Table 2.6):

- well-being and greater resilience – enhance protective factors;
- problem-solving to deal with their triggers for suicidal thoughts or adverse events;
- flexibility and broader perspective taking ("helicopter view");
- self-efficacy – skills and strategies for surfing or tackling suicidal thoughts.

Table 2.6 Ghahramanlou-Holloway et al (2014) recommend the following aims

Provide psychoeducation	To educate the patient about the association between one's suicidal thoughts, urges, and feelings and subsequent behaviours
Reduce suicide risk factors	To reduce the severity of established suicide risk factors (depression, hopelessness, suicidal ideation, etc.)
Enhance effective coping	To enhance effective coping, emotion regulation and problem-solving skills, such that suicide is no longer viewed as the only solution to one's life problems
Minimise social isolation	To help the patient gradually establish a new social support network or more adaptively use an existing social support network
Increase treatment adherence	To increase adherence to medical care, including mental health and treatment for substance-related disorders
Plan for safety	To prepare patients, family members and friends to implement emergency safety plan procedures when suicidal urges are high

Table 2.7 Skill-deficit domains, with examples of underdeveloped and overdeveloped skills (Ghahramanlou-Holloway et al 2014)

Skill-deficit domain	*Underdeveloped skill*	*Overdeveloped skill*
Coping strategies, self-efficacy, problem-solving	Self-soothing	Self-blame
Hopelessness Reasons for dying > reasons for living	Optimism	Catastrophising
Social support	Assertive communication	Social avoidance
Acquired capability for suicidal behaviour and motivation to repeat	Inhibition of urges to kill oneself	Pain endurance
Help-seeking	Skilful help-seeking and seeking when you are more likely to use it	Emotional blocking or struggling on alone

A helpful way of formulating skills development with an individual is to see the client as underutilising or over-utilising certain skills. This is less invalidating than suggesting clients are doing the wrong thing or not doing what would be more effective (Table 2.7).

Any SFI will involve coaching in the use and development of specific skills and strategies tailored to the needs of the patient. These include:

- coping strategies;
- problem-solving;
- emotion regulation/DBT skills;*
- effective social skills and increased social engagement;
- treatment adherence skills;
- skills for managing specific emotions.

*Any of these could be helpful: Mindfulness skills (especially Beginners mind and Wise Mind); STOP & TIP; Opposite-to-emotion action; Self-soothe; Willingness; Surfing urges; Skilful occupation; Pros and Cons; Checking the facts; Build mastery or positive experiences; Reducing vulnerability (eating, sleeping, exercise; taking medication).

Strategies for specific emotions and states: *Anger*: Deep breathing, counting, exercise, hitting cushions, shouting, dancing, biting on scrunched up material, going for a long run.

Sadness/fear: Wrapping up in a blanket, spending time with pets, walking in nature noticing surroundings, soothing music, crying, talking to someone, relaxation, dancing or smiling to introduce positive feelings.

Numb, disconnected state: Flicking an elastic band on your wrist, holding ice cubes, experiencing strong tastes (chilli, peppermint) or smells, having a cold shower, something that reconnects you.

Shame: Stop spending time with anyone who treats you unkindly, recognise that it is normal and human to make mistakes, remind yourself that there are reasons for how you behave – it is not because you are bad.

Self-hatred: Write a letter from the part of you that feels the self-hatred, and then write back with as much compassion and acceptance as you can. Find creative ways to express these painful feelings, for example in poetry, song or drawing or physical exercise such as running or going to the gym.

(based on https://www.healthyminds.services/content-article/zjkek4v6p1fcfawo7mop.)

When shaping behaviour, we reinforce *gradual approximations* of a targeted, desired or skilful behaviour. It is important to pace it in realistic steps and know where to pitch our expectations.

Shaping comes with:

- carefully paced goal setting and monitoring how this goes;
- cheerleading and positively reinforcing steps taken and achieved;
- rehearsing skills in session (in imagination or role play);
- generalising this to natural environments through "homework" tasks.

Shaping effective help-seeking

Part of the role of anyone delivering an SFI is to "shape" appropriate help-seeking. Shaping is a process of working in small successive steps that approximate the ultimate action you want, which is help-seeking in a timely manner with willingness to participate in skills-coaching. This needs to be explained and openly discussed. For the great majority of service users, help-seeking behaviour for suicidality is low (Calear et al 2014) and suicide prevention services are underutilised (Mann et al 2005;

McCarty et al 2011). Even when people have been assessed and made an initial engagement with services, their use of emergency services or telephone help lines within those services is often low. When patients do contact services, typically this will be in the height of the crisis, so effective skills-coaching is harder for both the patient and the professional seeking to help them.

Barriers to help-seeking include:

- depressed mood leading to passivity and impaired problem-solving;
- not recognising you need emotional support or professional help;
- stigma and shame;
- ambivalence and fear that others will intervene and take control (this is likely to be a factor in those who are most suicidal);
- cultural traditions that value individual independence or frown on seeking help outside of the family;
- hopelessness;
- feeling unimportant compared to others perceived as more in need or deserving of help;
- mistrust or previous experience of services being unhelpful;
- over-reliance on distraction; continuously trying to put off addressing suicidal thoughts and urges until they "hit you in the face".

As suicidal risk fluctuates and is likely to peak when the person is in their own environment or during out-of-hours, encouraging appropriate use of in-hours and out-of-hours support is vital. You can use a rating scale of suicidality (as in CAMS or DBT) and agree a number on that scale at which the person phones for help. (This is particularly helpful if you want to encourage the person to seek help earlier.) If the client is reluctant to do this, it can be role-played in the session. It can be helpful to practise a script of what to say when they seek help, which people may not know how to do. Practice steps could involve getting the patient to phone you for other reasons such as reporting on homework or telling you good news, just to practise contacting you outside your regular appointments. The skills which the practitioner wants the person to use can be made clear in their care plan. Since notes are recorded electronically, care plans are now accessible by the whole service, so the individual may also be also coached by "out of hours" crisis teams.

2.11 Ending the intervention

Ideally the intervention ends when the person is able to manage their suicidal thoughts and feelings. CAMS recommends ending the intervention only when there has been three consecutive sessions with self-rated risk below 3, the person is managing suicidal thoughts and feelings, and there has been no suicidal behaviour for three weeks (Jobes 2016).

Research has shown that people at risk of suicide are particularly vulnerable when they lose contact with or are transitioning between services (Bickley et al 2013; NCISH 2013, 2017; NCCMH 2018). Ideally contact should be faded and telephone booster sessions, outstanding needs and any signposting considered. If other interventions are indicated, within or outside the service, these may be planned. Finally, the safety plan should be revised as needed before discharge.

2.12 Training, support and supervision for staff

The first responsibility of any health professional is to do no harm and the second is to keep patients alive. Working with people who are suicidal is the most challenging and yet the most important role in mental health care. No other treatment will work unless we can keep people alive so they can participate and benefit from those treatments. Despite this, studies suggest mental health staff receive insufficient training (Awenat et al 2017) in how to respond to suicidal patients and helping them to address and reduce their suicidality. Although approximately 90% of mental health professionals report having an actively suicidal patient on their caseload, fewer than half receive suicide-specific training (Schmitz et al 2012). Dealing with patients who self-harm and/or are suicidal is perhaps one of the most difficult challenges faced by clinicians (Brown et al 2020). The limited training that mental health professionals receive relating to the assessment and management of suicidality may contribute to the burden felt by clinicians working in health care settings (Pope & Tabachnick 1993).

Losing a patient by suicide can impact on professional practice and even result in the avoidance of treating suicidal patients (Rothes et al 2014; Séguin et al 2014), almost a form of learned helplessness where reliance on the same systems for assessment and treatment continues. In a sample of 289 mental health practitioners, Jahn et al (2016) found 88% of mental health professionals had at least some level of fear relating to a patient dying by suicide, as well as discomfort around working with suicidal patients. Practitioners who felt their training was sufficient reported significantly greater comfort and skills in working with suicidal patients, as well as greater knowledge of suicide risk and protective factors.

Awenat et al (2017) interviewed 20 inpatient nursing staff, some of whom reported being reluctant to initiate or pursue discussions with patients about suicidality. Further, junior staff, with the least training or opportunities for clinical supervision, spent the most time with patients, but felt that engaging in conversations about distress and suicidality was beyond their remit, might harm the patient and leave themselves professionally and personally vulnerable. Awenat et al noted:

> the range of staff beliefs about suicidality had an impact on attitudes to patients and how this influenced patient care. For example, conceptualising suicidality as part of an illness resulted in some staff

> not addressing suicidality directly but in treating the underlying illness. Some staff viewed suicidality as an inevitable (and hence untreatable) feature of a condition. In contrast, a psychological conceptualisation that viewed suicidality as a response to modifiable thoughts resulted in more positive approaches and greater optimism for intervention.

Awenat et al urge service providers to recognise the emotional labour of caring for patients who are suicidal by actively encouraging staff uptake of training and clinical supervision and recommend that training and support should extend beyond risk assessment to improving staff skills in developing therapeutic interactions with inpatients who are suicidal. A systematic review by Sandford et al (2020) found the experience of losing a patient through suicide can have a significant impact on mental health professionals, both in terms of their personal reactions and subsequent changes to professional practice. The negative impact, however, may be moderated in particular by staff receiving support.

To conclude, training health professionals can help reduce suicide (Mann et al 2005; Beautrais et al 2007; Osteen et al 2014). If we agree that mental health services should provide SFIs then it follows that staff will need training in this as well as ongoing supervision. Whilst we may not be able to prevent a small number of people who are determined to end their life, we can ensure we have thoroughly assessed them, communicated our concern, treated them with empathy and compassion, and offered them appropriate help and intervention. In doing so we will also engage those people who are ambivalent and able to work with us to restore their hope (Hendin et al 2000).

Good practice point

All mental health services should provide suicide-specific interventions. All EDs in general hospitals should provide mental health assessment, safety planning and ideally BIC, a WHO-recommended evidence-based follow-up intervention for patients assessed as at risk of suicide. These require staff training and supervision to start up and support their ongoing delivery and efficacy.

Any staff member that has lost a patient to suicide will benefit from talking about their feelings and experience (Alexander et al 2000; Welton & Blackman 2006).

> ***Good practice point***
>
> All staff in secondary mental health services and liaison psychiatry services should be trained to deliver an evidence-based SFI. This will require leadership and ongoing investment. Any staff working with individuals at risk of suicide should receive training, supervision and support (especially when losing a client or patient from suicide).

The following are all well-established and academically evaluated skills-based training packages:

www.stormskillstraining.co.uk
www.livingworks.net
https://www.suicidefirstaid.uk/
https://cams-care.com
https://www.4mentalhealth.com/courses

References

Alexander DA, Klein S, Gray NM, Dewar IG, Eagles JM. Suicide by patients: Questionnaire study of its effect on consultant psychiatrists. *BMJ*. 2000;320(7249):1571–1574. doi:10.1136/bmj.320.7249.1571

Alonzo D. Suicidal individuals and mental health treatment: A novel approach to engagement. *Community Ment Health J*. 2016;52(5):527–533. doi:10.1007/s10597-015-9980-3

Alonzo D, Stanley B. A novel intervention for treatment of suicidal individuals. *Psychiatr Serv*. 2013;64(5):494. doi:10.1176/appi.ps.640105

Andreasson K, Krogh J, Bech P, Frandsen H, Buus N, Stanley B, Kerkhof A, Nordentoft M, Erlangsen A. MYPLAN - mobile phone application to manage crisis of persons at risk of suicide: Study protocol for a randomized controlled trial. *Trials*. 2017;18(1):171. doi:10.1186/s13063-017-1876-9

Armey MF, Schatten HT, Haradhvala N, Miller IW. Ecological momentary assessment (EMA) of depression-related phenomena. *Curr Opin Psychol*. 2015 Aug 1;4:21–25. doi:10.1016/j.copsyc.2015.01.002

Awenat Y, Peters S, Shaw-Nunez E, Gooding P, Pratt D, Haddock G. Staff experiences and perceptions of working with in-patients who are suicidal: Qualitative analysis. *Br J Psychiatry*. 2017;211(2):103–108. doi:10.1192/bjp.bp.116.191817

Bagge CL, Littlefield AK, Conner KR, Schumacher JA, Lee HJ. Near-term predictors of the intensity of suicidal ideation: An examination of the 24 h prior to a recent suicide attempt. *J Affect Disord.* 2014;165:53–58. doi:10.1016/j.jad.2014.04.010

Bagge CL, Littlefield AK, Glenn CR. Trajectories of affective response as warning signs for suicide attempts: An examination of the 48 hours prior to a recent suicide attempt. *Clin Psychol Sci.* 2017;5(2):259–271. doi:10.1177/2167702616681628

Bakker D, Kazantzis N, Rickwood D, Rickard N. Mental health smartphone apps: Review and evidence-based recommendations for future developments. *JMIR Ment Health.* 2016;3(1):e7. doi:10.2196/mental.4984

Beautrais A, Fergusson D, Coggan C, et al. Effective strategies for suicide prevention in New Zealand: A review of the evidence. *N Z Med J.* 2007;120(1251):U2459.

Beck AT, Brown GK, Steer RA, Dahlsgaard KK, Grisham JR. Suicide ideation at its worst point: A predictor of eventual suicide in psychiatric outpatients. *Suicide Life Threat Behav.* 1999;29(1):1–9.

Berk MS, Henriques GR, Warman DM, Brown GK, Beck AT. A cognitive therapy intervention for suicide attempters: An overview of the treatment and case examples. *Cogn Behav Pract.* 2004;11(3):265–277.

Berman AL, Silverman MM. How to ask about suicide? A question in need of an empirical answer. *Crisis.* 2017;38(4):213–216. doi:10.1027/0227-5910/a000501

Berrouiguet S, Courtet P, Larsen ME, Walter M, Vaiva G. Suicide prevention: Towards integrative, innovative and individualized brief contact interventions. *Eur Psychiatry.* 2018;47:25–26. doi:10.1016/j.eurpsy.2017.09.006

Bickley H, Hunt IM, Windfuhr K, Shaw J, Appleby L, Kapur N. Suicide within two weeks of discharge from psychiatric inpatient care: A case-control study. *Psychiatr Serv.* 2013;64(7):653–659. doi:10.1176/appi.ps.201200026

Britton PC, Conner KR, Maisto SA. An open trial of motivational interviewing to address suicidal ideation with hospitalized veterans. *J Clin Psychol.* 2012;68(9):961–971. doi:10.1002/jclp.21885

Britton PC, Patrick H, Wenzel A, Williams GC. Integrating motivational interviewing and self-determination theory with cognitive behavioral therapy to prevent suicide. *Cogn Behav Pract.* 2011;18(1):16–27. doi:10.1016/j.cbpra.2009.06.004

Britton PC, Williams GC, Conner KR. Self-determination theory, motivational interviewing, and the treatment of clients with acute suicidal ideation. *J Clin Psychol.* 2008;64(1):52–66. doi:10.1002/jclp.20430

Brodsky BS, Spruch-Feiner A, Stanley B. The zero suicide model: Applying evidence-based suicide prevention practices to clinical care. *Front Psychiatry.* 2018;9:33. doi:10.3389/fpsyt.2018.00033

Brown GK, Have T, Henriques GR, Xie SX, Hollander JE, Beck AT. Cognitive therapy for the prevention of suicide attempts: A randomized controlled trial. *JAMA.* 2005;294(5):563–570. doi:10.1001/jama.294.5.563

Brown GK, Henriques G, Ratto C, Beck AT. *Cognitive behavior therapy for adult suicide attempters.* Philadelphia: University of Pennsylvania; 2002.

Brown GK, Steer RA, Henriques GR, Beck AT. The internal struggle between the wish to die and the wish to live: A risk factor for suicide. *Am J Psychiatry.* 2005;162(10):1977–1979. doi:10.1176/appi.ajp.162.10.1977

Brown S, Iqbal Z, Burbidge F, Sajjad A, Reeve M, Ayres V, Melling R, Jobes D. Embedding an evidence-based model for suicide prevention in the national health service: A service improvement initiative. *Int J Environ Res Public Health.* 2020;17(14):E4920. doi:10.3390/ijerph17144920

Bryan C, ed. *Cognitive behavioral therapy for preventing suicide attempts: A guide to brief treatments across clinical settings.* New York: Routledge; 2015.

Bryan CJ, Mintz J, Clemans TA, et al. Effect of crisis response planning vs. contracts for safety on suicide risk in U.S. Army Soldiers: A randomized clinical trial. *J Affect Disord.* 2017;212:64–72. doi:10.1016/j.jad.2017.01.028

Bryan CJ, Rudd MD. *Brief cognitive-behavioral therapy for suicide prevention.* New York: Guilford Press; 2018.

Bush NE, Smolenski DJ, Denneson LM, Williams HB, Thomas EK, Dobscha SK. A virtual hope box: Randomized controlled trial of a smartphone app for emotional regulation and coping with distress. *Psychiatr Serv.* 2017;68(4):330–336. doi:10.1176/appi.ps.201600283

Buus N, Juel A, Haskelberg H, Frandsen H, Larsen JLS, River J, Andreasson K, Nordentoft M, Davenport T, Erlangsen A. User Involvement in developing the MYPLAN mobile phone safety plan app for people in suicidal crisis: Case study. *JMIR Ment Health* 2019;6(4):e11965. doi:10.2196/11965

Calati R, Courtet P. Is psychotherapy effective for reducing suicide attempt and non-suicidal self-injury rates? Meta-analysis and meta-regression of literature data. *J Psychiatr Res.* 2016;79:8–20. doi:10.1016/j.jpsychires.2016.04.003

Calear AL, Batterham PJ, Christensen H. Predictors of help-seeking for suicidal ideation in the community: Risks and opportunities for public suicide prevention campaigns. *Psychiatry Res.* 2014;219(3):525–530. doi:10.1016/j.psychres.2014.06.027

Carter GL, Clover K, Whyte IM, Dawson AH, D'Este C. Postcards from the EDge project: Randomised controlled trial of an intervention using postcards to reduce repetition of hospital treated deliberate self poisoning. *BMJ.* 2005;331(7520):805. doi:10.1136/bmj.38579.455266.E0

Centre for mental health. *Strengthening the front line.* London: April 2019.

Chan MK, Bhatti H, Meader N, Stockton S, Evans J, O'Connor RC, Kapur N, Kendall T. Predicting suicide following self-harm: Systematic review of risk factors and risk scales. *Br J Psychiatry.* 2016;209(4):277–283. doi:10.1192/bjp.bp.115.170050

Cole-King A, Green G, Gask L, Hines K, Platt S. Suicide mitigation: A compassionate approach to suicide prevention. *Advances in Psychiatric Treatment.* 2013;19:276–283. doi:10.1192/apt.bp.110.008763

Cole-King A, Lepping P. Suicide mitigation: Time for a more realistic approach. *Br J Gen Pract.* 2010;60(570):e1–e3. doi:10.3399/bjgp10X482022

Collins S, Cutcliffe JR. Addressing hopelessness in people with suicidal ideation: Building upon the therapeutic relationship utilizing a cognitive behavioural approach. *J Psychiatr Ment Health Nurs.* 2003;10(2):175–185. doi:10.1046/j.1365-2850.2003.00573.x

Jobes DA, Comtois KA, Gutierrez PM, Brenner LA, Huh D, Chalker SA, Ruhe G, Kerbrat AH, Atkins DC, Jennings K, Crumlish J, Corona CD, Connor SO, Hendricks KE, Schembari B, Singer B, Crow B. Collaborative assessment and management of suicidality (CAMS): Feasibility trial for next-day appointment services. *Depress Anxiety.* 2011;28(11):963–972. doi:10.1002/da.20895

Cooper J, Hunter C, Owen-Smith A, et al. "Well it's like someone at the other end cares about you." A qualitative study exploring the views of users and providers of care of contact-based interventions following self-harm. *Gen Hosp Psychiatry.* 2011;33(2):166–176. doi:10.1016/j.genhosppsych.2011.01.009

D'Anci KE, Uhl S, Giradi G, Martin C. Treatments for the prevention and management of suicide: A systematic review. *Ann Intern Med.* 2019;171(5):334–342. doi:10.7326/M19-0869

Davidson CL, Anestis MD, Gutierrez PM. Ecological momentary assessment is a neglected methodology in suicidology. *Arch Suicide Res.* 2017;21(1):1–11. doi:10.1080/13811118.2015.1004482

Dazzi T, Gribble R, Wessely S, Fear NT. Does asking about suicide and related behaviours induce suicidal ideation? What is the evidence? *Psychol Med.* 2014;44(16):3361–3363. doi:10.1017/S0033291714001299

de la Torre I, Castillo G, Arambarri J, López-Coronado M, Franco MA. Mobile apps for suicide prevention: Review of virtual stores and literature. *JMIR mHealth uHealth.* 2017;5(10):e130.

Devries K, Watts C, Yoshihama M, et al. Violence against women is strongly associated with suicide attempts: Evidence from the WHO multi-country study on women's health and domestic violence against women. *Soc Sci Med.* 2011;73(1):79–86. doi:10.1016/j.socscimed.2011.05.006

Donker T, Petrie K, Proudfoot J, Clarke J, Birch MR, Christensen H. Smartphones for smarter delivery of mental health programs: A systematic review. *J Med Internet Res.* 2013;15(11):e247. doi:10.2196/jmir.2791

Ducasse D, René E, Béziat S, Guillaume S, Courtet P, Olié E. Acceptance and commitment therapy for management of suicidal patients: A pilot study. *Psychother Psychosom.* 2014;83(6):374–376. doi:10.1159/000365974

Ellis TE, Rufino KA, Allen JG, Fowler JC, Jobes DA. Impact of a suicide-specific intervention within inpatient psychiatric care: The collaborative assessment and management of suicidality. *Suicide Life Threat Behav.* 2015;45(5):556–566. doi:10.1111/sltb.12151

Erlangsen A, Lind BD, Stuart EA, et al. Short-term and long-term effects of psychosocial therapy for people after deliberate self-harm: A register-based, nationwide multicentre study using propensity score matching. *Lancet Psychiatry.* 2015;2(1):49–58. doi:10.1016/S2215-0366(14)00083-2

Evans J, Evans M, Morgan HG, Hayward A, Gunnell D. Crisis card following self-harm: 12-month follow-up of a randomised controlled trial. Br J Psychiatry. 2005 Aug;187:186-7. doi: 10.1192/bjp.187.2.186. PMID: 16055834.

Fazel S, Runeson B. Suicide. *N Engl J Med.* 2020;382(3):266–274. doi:10.1056/NEJMra1902944

Fleischmann A, Bertolote JM, Wasserman D, et al. Effectiveness of brief intervention and contact for suicide attempters: A randomized controlled trial in five countries. *Bull World Health Organ.* 2008;86(9):703–709. doi:10.2471/blt.07.046995

Ghahramanlou-Holloway M, Cox D, Greene F. Post-admission cognitive therapy: A brief intervention for psychiatric inpatients admitted after a suicide attempt. *Cognitive and Behavioral Practice.* 2012;19:233–244.

Ghahramanlou-Holloway M, Neely LL, Tucker J. A cognitive-behavioral strategy for preventing suicide. *Current Psychiatry.* 2014;13(8):18–25,

Ghahramanlou-Holloway M, Neely LL, Tucker J, et al. Inpatient cognitive behavior therapy approaches for suicide prevention. *Curr Treat Options Psych.* 2015;2:371–382 doi:10.1007/s40501-015-0063-4

Gilburt H, Rose D, Slade M. The importance of relationships in mental health care: A qualitative study of service users' experiences of psychiatric hospital admission in the UK. *BMC Health Serv Res.* 2008;8:92. doi:10.1186/1472-6963-8-92

Gøtzsche PC, Gøtzsche PK. Cognitive behavioural therapy halves the risk of repeated suicide attempts: Systematic review. *J R Soc Med.* 2017;110(10):404–410. doi:10.1177/0141076817731904

Gould MS, Marrocco FA, Kleinman M, Thomas JG, Mostkoff K, Cote J, Davies M. Evaluating iatrogenic risk of youth suicide screening programs: A randomized controlled trial. *JAMA.* 2005;293(13):1635–1643. doi:10.1001/jama.293.13.1635

Guthrie E, Kapur N, Mackway-Jones K, Chew-Graham C, Moorey J, Mendel E, Marino-Francis F, Sanderson S, Turpin C, Boddy G, Tomenson B. Randomised controlled trial of brief psychological intervention after deliberate self-poisoning. *BMJ.* 2001;323(7305):135–138. doi:10.1136/bmj.323.7305.135

Gysin-Maillart A, Schwab S, Soravia L, Megert M, Michel K. A novel brief therapy for patients who attempt suicide: A 24-months follow-up randomized controlled study of the attempted suicide short intervention program (ASSIP). *PLoS Med.* 2016;13(3):e1001968. doi:10.1371/journal.pmed.1001968

Hallensleben N, Glaesmer H, Forkmann T, Rath D, Strauss M, Kersting A, Spangenberg L. Predicting suicidal ideation by interpersonal variables, hopelessness and depression in real-time. An ecological momentary assessment study in psychiatric inpatients with depression. *Eur Psychiatry.* 2019;56:43–50. doi:10.1016/j.eurpsy.2018.11.003

Hawton K. Suicide risk assessment psychiatry for general practitioners study days. December 2017. https://pdfs.semanticscholar.org/afb5/aeb33664477c98d8941cf6a17df441e02f1b.pdf

Hendin H, Lipschitz A, Maltsberger JT, Haas AP, Wynecoop S. Therapists' reactions to patients' suicides. *Am J Psychiatry*. 2000;157(12):2022–2027. doi:10.1176/appi.ajp.157.12.2022

Husky M, Olié E, Guillaume S, Genty C, Swendsen J, Courtet P. Feasibility and validity of ecological momentary assessment in the investigation of suicide risk. *Psychiatry Res*. 2014;220(1–2):564–570. doi:10.1016/j.psychres.2014.08.019

Inagaki M, Kawashima Y, Yonemoto N, Yamada M. Active contact and follow-up interventions to prevent repeat suicide attempts during high-risk periods among patients admitted to emergency departments for suicidal behavior: A systematic review and meta-analysis. *BMC Psychiatry*. 2019;19(1):44. doi:10.1186/s12888-019-2017-7

Institute of Medicine (US). Committee on pathophysiology and prevention of adolescent and adult suicide. In: Goldsmith SK, Pellmar TC, Kleinman AM, Bunney WE, editors. *Reducing suicide: A national imperative*. Washington, DC: National Academies Press; 2002.

Jahn DR, Quinnett P, Ries R. The influence of training and experience on mental health practitioners' comfort working with suicidal individuals. *Prof Psychol Res Pract*. 2016;47:130–138.

Jaroszewski AC, Morris RR, Nock MK. Randomized controlled trial of an online machine learning-driven risk assessment and intervention platform for increasing the use of crisis services. *J Consult Clin Psychol*. 2019;87(4):370–379. doi:10.1037/ccp0000389

Jobes D. *Managing suicidal risk, a collaborative approach*. New York: Guilford Press; 1st ed., 2006, 2nd ed., 2016.

Jobes DA, Chalker SA. One size does not fit all: A comprehensive clinical approach to reducing suicidal ideation, attempts, and deaths. *Int J Environ Res Public Health*. 2019;16(19):3606. doi:10.3390/ijerph16193606

Jobes DA, Comtois KA, Gutierrez PM, Brenner LA, Huh D, Chalker SA, Ruhe G, Kerbrat AH, Atkins DC, Jennings K, Crumlish J, Corona CD, Connor SO, Hendricks KE, Schembari B, Singer B, Crow B. A randomized controlled trial of the collaborative assessment and management of suicidality versus enhanced care as usual with suicidal soldiers. *Psychiatry*. 2017;80(4):339–356. doi:10.1080/00332747.2017.1354607

Jobes DA, Wong SA, Conrad AK, Drozd JF, Neal-Walden T. The collaborative assessment and management of suicidality versus treatment as usual: A retrospective study with suicidal outpatients. *Suicide Life Threat Behav*. 2005;35(5):483–497. doi:10.1521/suli.2005.35.5.483

Kapur N, Cooper J, Bennewith O, Gunnell D, Hawton K. Postcards, green cards and telephone calls: Therapeutic contact with individuals following self-harm. *Br J Psychiatry*. 2010;197(1):5–7. doi:10.1192/bjp.bp.109.072496

King K, Bassilios B, Reifels L, Fletcher J, Ftanou M, Blashki G, Burgess P, Pirkis J. Suicide prevention: Evaluation of a pilot intervention in a primary care context. *J Ment Health*. 2013;22(5):439–448. doi:10.3109/09638237.2013.815334

Kleiman EM, Nock MK. Real-time assessment of suicidal thoughts and behaviors. *Curr Opin Psychol*. 2018;22:33–37. doi:10.1016/j.copsyc.2017.07.026

Kleiman EM, Turner BJ, Fedor S, Beale EE, Huffman JC, Nock MK. Examination of real-time fluctuations in suicidal ideation and its risk factors: Results from two ecological momentary assessment studies. *J Abnorm Psychol*. 2017;126(6):726–738. doi:10.1037/abn0000273

Kleiman EM, Turner BJ, Fedor S, Beale EE, Picard RW, Huffman JC, Nock MK. Digital phenotyping of suicidal thoughts. *Depress Anxiety*. 2018;35(7):601–608. doi:10.1002/da.22730

Kreuze E, Jenkins C, Gregoski M, York J, Mueller M, Lamis DA, Ruggiero KJ. Technology-enhanced suicide prevention interventions: A systematic review. *J Telemed Telecare*. 2017;23(6):605–617. doi:10.1177/1357633X16657928

Krysinska K. ASSIP – Attempted suicide short intervention program. A manual for clinicians. *Advances in Mental Health.* 2016;14:1–3. doi:10.1080/18387357.2015.1123514

LaCroix JM, Perera KU, Neely LL, Grammer G, Weaver J, Ghahramanlou-Holloway M. Pilot trial of post-admission cognitive therapy: Inpatient program for suicide prevention. *Psychol Serv.* 2018;15(3):279–288. doi:10.1037/ser0000224

Landeweer E, Molewijk B, Hem MH, Pedersen R. Worlds apart? A scoping review addressing different stakeholder perspectives on barriers to family involvement in the care for persons with severe mental illness. *BMC Health Serv Res.* 2017;17(1):349. doi:10.1186/s12913-017-2213-2214

Larsen ME, Nicholas J, Christensen H. A Systematic assessment of smartphone tools for suicide prevention. *PLoS One.* 2016;11(4):e0152285. doi:10.1371/journal.pone.0152285

Larsen ME, Shand F, Morley K, Batterham PJ, Petrie K, Reda B, Berrouiguet S, Haber PS, Carter G, Christensen H. A Mobile text message intervention to reduce repeat suicidal episodes: Design and development of reconnecting after a suicide attempt (RAFT). *JMIR Ment Health.* 2017;4(4):e56. doi:10.2196/mental.7500

Larson EB, Yao X. Clinical empathy as emotional labor in the patient-physician relationship. *JAMA.* 2005;293(9):1100–1106. doi:10.1001/jama.293.9.1100

Law MK, Furr RM, Arnold EM, Mneimne M, Jaquett C, Fleeson W. Does assessing suicidality frequently and repeatedly cause harm? A randomized control study. *Psychol Assess.* 2015;27(4):1171–1181. doi:10.1037/pas0000118

Leavey K, Hawkins R. Is cognitive behavioural therapy effective in reducing suicidal ideation and behaviour when delivered face-to-face or via e-health? A systematic review and meta-analysis. *Cogn Behav Ther.* 2017;46(5):353–374. doi:10.1080/16506073.2017.1332095

Linehan MM. *Cognitive-behavioral treatment of borderline personality disorder.* New York: Guilford Press; 1993.

Littlewood DL, Quinlivan L, Graney J, Appleby L, Turnbull P, Webb RT, Kapur N. Learning from clinicians' views of good quality practice in mental healthcare services in the context of suicide prevention: A qualitative study. *BMC Psychiatry.* 2019;19(1):346. doi:10.1186/s12888-019-2336-8

LoParo D, Florez IA, Valentine N, Lamis DA. Associations of suicide prevention trainings with practices and confidence among clinicians at community mental health centers. *Suicide Life Threat Behav.* 2019;49(4):1148–1156. doi:10.1111/sltb.12498

Luxton DD, June JD, Comtois KA. Can post-discharge follow-up contacts prevent suicide and suicidal behavior? A review of the evidence. *Crisis.* 2013;34(1):32–41. doi:10.1027/0227-5910/a000158

Mann JJ, Apter A, Bertolote J, Beautrais A, Currier D, Haas A, Hegerl U, Lonnqvist J, Malone K, Marusic A, Mehlum L, Patton G, Phillips M, Rutz W, Rihmer Z, Schmidtke A, Shaffer D, Silverman M, Takahashi Y, Varnik A, Wasserman D, Yip P, Hendin H. Suicide prevention strategies: A systematic review. *JAMA.* 2005;294(16):2064–2074. doi:10.1001/jama.294.16.2064

Manuel J, Crowe M, Inder M, Henaghan M. Suicide prevention in mental health services: A qualitative analysis of coroners' reports. *Int J Ment Health Nurs.* 2018;27(2):642–651. doi:10.1111/inm.12349

Martinengo L, Van Galen L, Lum E, Kowalski M, Subramaniam M, Car J. Suicide prevention and depression apps' suicide risk assessment and management: a systematic assessment of adherence to clinical guidelines. BMC Med. 2019 Dec 19;17(1):231. doi: 10.1186/s12916-019-1461-z. PMID: 31852455; PMCID: PMC6921471

McBride CM, Emmons KM, Lipkus IM. Understanding the potential of teachable moments: The case of smoking cessation. *Health Educ Res.* 2003;18(2):156–170. doi:10.1093/her/18.2.156

McCabe R, Sterno I, Priebe S, Barnes R, Byng R. How do healthcare professionals interview patients to assess suicide risk? *BMC Psychiatry*. 2017;17(1):122. doi:10.1186/s12888-017-1212-7

McCarty CA, Russo J, Grossman DC, Katon W, Rockhill C, McCauley E, Richards J, Richardson L. Adolescents with suicidal ideation: Health care use and functioning. *Acad Pediatr*. 2011;11(5):422–426. doi:10.1016/j.acap.2011.01.004

Meehan J, Kapur N, Hunt IM, Turnbull P, Robinson J, Bickley H, Parsons R, Flynn S, Burns J, Amos T, Shaw J, Appleby L. Suicide in mental health in-patients and within 3 months of discharge. National clinical survey. *Br J Psychiatry*. 2006;188:129–134. doi:10.1192/bjp.188.2.129

Meerwijk EL, Parekh A, Oquendo MA, Allen IE, Franck LS, Lee KA. Direct versus indirect psychosocial and behavioural interventions to prevent suicide and suicide attempts: A systematic review and meta-analysis. *Lancet Psychiatry*. 2016;3(6): 544–554. doi:10.1016/S2215-0366(16)00064-X

Méndez-Bustos P, Calati R, Rubio-Ramírez F, Olié E, Courtet P, Lopez-Castroman J. Effectiveness of psychotherapy on suicidal risk: A systematic review of observational studies. *Front Psychol*. 2019;10:277. doi:10.3389/fpsyg.2019.00277

Mewton L, Andrews G. Cognitive behavioral therapy for suicidal behaviors: Improving patient outcomes. *Psychol Res Behav Manag*. 2016;9:21–29. doi:10.2147/PRBM.S84589

Mewton L, Andrews G. Cognitive behaviour therapy via the internet for depression: A useful strategy to reduce suicidal ideation. *J Affect Disord*. 2015;170:78–84. doi:10.1016/j.jad.2014.08.038

Michel K, Gysin-Maillart A. *ASSIP – Attempted suicide short intervention program: A manual for clinicians*. Göttingen: Hogrefe Publishing; 2015.

Miller IW, Camargo CA Jr, Arias SA, et al; ED-SAFE Investigators. Suicide prevention in an emergency department population: The ED-SAFE study. *JAMA Psychiatry*. 2017;74:563–570.

Milner A, Spittal MJ, Kapur N, Witt K, Pirkis J, Carter G. Mechanisms of brief contact interventions in clinical populations: A systematic review. *BMC Psychiatry*. 2016;16:194. doi:10.1186/s12888-016-0896-4

Milner AJ, Carter G, Pirkis J, Robinson J, Spittal MJ. Letters, green cards, telephone calls and postcards: Systematic and meta-analytic review of brief contact interventions for reducing self-harm, suicide attempts and suicide. *Br J Psychiatry*. 2015;206(3): 184–190. doi:10.1192/bjp.bp.114.147819

Millner AJ, Lee MD, Nock MK. Describing and measuring the pathway to suicide attempts: A preliminary study. *Suicide Life Threat Behav*. 2017;47(3):353–369. doi:10.1111/sltb.12284

Motto JA, Bostrom AG. A randomized controlled trial of postcrisis suicide prevention. *Psychiatr Serv*. 2001;52(6):828–833. doi:10.1176/appi.ps.52.6.828

Munro VE, Aitken R. From hoping to help: Identifying and responding to suicidality amongst victims of domestic abuse. *International Review of Victimology*. 2020;26(1):29-49. doi:10.1177/0269758018824160

National Collaborating Centre for Mental Health. *Self-harm and suicide prevention competence framework: Community and public health*. London: October 2018.

NHS Resolution. *Learning from suicide related claims: A thematic review of NHS resolution data*. 2018. https://resolution.nhs.uk/resources/learning-from-suicide-related-claims/

Noh D, Park YS, Oh EG. Effectiveness of telephone-delivered interventions following suicide attempts: A systematic review. *Arch Psychiatr Nurs*. 2016;30(1):114–119. doi:10.1016/j.apnu.2015.10.012

Nuij C, van Ballegooijen W, Ruwaard J, de Beurs D, Mokkenstorm J, van Duijn E, de Winter RFP, O'Connor RC, Smit JH, Riper H, Kerkhof A. Smartphone-based safety planning and self-monitoring for suicidal patients: Rationale and study protocol of the CASPAR (Continuous Assessment for Suicide Prevention and Research) study. *Internet Interventions.* 2018;13:16–23.

O'Connor RC, Ferguson E, Scott F, Smyth R, McDaid D, Park AL, Beautrais A, Armitage CJ. A brief psychological intervention to reduce repetition of self-harm in patients admitted to hospital following a suicide attempt: a randomised controlled trial. Lancet Psychiatry. 2017 Jun;4(6):451-460. doi: 10.1016/S2215-0366(17)30129-3. Epub 2017 Apr 20. PMID: 28434871; PMCID: PMC5447136.

O'Connor SS, Mcclay MM, Choudhry S, Shields AD, Carlson R, Alonso Y, Lavin K, Venanzi L, Comtois KA, Wilson JE, Nicolson SE. Pilot randomized clinical trial of the Teachable Moment Brief Intervention for hospitalized suicide attempt survivors. Gen Hosp Psychiatry. 2020 Mar-Apr;63:111-118. doi: 10.1016/j.genhosppsych.2018.08.001. Epub 2018 Aug 10. PMID: 30389316.

O'Connor RC, Nock MK. The psychology of suicidal behaviour. *Lancet Psychiatry.* 2014;1(1):73–85. doi:10.1016/S2215-0366(14)70222-6

O'Connor SS, Comtois KA, Wang J, Russo J, Peterson R, Lapping-Carr L, Zatzick D. The development and implementation of a brief intervention for medically admitted suicide attempt survivors. *Gen Hosp Psychiatry.* 2015;37(5):427–433. doi:10.1016/j.genhosppsych.2015.05.001

Oordt MS, Jobes DA, Fonseca VP, Schmidt SM. Training mental health professionals to assess and manage suicidal behavior: Can provider confidence and practice behaviors be altered? *Suicide Life Threat Behav.* 2009;39(1):21–32. doi:10.1521/suli.2009.39.1.21

Osteen PJ, Frey JJ, Ko J. Advancing training to identify, intervene, and follow up with individuals at risk for suicide through research. *Am J Prev Med.* 2014;47(3 Suppl 2): S216–S221. doi:10.1016/j.amepre.2014.05.033

Pauwels K, Aerts S, Muijzers E, De Jaegere E, van Heeringen K, Portzky G. BackUp: Development and evaluation of a smartphone application for coping with suicidal crises. *PLoS One.* 2017;12(6):e0178144.

Pope KS, Tabachnick BG. Therapists' anger, hate, fear, and sexual feelings: National survey of therapist responses, client characteristics, critical events, formal complaints, and training. *Prof Psychol Res Pract.*1993;24:142–152.

Power PJ, Bell RJ, Mills R, Herrman-Doig T, Davern M, Henry L, Yuen HP, Khademy-Deljo A, McGorry PD. Suicide prevention in first episode psychosis: The development of a randomised controlled trial of cognitive therapy for acutely suicidal patients with early psychosis. *Aust N Z J Psychiatry.* 2003;37(4):414–420. doi:10.1046/j.1440-1614.2003.01209.x

Quinlivan L, Cooper J, Meehan D, Longson D, Potokar J, Hulme T, Marsden J, Brand F, Lange K, Riseborough E, Page L, Metcalfe C, Davies L, O'Connor R, Hawton K, Gunnell D, Kapur N. Predictive accuracy of risk scales following self-harm: Multicentre, prospective cohort study. *Br J Psychiatry.* 2017;210(6):429–436. doi:10.1192/bjp.bp.116.189993

Riblet NB, Shiner B, Schnurr P, Bruce ML, Wasserman D, Cornelius S, Scott R, Watts BV. A pilot study of an intervention to prevent suicide after psychiatric hospitalization. *J Nerv Ment Dis.* 2019;207(12):1031–1038. doi:10.1097/NMD.0000000000001061

Riblet NBV, Shiner B, Young-Xu Y, Watts BV. Strategies to prevent death by suicide: Meta-analysis of randomised controlled trials. *Br J Psychiatry.* 2017;210(6):396–402. doi:10.1192/bjp.bp.116.187799

Rizvi SL, Ritschel LA. Mastering the art of chain analysis in dialectical behavior therapy. *Cognitive and Behavioral Practice.* 2014 Aug;21(3):335–349. doi:10.1016/j.cbpra.2013.09.002

Rothes IA, Henriques MR, Leal JB, Lemos MS. Facing a patient who seeks help after a suicide attempt: The difficulties of health professionals. *Crisis.* 2014;35(2):110–122. doi:10.1027/0227-5910/a000242

Royal College of Psychiatrists. *Self-harm, suicide and risk: Helping people who self-harm: Final report of a working group* (College Report CR158); 2010.

Rudd MD. Psychological treatments for suicidal behavior: What are the common elements of treatments that work? In: Wasserman D, editor, *Oxford Textbook of suicidology*. Oxford: Oxford University Press; 2009. pp. 427–438.

Rudd MD. The suicidal mode: A cognitive-behavioral model of suicidality. *Suicide Life Threat Behav*. 2000;30(1):18–33.

Rudd MD, Bryan CJ, Wertenberger EG, Peterson AL, Young-McCaughan S, Mintz J, Williams SR, Arne KA, Breitbach J, Delano K, Wilkinson E, Bruce TO. Brief cognitive-behavioral therapy effects on post-treatment suicide attempts in a military sample: Results of a randomized clinical trial with 2-year follow-up. *Am J Psychiatry*. 2015;172(5):441–449. doi:10.1176/appi.ajp.2014.14070843

Ryberg W, Zahl PH, Diep LM, Landrø NI, Fosse R. Managing suicidality within specialized care: A randomized controlled trial. *J Affect Disord*. 2019;249:112–120. doi:10.1016/j.jad.2019.02.022

Salvatore T. *Intimate partner violence: A pathway to suicide*. 2018. https://www.researchgate.net/publication/325880393_Intimate_Partner_Violence_A_Pathway_to_Suicide

Samaritans. *Dying from inequality. Socioeconomic disadvantage and suicidal behaviour*. Summary Report; 2017.

Sandford DM, Kirtley OJ, Thwaites R, O'Connor RC. The impact on mental health practitioners of the death of a patient by suicide: a systematic review. *Clin Psychol Psychother*. 2020 Sep 10. doi: 10.1002/cpp.2515. Epub ahead of print. PMID: 32914489.

Schmitz WM Jr, Allen MH, Feldman BN, Gutin NJ, Jahn DR, Kleespies PM, Quinnett P, Simpson S. Preventing suicide through improved training in suicide risk assessment and care: An American Association of Suicidology Task Force report addressing serious gaps in U.S. mental health training. *Suicide Life Threat Behav*. 2012;42(3):292–304.

Schuberg K, Jobes DA, Ballard E, Kraft TL, Kerr NA, Hyland CA, Friemuth J, Seaman K, Guidry E, Knyazev E. Pre/post/post evaluations of CAMS-trained VA clinicians. In *Proceedings of the American Association of Suicidology Conference*, San Francisco, CA, USA. April 2009.

Séguin M, Bordeleau V, Drouin MS, Castelli-Dransart DA, Giasson F. Professionals' reactions following a patient's suicide: Review and future investigation. *Arch Suicide Res*. 2014;18(4):340–362. doi:10.1080/13811118.2013.833151

Selby EA, Yen S, Spirito A. Time varying prediction of thoughts of death and suicidal ideation in adolescents: Weekly ratings over 6-month follow-up. *Journal of Clinical Child & Adolescent Psychology*. 2013;42(4):481–495.

Shand FL, Ridani R, Tighe J, Christensen H. The effectiveness of a suicide prevention app for indigenous Australian youths: Study protocol for a randomized controlled trial. *Trials*. 2013;14:396. doi:10.1186/1745-6215-14-396

Skovgaard Larsen JL, Frandsen H, Erlangsen A. MYPLAN–A mobile phone application for supporting people at risk of suicide. *Crisis*. 2016;37(3):236–240. doi:10.1027/0227-5910/a000371

Smith P, Poindexter E, Cukrowicz K. The effect of participating in suicide research: Does participating in a research protocol on suicide and psychiatric symptoms increase suicide ideation and attempts? *Suicide and Life-Threatening Behavior*. 2010;40(6):535–543.

Stanley B, Brown GK. Safety planning intervention: A brief intervention to mitigate suicide risk. *Cognitive and Behavioral Practice*. 2012;19(2):256–264.

Stanley B, Brown G, Brent DA, Wells K, Poling K, Curry J, Kennard BD, Wagner A, Cwik MF, Klomek AB, Goldstein T, Vitiello B, Barnett S, Daniel S, Hughes J. Cognitive-behavioral therapy for suicide prevention (CBT-SP): Treatment model, feasibility, and acceptability. *J Am Acad Child Adolesc Psychiatry*. 2009;48(10): 1005–1013. doi:10.1097/CHI.0b013e3181b5dbfe

Stanley B, Brown GK, Brenner LA, et al. Comparison of the safety planning intervention with follow-up vs usual care of suicidal patients treated in the emergency department. *JAMA Psychiatry*. 2018;75:894–900.

Steeg S, Quinlivan L, Nowland R, Carroll R, Casey D, Clements C, Cooper J, Davies L, Knipe D, Ness J, O'Connor RC, Hawton K, Gunnell D, Kapur N. Accuracy of risk scales for predicting repeat self-harm and suicide: A multicentre, population-level cohort study using routine clinical data. *BMC Psychiatry*. 2018;18(1):113. doi:10.1186/s12888-018-1693-z

Stoddard JA, Afari N. *The big book of ACT metaphors: A practitioner's guide to experiential exercises and metaphors in acceptance and commitment therapy*. Oakland, CA: New Harbinger Publications; 2014.

Sudak DM, Rajyalakshmi AK. Reducing suicide risk: The role of psychotherapy. *Psychiatric Times*. 2018;35(12):12–13.

Tarrier N, Taylor K, Gooding P. *Cognitive-behavioral interventions to reduce suicide behavior: A systematic review and meta-analysis*. In: Database of Abstracts of Reviews of Effects (DARE): Quality-assessed Reviews [Internet]. York, UK: Centre for Reviews and Dissemination; 2008.

The National Confidential Inquiry into Suicide and Homicide by People with Mental Illness. *Annual report: England, Northern Ireland, Scotland and Wales*. Manchester: University of Manchester; July 2013.

The National Confidential Inquiry into Suicide and Homicide by People with Mental Illness. *Annual report: England, Northern Ireland, Scotland and Wales*. Manchester: University of Manchester; 2017. https://sites.manchester.ac.uk/ncish/reports/annual-report-2017-england-northern-ireland-scotland-and-wales/

The National Confidential Inquiry into Suicide and Safety in Mental Health (NCISH). *Annual report 2018*. https://sites.manchester.ac.uk/ncish/.

Thompson AR, Powis J, Carradice A. Community psychiatric nurses' experience of working with people who engage in deliberate self-harm. *Int J Ment Health Nurs*. 2008;17(3):153–161. doi:10.1111/j.1447-0349.2008.00533.x

Tighe J, Shand F, Ridani R, Mackinnon A, De La Mata N, Christensen H. Ibobbly mobile health intervention for suicide prevention in Australian Indigenous youth: A pilot randomised controlled trial. *BMJ Open*. 2017 Dec 27;7(1):e013518. doi:10.1136/bmjopen-2016-013518

Tucker RP, Crowley KJ, Davidson CL, Gutierrez PM. Risk factors, warning signs, and drivers of suicide: What are they, how do they differ, and why does it matter? *Suicide Life Threat Behav*. 2015;45(6):679–689. doi:10.1111/sltb.12161

Vaiva G, Berrouiguet S, Walter M, Courtet P, Ducrocq F, Jardon V, Larsen ME, Cailhol L, Godesense C, Couturier C, Mathur A, Lagree V, Pichene C, Travers D, Lemogne C, Henry JM, Jover F, Chastang F, Prudhomme O, Lestavel P, Gignac CT, Duhem S, Demarty AL, Mesmeur C, Bellivier F, Labreuche J, Duhamel A, Goldstein P. Combining postcards, crisis cards, and telephone contact into a decision-making algorithm to reduce suicide reattempt: A randomized clinical trial of a personalized brief contact intervention. *J Clin Psychiatry*. 2018;79(6):17m11631. doi:10.4088/JCP.17m1163

Vaiva G, Vaiva G, Ducrocq F, Meyer P, Mathieu D, Philippe A, Libersa C, Goudemand M. Effect of telephone contact on further suicide attempts in patients discharged from an emergency department: Randomised controlled study. *BMJ*. 2006;332(7552):1241–1245. doi:10.1136/bmj.332.7552.1241

Vijayakumar L, Umamaheswari C, Shujaath Ali ZS, Devaraj P, Kesavan K. Intervention for suicide attempters: A randomized controlled study. *Indian J Psychiatry*. 2011;53(3):244–248. doi:10.4103/0019-5545.86817

Wang YC, Hsieh LY, Wang MY, Chou CH, Huang MW, Ko HC. Coping card usage can further reduce suicide reattempt in suicide attempter case management within 3-month intervention. *Suicide Life Threat Behav*. 2016;46(1):106–120. doi:10.1111/sltb.12177

Watts S, Newby JM, Mewton L, Andrews G. A clinical audit of changes in suicide ideas with internet treatment for depression. *BMJ Open*. 2012;2(5):e001558. doi:10.1136/bmjopen-2012-001558

Welton RS. The management of suicidality: Assessment and intervention. *Psychiatry (Edgmont)*. 2007;4(5):24–34.

Welton RS, Blackman LR. Suicide and the air force mental health provider: Frequency and impact. *Mil Med*. 2006;171(9):844–848. doi:10.7205/milmed.171.9.844

Wenzel A, Brown GK, Beck AT. *Cognitive therapy for suicidal patients: Scientific and clinical applications*. Washington, DC: APA Books; 2009.

Wenzel A, Jager-Hyman S. Cognitive therapy for suicidal patients: Current status. *Behav Ther*. 2012;35(7):121–130.

Whiteside U, Richards J, Huh D, Hidalgo R, Nordhauser R, Wong AJ, Zhang X, Luxton DD, Ellsworth M, Lezine D. Development and evaluation of a web-based resource for suicidal thoughts: NowMattersNow.org. *J Med Internet Res*. 2019;21(5):e13183. doi:10.2196/13183

Winter D, Bradshaw S, Bunn F, Wellsted D. A systematic review of the literature on counselling and psychotherapy for the prevention of suicide: 1. Quantitative outcome and process studies. *Couns Psychother Res*. 2013;13(3):164–183. doi:10.1080/14733145.2012.761717

Wu CY, Chang CK, Hayes RD, Broadbent M, Hotopf M, Stewart R. Clinical risk assessment rating and all-cause mortality in secondary mental healthcare: The South London and Maudsley NHS Foundation Trust Biomedical Research Centre (SLAM BRC) Case Register. *Psychol Med*. 2012;42(8):1581–1590.

Zalsman G, Hawton K, Wasserman D, van Heeringen K, Arensman E, Sarchiapone M, Carli V, Höschl C, Barzilay R, Balazs J, Purebl G, Kahn JP, Sáiz PA, Lipsicas CB, Bobes J, Cozman D, Hegerl U, Zohar J. Suicide prevention strategies revisited: 10-year systematic review. *Lancet Psychiatry*. 2016;3(7):646–659. doi:10.1016/S2215-0366(16)30030-X

PART 3

KEY SUICIDE INTERVENTION SKILLS

Some suicide-focused interventions are manualised in which, typically, topics to be discussed are pre-set. The advantages of this is that it is easier to train staff to deliver such a protocol and in particular to assess its efficacy in research trials. However, people presenting with suicide risk have diverse motivation and may have complex needs such as homelessness, substance misuse or a relationship crisis. A pre-ordained agenda is likely to be inappropriate or too insensitive and many patients would not engage in such highly structured protocols. The pacing and timing of subjects which may be critical to tackle such as reduction in means may need to be adapted according to the person's ambivalence, willingness and level of engagement at that time. I would therefore advocate the use of evidence-based psychological interventions and strategies within a structured framework such as CAMS. The framework should always include a robust and ongoing risk assessment as well as a treatment contract and safety plan. Here are ten key skills for practitioners to employ within such an SFI. They are drawn from evidence-based interventions:

3.1 Validation

Validation is a skill identified and developed within DBT for use by therapists and clients. Whilst DBT was developed for people with a specific disorder who self-harm and attempt suicide, the skills are being researched for wider application and definitely relevant for anyone who is considering ending their life. Validating your client helps them to know you have "heard" them and have some awareness of their pain and their struggle in tolerating it. It is the expression of genuine understanding of someone's experience or behaviour (emotion, want, thought, sensation, action), and how that "makes sense" (Linehan 1993). The practitioner takes the client's experience or behaviour seriously and communicates that it is understandable and legitimate in one or more ways. It is important to be sincere and not patronising. We aim to *validate the valid*, i.e. what is legitimate in context, i.e. taking account of the person's history and current situation.

The purpose of validation by clinicians or practitioners is to:

1. increase therapist-client rapport and strengthen the therapeutic alliance;
2. model and strengthen self-validation;
3. facilitate change by using validation as a reinforcer for shaping skilful behaviour in the desired direction of change.

When validation is employed as a reinforcer, it should be contingent on the client being skilful or making progress. The clinician highlights what is understandable or legitimate (valid). By targeting what we validate, we can communicate acceptance and understanding, *and* facilitate change. In DBT the therapist is typically validating a specific behaviour or experience of the person. Fruzzetti and Rourke (2018) explain:

> Thinking, especially non-judgmental thinking and accurate appraisals are all easily validated because they are not likely provocative and are easy to understand. Of course, judgments, misappraisals, and problematic thinking can be validated, but it is trickier, and these must be validated in quite different ways. If a client says, *I know I'm just a terrible, awful person*, the therapist can validate what is actually valid about this kind of self-invalidating

thinking and statement: *I know you often think very judgmentally about yourself.* The therapist might add additional, more change-oriented interventions immediately, of course (e.g. *What actually happened? What did you do? Can you be more descriptive*? or, simply, *Can you say that again, without the judgments*?). But, leading with the validating statement may be essential to let the client know that the therapist does understand his or her experience, and its importance to the client, prior to targeting it for change.

Linehan (1993) identified six levels of validation. Each level increases in complexity but all are valuable. Higher levels of validation may presuppose the earlier levels. The most effective validation is the level that fits the situation and the therapeutic goals.

1. The first level of validation is providing **openness, paying attention and active listening**. When someone is considering ending their life, responding in this way may not come readily as we have a built-in aversion to suicide. So this skill requires us to be willing to push through that and just stay open, listen and be interested. Show interest in the other person (through verbal and nonverbal cues), and demonstrate you are paying attention (nodding, eye contact, etc.)

   Ask questions and give prompts – "Tell me more", "uh-huh".
2. The second level of validation is **acknowledging and accurately reflecting the experience of the client**. "So, right now you have no other solutions for managing this pain". (This could be a segue into that becoming a potential agenda for working together.) Summarise what the person is sharing, then ask, "Is that right?" Take a non-judgemental stance towards the person. Even if you think their perception is exaggerated or personalised you can still validate that how they feel. Notice this is also an important quality when practising motivational interviewing (MI) (see below)
3. The third level of validation is **articulating unverbalised experiences or behaviours**. Although we are usually discouraged from mind reading it may be necessary to guess at what the person is feeling but struggling to say, "I wonder if you're feeling…?" Be careful not to make assumptions and do ask your client if that seems to fit for them or not.

4. The fourth level of validation is **validating in terms of the person's previous learning or** biology. We react to the world based on our previous experiences and biological wiring. If we have had a negative experience, future situations similar to the previous experience may trigger difficult thoughts and feelings. "It makes sense why you would think your life can never get better given how many times life has knocked you back".
5. The fifth level of validation is **normalising the client's behaviour or experience** by recognising emotional reactions that most people would have. Knowing that other people would have similar reactions to a situation helps to reduce the critical self-judgements of oneself or one's sense of isolation. This might sound like, "When you lose someone from suicide it is entirely natural that you feel angry toward that person. This is a difficult set of emotions and thoughts to process because you are also feeing sad and loving toward them".
6. The sixth level of validation is **radical genuineness**. This could be a validation of a very negative experience or state (e.g. "losing contact with your children is one of the most painful things that can happen to a parent. I can't imagine how bad that feels") or an expression of your commitment to help them move forward. You can express that you believe they have resources even if they are not easily accessible at the moment. "Right now, you don't how else to manage this pain. I would really like to help you find other solutions or at least consider them". When someone has lost all hope or is without hope, you can *hold the hope for them* until they are able to pick it up again.

3.2 Chain or functional analysis of suicidal behaviour

Functional analysis is a step-by-step examination of the triggers, events, thoughts, feelings, body sensations and behaviours that lead to suicidal urges and behaviours. It is a collaborative structured mapping which is then used to indicate relevant problem-solving strategies that can help stop clients from attempting suicide in the future.

Doing a functional or chain analysis before your safety plan will enable you to develop a much more personalised plan which targets key factors for that individual's suicidal "mode". Initial questions could be:

> Please tell me about what happened on the day of your last suicide attempt. I would like to hear about the triggers, thoughts, feelings, and actions that resulted in your decision to attempt suicide. I'd like to know the key thought, emotions, physical sensations you had and what actions you took. Let's start with when you decided to end your life or attempt to end your life. When did you make that decision? What led up to it?

Steps in doing a functional or chain analysis:

1. Name the behaviour being analysed in the analysis, e.g. took 50 sertraline; went to the railway bridge, and then work backwards and forwards from that point

Then identify:

2. Vulnerability factors relevant in the preceding hours. (Keep to a maximum of 24 hours as otherwise the chain can become too unwieldy.) Include physical illness or injury, drugs and alcohol; intense emotions; inadequate eating or sleeping or stressful events.
3. Events, thoughts, feelings and body sensations that lead up to the suicidal act. Significant earlier life events such as major loss can be identified in current thoughts and emotions.
4. The consequences for the person and their environment; short term and perhaps (later in an intervention for example) longer term.

Identifying consequences of suicidal thinking and behaviour is important (Table 3.1).

Table 3.1 Possible consequences of suicidal behaviour

	In self	*In environment*
Short-term	(usually immediate) "relief" – reduction in negative affect and physical tension, such as intense chronic emptiness and anger	(often some delay) Perhaps concern from others
Medium-term	Either regret I didn't die or regret I attempted suicide, i.e. shame	Those who know may treat the person differently
Longer-term	Feeling I've failed at ending my life; possible scars shame	There may be an impact on the person's close relationships

Don't at this stage judge whether consequences are good or bad for the person but rather try to identify and name them non-judgementally. In behavioural psychology or operant conditioning, reinforcement is a consequence that will strengthen a future response or behaviour. Reinforcement is anything delivered contingent on a behaviour that makes the behaviour likely to happen again. Positive reinforcement adds a desirable or favourable outcome, event or reward after an action. One of the easiest ways to remember positive reinforcement is to think of it as something being *added*; e.g. endorphins after self-harm can feel pleasant. Negative reinforcement also increases the chance of behaviour re-occurring but by *reducing an undesirable or aversive stimulus*. Suicidal thinking may be followed by a decrease in negative affect or an increase in positive affect. In a sample of 217 patients with a history of recurrent depression and suicidality, Crane et al (2014) found 15% reported experiencing comfort from suicidal cognitions and that comfort was associated with several markers of a more severe clinical profile including both worst-ever prior suicidal ideation and worst suicidal ideation over a 12-month follow-up period. Ruminating about suicide may give the person a sense of relief as it confers a sense of control over their psychological pain; they believe the pain will go away if they die. So contemplating suicide is both positively and negatively reinforced but as it represents an escape from intolerable pain or circumstances it is mostly negatively reinforced. Both non-suicidal self-injury (Nock 2010) and suicidal behaviour (Kleiman et al 2018) are mostly negatively reinforced – they bring a reduction in aversive or dysphoric states or affect.

So do consider what is reinforcing or maintaining suicidal thoughts and specific suicide-related behaviours (e.g. keeping the means to end one's life). Reinforcers may be different for thoughts and actions and across individuals. Reinforcers can be responses from others (social reinforcement of suicidal behaviour would usually be in the context of emotionally unstable personality disorder). They can also be physiological, such as an increase in endorphins or reduction in arousal). Please note that what psychologists mean by negative reinforcement and what a lay person may understand to be negative reinforcement are very different.

Some clients will be able to give you a clear temporal account starting with triggers and any vulnerability factors. Then you can write down what happened in a temporal order using the four domains (thoughts and beliefs; physical sensations; actions or behaviour; and emotions). To these we can also add (in one or two words) events or vulnerability factors.

Example of a suicide chain analysis:

Vulnerability factors: worry over being unemployed band in debt; only got 4 or 5 hours sleep

Thoughts "I am a failure. I can't provide for my family"

Emotions Shame Hopelessness

Thought "I can no longer do this to my family. They would be better off without me"

Action took all the tablets I had (around 50 sertraline)

Event: my wife found me and called an ambulance & I was taken to 'A & E'

Thoughts I've failed again

Emotion guilt

Notice I have written the thoughts (or beliefs) in italics. This is because you don't want to reify them as if they have equivalent factual status to real events like being unemployed or going to an emergency department (ED). This is an example of shaping (see p ....).

Other clients will have a less clear memory of what happened in any clear order. Then you can use a more phenomenological approach and put the key elements in these four areas. Once you've done this you do want a sense of what came in what order (Figure 3.1).

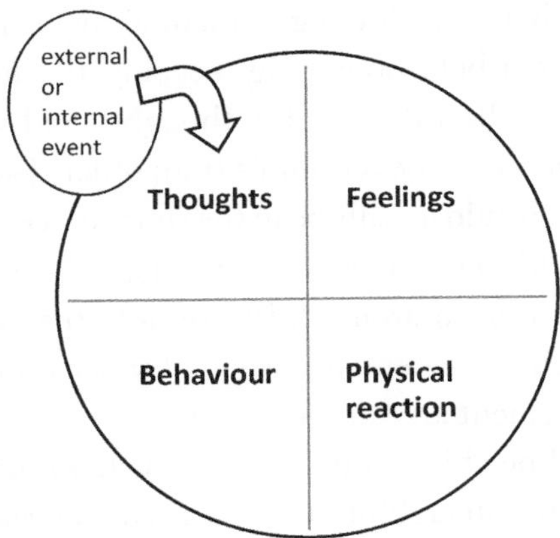

Figure 3.1 Hot cross bun.

General principles for "chaining" are:

- Keep it simple.
- Help the person take an active part – get them to write it or co-write it.
- Focus on the few hours before the suicide attempt.
- Validate whenever you have the opportunity or prompt based on your knowledge of the person and their risk factors or drivers, e.g. regarding distal or stable risk factors which may not necessarily appear in the chain.
- Elucidate the personal meaning (which will be in "thoughts" quadrant) of direct drivers (see p…).
- Identifying factors as thoughts or beliefs, emotions, actions or physical sensations is helpful for making an accurate formulation as well as providing teaching points for the client. Hopelessness, for example, is a combination of an emotion (sadness) and a thought ("I have no future"; "my life is over", etc.). Thoughts and emotions indicate different skills for managing them. Sadness will probably need acceptance-based skills such as distress tolerance whereas thoughts can be modified (change skills) or defused from.

Applying what you've learnt in the chain

Once you've established vulnerability factors and key suicide "drivers" then this indicates what needs to be targeted in the safety plan and/or skills building, for example, help people tackle sleep problems; addressing

> ***Good practice point***
>
> People with poor mental states tend either to ruminate or, if ambivalent about suicide, put off acting on suicidal thoughts or urges and over-rely on distraction to cope. This typically results in them trying to intervene too late when their thoughts and urges are then so high, they are hard to resist. Targeting alternative coping responses earlier in the chain is more likely to avert suicidal behaviour and build resilience. Using a metaphor can help clients remember this, such as "taking action before you fall off the cliff". This is also a compassionate way of urging them to seek professional help before self-harming or taking steps towards a suicide plan such as going to a train track or bridge.

indirect drivers such as debt and unemployment and also tackle direct drivers such as perceived failure.

Agree two or three key areas to target. Consider their order of priority in terms of risk (based on how much they recur for the client and your knowledge of risk factors). Also prioritise them according to what the person themselves wants to prioritise and what they are most willing to tackle first. ***Push it where it moves.*** *Early wins* can help rebuild optimism and therapeutic rapport.

As health professionals, we are in the business of shaping healthier behaviours – increasing and strengthening skilful behaviour and decreasing unskilful behaviour. Which behaviours do you want to increase and which behaviours do you want to decrease? Consider the following concepts to help you do this:

Stimulus control is a term used to describe situations in which behaviour is triggered by the *presence or absence of a stimulus*. For example, if you always eat when you watch TV, your eating behaviour is "cued" by the stimulus of watching TV. Cues for suicidal states or modes can include anniversaries or deaths. This can be an important aspect that contributes to repetitive behaviours and can be helpful to address when trying to reduce unskilful behaviour. *Shaping* is a behaviour modification technique in which *successive approximations* to the desired behaviour is rewarded. Any behaviour leading to the desired behaviour (e.g. help-seeking before a suicidal act) is rewarded. Another behavioural process is habituation. Suicidal individuals may build a tolerance for the negative aspects of suicide (e.g. physical pain or fear) through repeated exposure to painful stimuli or fear (Joiner 2005).

3.3 Safety planning and promoting adherence to the plan

Safety planning is a structured and proactive way to help people plan effective strategies, activities and sources of support they can use to help them prevent or manage a developing crisis and keep them safe from self-harm. Suicidal urges fluctuate, so if the person can delay acting on suicidal impulses, it could be lifesaving.

> ***Good practice point***
> Everyone at risk of suicide should have a safety plan with strategies for keeping themselves safe, Reasons for living (RFL) and who to contact for support.

A safety plan should include:

- RFL and reasons not to harm themselves, with a gentle request to consider these.
- A plan to keep the person's environment safe, including any agreement to remove or distance from self-harm or suicidal means.
- Activities to lift their mood or help to calm them. I don't encourage distraction as people are usually already over-reliant on this and distraction doesn't transform mood or mental state. Buying time is a valid goal, as suicidal thoughts fluctuate but ideally this is done with activities in line with values or activities that *improve the movement* (Linehan 1993) or provide skilful occupation.
- People to talk to if distressed. It is important to build a network of support that can be mobilised in the event of a crisis. This might include both personal contacts and third-sector organisations such as the Samaritans. Cole-King et al (2013) suggest a "key contact" from the person's immediate circle of family and friends should be identified. This needs to be someone the person can trust who can support them and, if helpful, to attend appointments.
- Professional support, such as 24-hour crisis telephone lines.
- Emergency NHS contact details.
- Names and all phone numbers for people to be contacted; personal agreement to use the plan and review it together at intervals.

Stanley and Brown (2008) suggest the following the following principles:

1. Recognising warning signs that are proximal to an impending suicidal crisis

   By reflecting back on previous crises, using timelines or chain analysis, we identify warning signs for the client to watch out for.

   Helpful questions to assist recognition of warning signs include:

   "How will you know when you need to start using your safety plan?"

   "Looking back, what events, thoughts and feelings have triggered previous suicidal states?"

2. Identifying and employing internal coping strategies without needing to contact another person

   a. Identify coping strategies – "what has worked before?"
   b. Discuss the likelihood of using such strategies "How likely do you think you would be able to do this during a time of crisis?"
   c. Identify barriers and problem-solve: "What might prevent you from thinking of or doing these activities or skills?" Problem-solve together to address barriers and discuss alternatives and strategies.

3. Naming people to contact (friends and family) without discussing suicidal thoughts, to optimise social connectedness or belongingness. Consider social settings the person can attend (e.g. church group or place of worship, day centres, gyms, clubs) and identify friends and family members that the service user might feel able to contact to do some activity with. Include contacts for "kindly interaction" (not necessarily confiding their suicidal thoughts). Getting social interaction through an activity can have a double benefit by meeting interpersonal needs and improving mood through behavioural activation.
4. Contact family members or friends who may help to resolve a crisis and with whom suicidality *can* be discussed. Ideally these will be people who are willing and have agreed to help. The client may, for example, have shared their crisis plan with them. These need

to be appropriate adults rather than young carers (as can happen when a young person is supporting a parent with mental health problems or suicidal crises).

5. Contacting mental health professionals

   It is helpful to clarify and agree the purpose of this, how long the call is likely to last and what the focus will be. In order to address suicide risk effectively, an unplanned crisis call will typically take 15–30 minutes. As in DBT, it is a good idea to keep these calls short and focused. Don't simply instruct the patient to contact services (sadly this is common practice). Enquire if they are likely to and, if not, what will get in the way of them contacting services. Discuss their expectations of what will happen and if necessary previous experiences. Crisis or out-of-hours services can have low satisfaction with service users. There are a number of reasons for this such as high staff turnover or inadequate training. It may be helpful to give the patient some context about the crisis service, e.g. how pressured they are so can end up giving out suggestions which can seem unhelpful or too generalised. I often explain that we have staff shortages and may have to rely on less experienced temporary staff. If there is a specific practitioner they do not want to talk to again, it can be helpful to explain the size of the team and ask the patient to estimate the chances of getting that individual again. They may even have avoided contacting the crisis service because of one practitioner they fell out with who in fact left the service. If the person knows DBT skills you can invite them to practise *willingness* or *beginner's mind.*

6. Reducing the potential for using lethal means

   Discuss and reduce access to means and strategies to reduce risk. Service users should be encouraged to take responsibility for disposing of or handing in means that they are in possession of and are thinking of using to self-harm in the immediate or distant future. It is important to explore ambivalence here; discussing their suicidality is evidence of ambivalence and provides opportunities to look for RFL.

In addition to this I would add that

- Ideally a person should write their own safety plan with support, as practised in CAMS (Jobes 2006, 2016) or it can be co-written with a clinician or practitioner. StayingSafe.net has a downloadable blank safety plan template.
- The safety plan should be rooted in and informed by your assessment of that individual and their personal formulation of suicidality. For example, Sudak and Rajyalakshmi (2018) suggest patients can be asked to reflect on the things that will be missed if they die, year by year. This can bring to mind the reality of what the patient will miss. However, this would not be a wise suggestion if you had established that the person saw themselves as a burden to their family and friends as thinking about future events could trigger thoughts that the suicidal person would spoil them if they were there.
- Target key factors identified from your chain analysis, such as the need to reduce physical arousal or agitation or connect to feeling loved. If someone feels suicidal when problems feel overwhelming, you may want to suggest they write a worry list which they can then break down into manageable steps and just focus on one at a time or seek help in tackling the problems. If they become emotionally dysregulated then recording their feelings in a diary, letter, blog or video could be helpful.
- Consider the context of where people are likely to be. Are they living alone? with supportive others? with others who may trigger them? Are they most likely to feel suicidal late at night?
- Be sensitive when listing supportive others lest people have limited or even no supportive relationships or people they would trust. If this is the case, then contact with animals and pets can also be very beneficial. I have known clients who even have an important affiliation with someone else's pet if they are unable to have pets themselves.
- Always have a small range of agreed options as no one skill works all the time or fits every situation.
- Address obstacles. Troubleshoot what stops people seeking help or connecting to others. Consider doing a "hot cross bun" and identifying core beliefs. For example, people may feel they are burden or not

know how to ask for help with words. These obstacles can then be addressed in your SFI, by shaping and role-play for example. You can write a script together of how to ask for help; what to say to whom and role-play doing this.

- Rather than aiming to write the perfect safety plan in one go, include elements which the client has some experience of working for them and confidence they can help so are likely to use. If this doesn't apply, then don't include those elements until and unless the client acquires this with coaching and practice.
- Everyone can benefit from having the Samaritans contact details (telephone 116 123). This is especially important for clients who are unlikely to contact professional services. Invite the client to enter this and mental health service numbers into their mobile.

Safety planning is a process, not an end in itself. A common deficiency or error in mental health practice when staff are under pressure to complete tasks or have high caseloads or throughput of patients is to prescribe a safety plan which the patient may or may not be able or willing to participate in. If you have significant suicidal thoughts and urges, maintaining one's own safety requires a set of skills which need guidance, fostering, practice, shaping and reviewing. The process of safety planning usually requires "shaping" self-care as well as shaping help-seeking behaviour before or after self-harm. A patient may not follow advice if requested too early within an intervention. Skills often need to be rehearsed and practised in session and then practised with "successive approximation" outside of session, i.e. in their natural environment with all its potential flux and triggers. In session you can use *imaginal* rehearsal in which you ask the patient again to take you through the sequence of events leading to the most recent episode of suicidal ideation or suicidal self-directed violence. Help your client using the skills you have learnt and practised together to respond cognitively, affectively and behaviourally to take positive steps towards staying alive. If the patient is moving too fast or neglecting important points, pause and ask about alternative ways of thinking, feeling and behaving. Use as much time as needed until the person can demonstrate solid learning of a few key strategies to prevent suicidal behaviour (Table 3.2).

Table 3.2 Creating a safety plan

Element of plan	*Sample questions*
Warning signs and personal triggers	• Are there any specific situations or people that you find stressful or triggering, or that contribute to your suicidal thoughts? • How will you know when your safety plan should be used? • What are some of the difficult thoughts, feelings or behaviours that you experience leading up to a crisis?
Reducing access to means ("making your situation safer"	• What things do you have access to that are likely to be used in a suicide attempt? • How can we develop a plan to limit your access to these things to help you stay safe?
Identifying reasons for living	• What's the best thing about your life? • What's the most important thing in your life? • Is there anything in your future you are looking forward to?
Internal coping strategies	• What can you do on your own if you have suicidal thoughts in the future, to avoid acting on those thoughts? • What has helped you in the past cope with suicidal thoughts?
Social contact	• Who helps you to feel good when you spend time with them? • Where can you go and be around other people in a safe environment?
Trusted contacts for assisting with a crisis	• Among your friends and family, who do you feel you could talk to when you're having suicidal thoughts? • Who do you feel you could contact to support you during a suicidal crisis? • Which services or professionals can you turn to for support?

Adapted from Stanley and Brown (2012).

It is important for the person to have a workable means of storing and accessing their safety plan. Mobile phones can help these days. You may want to consider multiple storage and then talk together about practicing accessing it. In addition to a detailed safety plan, you may want to develop a shorter coping card which can reduce suicide risk (Wang et al 2016). A trusted person could also keep a copy of the safety plan.

Sample coping card:
When I feel down I will
put on my trainers and walk outside for at least 10 minutes
practise my breathing
take a shower and relax

When I have the thought that life isn't worth living, I will
take out and reflect on the things in my Hope Box
text SHOUT* to 85258 or phone a friend who cares about me
If I'm still struggling, I will phone the mental health service.
*Shout is a free confidential 24/7 mental health text support in the UK giveusashout.org

3.4 Reducing access to means and 'shaping' skilful behaviour including appropriate help-seeking

Reducing access to suicide or self-harm means is one of the most effective ways to prevent suicide (DHSC 2019). WHO (2014) stated, "An effective strategy for preventing suicides and suicide attempts is to restrict access to the most common means, including pesticides, firearms and certain medications". Suicidal crises are often short-lived (fuelled by ambivalence or impulsiveness) and therefore means reduction can save lives, particularly in the prevention of highly lethal impulsive suicidal behaviours (Hawton 2001). One might imagine that if one suicide method is unavailable, it will be replaced with another (the substitution hypothesis). However, there is little support for this. Suicidal individuals tend to have a preference for a specific method. Depending on the individual, certain forms of death seem more terrifying, painful or shameful. Moreover, if access to highly lethal methods of suicide is reduced, even where substitution occurs, the proportion of people who survive suicide attempts will be increased (Hawton 2007). If individuals seem to have a preference for a specific means of suicide and if they essentially experience short-lived crises, restricting access to a specific method should not lead to the substitution by other means (Daigle 2005). The fundamental assumption underlying restricting access to means of suicide is that, in many cases, it may delay an attempt until the period of high-risk passes. Moreover, if access to highly lethal methods of suicide is reduced, even where substitution occurs, more people will survive (Hawton 2007).

Methods of suicide vary across world regions and cultures. According to the data derived from World Health Organization (WHO) mortality database:

- Self-poisoning by pesticide is common in many Asian countries and in Latin America. Over half of deaths by suicide in rural parts of China are by pesticides or rat poison; and in India (Chowdhury et al 2010), availability of pesticides partly accounted for higher rates of suicide in rural areas.
- Self-poisoning by drugs is common in both Nordic countries and the United Kingdom.

- Hanging is the most common method of suicide in Eastern Europe and the United Kingdom, as is suicide with firearms in the United States.

There is substantial support for the suggestion that ease of access influences the choice of method. For example, overdose survivors indicate that they chose overdose because drugs were readily available in the household (Sarchiapone et al 2011). Thomas and Gunnell (2010) noted the rapid rise in gas suicide deaths in the 1920s demonstrates how quickly a new method of suicide can be established in a population when it is easily available. According to a recent review of the literature on inpatient suicides, the methods used for suicide were linked to the availability of means (Bowers et al 2010).

In the United States, suicides with firearms are carried out by people with access to guns, and household firearm ownership levels are strongly associated with higher rates of suicide (Miller et al 2007). In rural areas people may have greater access to firearms, whereas in urban areas they may jump from a high building (Ajdacic-Gross et al 2008; Stark et al 2011). Following UK legislation in 1998 to reduce pack sizes of paracetamol, there were 765 fewer deaths due to paracetamol self-poisoning in England and Wales during the subsequent 11 years (Hawton et al 2013).

Means reduction can occur on a population or on an individual level. As quoted in Part 1, restriction of lethal means – creating barriers to jumping from bridges as well as reducing access to poisons, drugs and firearms – has demonstrated reductions in suicide risk (Daigle 2005; Mann et al 2005). Means restriction counselling is especially well suited for primary care settings because of its brevity and practicality (Table 3.3).

Table 3.3 Sample questions for reducing access to means

Elements	*Sample questions*
Identify a menu of options for restricting access to means.	*How could we reduce the likelihood of you using x when you are very distressed?*
Giving up the means is ideal or if not the impeding access or increasing distance	*My concern is that objects that are hidden can be found – can we think of any other options?*
If the person isn't ready or willing to give up the access then use a shaping approach, e.g. increasing distance between them and where the means are kept or addling something to the means such as a photo of their children, though you would need to be confident this will trigger reasons for living not reasons for dying.	*Now we have identified your options, what are the pros and cons of each?*
Develop a written plan.	*It sounds like you have come to a decision –shall we write this down so we are both clear what the plan is.* *Is there anyone who might help with the plan?* *Is there anyone you trust who could support you with the plan?*

3.5 Exploring ambivalence, reasons for living and reasons for dying

Individuals who contemplate suicide typically experience an internal struggle over whether to live or die. This is like an "internal suicide debate" between reasons for dying (RFD) and RFL (Jobes & Mann 1999; Harris et al 2010). People contemplating suicide may be difficult to engage in treatment because of reduced motivation to live and therefore lowered interest in and energy for treatment (Britton et al 2011). If people are experiencing extreme emotional pain and anguish, they may not be able to identify any RFL or see a future. This may be particularly evident if the patient has a severe mental illness such as psychosis (Cole-King et al 2013). Most individuals who think about suicide are ambivalent; they want to die, but they also want to live with less pain. This ambivalence suggests that the underlying issue for those contemplating suicide may be a desire to escape from psychological pain and suffering, and if that pain were resolved, the desire to die would diminish. Secondly, people who are thinking about suicide often have obstacles to participating in treatment or barriers to engaging in treatment such as hopelessness or poverty. The ability to overcome these hurdles may be compromised by the restricted cognitive functioning that is often associated with the suicidal state (see Baumeister 1990; Wenzel et al 2009). Further, many patients who are thinking about or have already engaged in suicidal behaviour are often seen in acute settings (acute mental health services or EDs) which may not provide the time or resources necessary for complex and expensive treatments. Clinicians from different settings, therefore, may benefit from having practical tools and methods to address motivation to live and motivation for treatment.

Kovacs and Beck identified the wish to live and wish to die as part of suicidal conflict as early as 1977, and this was elaborated by Linehan et al (1983), who developed a RFL scale. Jobes and Mann (1999) coined the terms "Reasons for Living" and "Reasons for Dying". RFL and RFD are important individual reasons for staying alive (e.g. family) or wanting to die (e.g. hopelessness) and reflect this internal motivational conflict of the suicidal mind. The ratio of the strength of the wish to live to the wish to die has been found to be a critical determinant of future suicide-related behaviour. When the wish to live is stronger than the wish to die, individuals who make a suicide attempt are less intent on dying and are less likely to die by suicide (Brown et al 2005). In addition to being associated with life-threatening behaviour, the ratio of the wish to live and the wish to die may also be related to engagement in life-sustaining behaviour, such as treatment.

Studies have shown that individuals with few RFL were at increased risk for developing suicidal thoughts (Zhang et al 2011) and attempting suicide (Galfalvy et al 2006). In a systematic review, Bakhiyi et al (2016) found RFL may protect against suicidal ideation and suicide attempts. The role of two specific RFL ("Moral Objections to Suicide" and "Survival and Coping Beliefs") were particularly emphasised. They concluded that RFL may moderate suicide risk factors and correlate with resilience factors. Clinicians could develop therapeutic strategies aimed at enhancing RFL, like dialectical behaviour therapy and cognitive behavioural therapies, to prevent suicidal thoughts and behaviours and improve the care of suicidal patients. A recent study by Cwik et al (2017) found those who reported more RFL experienced less suicidal ideation compared to participants with only a small number of RFL. However, Brüdern et al (2018) found the number of RFL did not correlate with suicide risk and, therefore, was not confirmed as a protective factor against suicidal ideation or further suicide attempts. They did find individuals with a high number of RFD were very prone to a suicidal crisis. They strongly recommend therefore that RFD, which serve as motives for someone to end their life, should be carefully assessed and treated. They also suggest psychological interventions for people in suicidal crisis should give priority to the reduction of RFD or to foster cognitive defusion from RFD, which could serve as motivational drivers in the suicidal process rather than the elaborating RFL.

Good practice point

Identify RFL and RFD in your assessment. This will inform your formulation of your patient's suicidality and indicate how they can be helped by addressing RFD and enhancing RFL.

Britton et al (2011) argue it is critical to address motivation for treatment because it may be associated with long-term risk for suicide-related behaviour and can be very different from the motivation to live. For example, a client's primary reason for thinking about suicide may be that they are tired of living with severe chronic pain, but their reason for living is that they value autonomy and have pushed through difficult times in the past. Their principal reason not to seek treatment is that they consider themselves autonomous and have always been able to resolve their problems on their own, but they are willing to consider treatment because of wanting to manage their severe chronic pain. In this scenario, the clients' reason for living is aligned with their reason not to seek treatment. So this client will need to be engaged on the basis of learning ways to manage chronic pain and treatment presented very much as a choice.

Given the significant ambivalence in individuals who are thinking about suicide, MI is uniquely suited for working with clients who are considering suicide. Although originally developed for individuals with substance use behaviours, MI has been applied to other health-related behaviour, such as diet, exercise, medication adherence and treatment engagement (Hettema et al 2005). MI has a natural "fit" with addressing suicidality as it was developed to help clients align with their reasons for stopping harmful behaviours, or engaging in a beneficial behaviour, and to increase the likelihood that they will behave skilfully (Britton et al 2011). MI can help resolve ambivalence. In MI, clinicians strategically attend to both sides of clients' ambivalence to ensure that client perceives that the clinician understands the complexity of their situation. If a clinician, for example, only encourages discussion about RFL, an ambivalent client may express his RFD to ensure that the clinician understands how he feels. Clinicians who use MI would elicit and reflect back clients' RFD which frees clients then to explain their RFL. To build their motivation to live, clinicians help clients explore their RFL in greater depth. After exploring their RFD and RFL, clients often come to the realisation that they want to live, but that they need to make some changes to ensure that their lives will be worth living. When clients are ready to talk about making changes, clinicians explore potential changes, including their participation in treatment that addresses their RFD.

MI is client-centred and builds on Carl Rogers' optimistic and humanistic theories about people's capabilities for change through a process of self-actualisation. MI is rooted in a trusting relationship established between you and your client. The therapeutic relationship for motivational interviewers is a democratic partnership. Your role in MI is directive, to elicit self-motivational statements and behavioural change from the client (Miller & Rollnick 1991, 2002). Clinicians have a desired outcome and they strategically guide their clients towards the desired outcome. Explicitly directive techniques, such as providing information and making recommendations, are appropriate from an MI perspective, but only with the client's permission. Miller and Rollnick wrote:

> The motivational interviewer must proceed with a strong sense of purpose, clear strategies and skills for pursuing that purpose, and a sense of timing to intervene in particular ways at incisive moments.
>
> (Miller & Rollnick 1991, pp. 51–52)

Principles of MI and how they apply to working with someone contemplating suicide

The fundamental principles of MI are:

1. Express empathy through reflective listening.
2. Develop discrepancy between clients' goals or values and their current behaviour.
3. Avoid argument and direct confrontation.
4. Roll with any client resistance rather than opposing it directly.
5. Support self-efficacy and optimism that change is achievable.

Express empathy

Empathy is the clinician's accurate understanding of the client's experience and it facilitates change. Empathy "is a specifiable and learnable skill for *understanding* another's meaning through the use of reflective listening. It requires sharp attention to each new client statement, and the continual generation of hypotheses as to the underlying meaning" (Miller & Rollnick 1991, p. 20). When practising MI, one has an attitude of acceptance but not necessarily approval or agreement. Although empathy is the foundation of a motivational counselling style, it is not *identification* with the client or the sharing of common past experiences (Miller & Rollnick 1991).

Develop discrepancy

MI aims to help clients examine the discrepancies between their current behaviour and future hopes. "Motivation for change occurs when people perceive a discrepancy between where they are and where they want to be" (Miller et al 1992). When someone can barely imagine a positive future, this needs to be addressed gently with open-ended question such as *When you think about suicide what has held you back from always acting on those thoughts?*

Suicide may well be in conflict with certain values the client has but may not always have articulated to themselves. This needs to be explored sensitively.

Roll with resistance and avoid arguing

In MI, the clinician does not fight client resistance, but "rolls with it". Statements demonstrating resistance are not challenged. We do need to be concerned about "resistance" because it is predictive of poor treatment outcomes and sub-optimal engagement. One view of resistance is that the client is behaving defiantly. Another, perhaps more constructive, viewpoint is that resistance is a signal that the client views the situation differently from the clinician. This requires you to understand your client's perspective and proceed from there. Resistance is a signal for you to change direction or listen more carefully. Try to avoid evoking resistance whenever possible and divert or deflect the energy the client is investing in resistance towards positive change. However tempting, resist trying to convince a client that suicide isn't a solution as that could precipitate resistance. When it is the client, not you, who voices reasons for change, progress can be made. Arguments are counterproductive and resistance is a signal to change strategies.

MI has some wonderful strategies for responding when a client is defensive.

These include:

Agreeing with a twist. For example: "You've got a good point there…"

Client: I know you want me to give you the rope, but I'm not going to do that.

Clinician: It sounds like that's a big step for you … Thank you for talking about this … Right now you don't feel ready to get rid of the rope.

The twist is the addition of "right now", i.e. hinting the client may feel differently in the future.

Others are:

Shifting focus – just simply change tack. "OK let's go back to…"

Emphasising personal choice and control I've got some ideas about how you could keep yourself safe but it's your decision whether to take those steps

Coming alongside – Right now that just doesn't seem doable

Values exploration (see p) – It sounds like it's really important for you to make this decision for yourself

Reframing – offering a new and positive interpretation of negative information provided by the client. Reframing "acknowledges the validity of the client's raw observations, but offers a new meaning … for them" (Miller & Rollnick 1991, p. 107). For example,

Client: My partner wants to get all the knives out the house which annoys me.

Clinician: It sounds like he really cares about you and is very concerned about what you might do.

Support self-efficacy

In MI we are aiming to foster in our client the belief that he or she can make positive changes. Engaging the client in the process of change is the fundamental task of MI. People who are considering suicide may not have a well-developed sense of self-efficacy and find it difficult to believe that they can manage their lives effectively. Enhancing self-efficacy requires eliciting and supporting hope, optimism and the feasibility of accomplishing change. This requires us to recognise their strengths and bring these to the forefront whenever possible. Because self-efficacy is a critical component of behaviour change, it is crucial that we "hold the hope", especially when your client struggles to have hope.

Ways of instilling hope can be:

- celebrating their engagement in your session or intervention, attending, talking about this difficult matter;
- identifying strengths they have that have enabled them to resist suicidal urges;
- identifying how current or future interventions may help.

When practising MI we use "OARS" to move the person forward by eliciting "change talk", or motivational statements.

- open-ended questions;
- affirmations;
- reflective listening;
- summaries.

Open-ended questions

An open-ended question cannot be answered with a single word or phrase. Asking open-ended questions helps us understand our clients' point of view and elicits their feelings about a given topic or situation. Open-ended questions facilitate dialogue and encourage the client to do most of the talking. They help us to avoid making premature judgements, and keep communication moving forward. Use open-ended questions wherever possible. Who/what/when/why/how/where? or tell me about….

So this week you've really struggled not to take an overdose. What helped you not take that final step?

Affirming

When it is done sincerely, affirming your client supports and promotes self-efficacy. More broadly, your affirmation acknowledges the difficulties the client has experienced. By affirming, you are validating the client's experiences and feelings. Affirming helps clients feel confident about coping and behaviour change. Highlighting their past experiences that demonstrate strength or success can be helpful. Examples of affirming statements (Miller & Rollnick 1991, 2002) include:

I appreciate how hard it must have been for you to decide to come here. You took a big step.

That must have been difficult for you to tell me. Thank you for your honesty.

Client: I could move the pills into the shed.

Clinician: That's a good idea.

Reflective listening

Reflective listening, a fundamental component of MI, is a skill in which you demonstrate that you have accurately heard and understood a client's communication by restating its meaning. "Reflective listening is a way of checking rather than assuming that you *know* what is meant" (Miller & Rollnick 1991, p. 75). It strengthens the empathic relationship between the clinician and the client and encourages further exploration of problems and solutions. It is particularly helpful in early sessions. Reflective listening helps the client by providing a synthesis of content and process. It reduces the likelihood of resistance, encourages the client to keep talking, communicates respect, cements the therapeutic alliance, clarifies exactly what the client means and reinforces motivation (Miller et al 1992).

Simple reflections repeat or slightly rephrase something you want to emphasise that a client has said, whilst *complex reflections* paraphrase meaning, or reflect a level of content or feeling not voiced. Complex reflections include:

Amplified reflection: The clinician amplifies or exaggerates the point to the point where the client may disavow or disagree with it. You can also understate a reflection.

Continuing anticipating the next statement not yet expressed.

Double-sided reflection: One response containing both sides of ambivalence (employing broad knowledge of the patient).

Culturally appropriate *similes, analogies, metaphors and stories* which can:

- capture the essential nature of an experience;
- express a complex idea in a few words and help a client to remember something;
- enhance rapport;
- enable clients to gain a new perspective on their problems;
- increase personal impact and clarity of meaning;
- be a less threatening way of exploring possibilities of change.

Summarising

It is helpful to periodically summarise what your client has shared. Summarising is a reflection of two or more client statements to:

- communicate your interest in a client;
- build rapport;
- call attention to salient elements of the discussion; or
- shift attention or direction.

"Summaries reinforce what has been said, show that you have been listening carefully, and prepare the client to move on" (Miller & Rollnick 1991, p. 78). Summarising can be helpful at the beginning and end of each session. Summarising can also be strategic, e.g. modulating up hope and modulating down hopelessness. You can select what information to emphasise and what can be minimised. If ambivalence was evident, this should be included in the summary.

There is a recency effect in memory and conversation, so it may be helpful (especially towards the end of a session) to start the summary with negatives and end the summary with something hopeful the client has given or indicated. Correction of a summary by the client should be invited, and this often leads to further comments and discussion. Summarising helps clients consider their own responses and contemplate their own experience. It also gives you and your client an opportunity to notice what might have been overlooked or misunderstood.

Elicit self-motivational statements

Our role is to encourage the client to voice personal concerns and intentions, not to convince him or her of what he or she should do. Successful MI requires that clients, not the clinician, ultimately argue for change and persuade themselves that they want to and can make changes.

There are four types of motivational statements (Miller & Rollnick 1991, 2002):

- recognition of the problem, for example "I guess this is serious".
- expression of concern about the perceived problem, for example "I'm really worried I might end up doing it".
- a direct or implicit intention to change behaviour, for example "I've got to do something about this".
- optimism about one's ability to change, for example "I know that if I try, I can really do it".

You can reinforce your client's self-motivational statements by reflecting them, nodding, or making approving facial expressions and affirming statements. Encourage clients to continue exploring the possibility of change. This can be done by asking for an elaboration, explicit examples, or more details about remaining concerns. Questions like "anything else?" are effective ways to invite further amplification.

3.6 Problem-solving

It is clear from the risk factors for suicide that people who consider suicide often have real and overwhelming problems. Problems that increase risk of suicide include debt; unemployment; chronic pain or illness; social isolation, being in trouble with the law; substance misuse; sleep deprivation; unresolved grief; having an abusive partner; or losing contact with children. People who become suicidal have challenging problems and, most likely, an impaired ability to solve them, due to their mental health and negative experiences and outcomes of learning and education. Problem-solving diminishes during crises, and deficits in problem-solving can increase vulnerability to suicide (Pollock & Williams 2004; Reinecke 2006). Gibbs et al (2009) found that perceiving problems as threatening and unsolvable, plus an impulsive approach to problem-solving, predisposed vulnerable elderly people to suicide attempts. Individuals at risk of suicide may not even be aware of their deficits in problem-solving and just skip this response altogether. Clients I have worked with, particularly those with enduring suicidal states, may have "go to" distraction activities such as cleaning, but when that doesn't reduce their emotional distress feel suicide or self-harm is their only escape. Theoretical modelling of suicide (problem-solving deficits and the desire to escape overwhelming problems) can help us formulate and understand how these patterns get established. Learning how to solve problems can take years of practise and may still not prepare one for major life events, which can trigger suicidal thoughts in people previously robust.

Problem-solving therapy (PST) is a cognitive behavioural intervention for people with depression that focuses on training in adaptive problem-solving attitudes and skills (Nezu et al 1989). It instructs patients on problem identification, efficient problem-solving and managing features of depression. Treatment length is 4–12 sessions. A meta-analysis of six studies of PST for self-harm concluded that PST is more effective than control treatments for depression, hopelessness and problem-improvement (Townsend et al 2001). In another study (Fitzpatrick et al 2005), young people with active suicidal ideation were randomly assigned to receive a brief problem-orientation intervention or a control procedure. Exposure to a brief video intervention on problem-solving and coping skills was sufficient to significantly decrease suicidal ideation and depression, though it did not improve problem orientation or other problem-solving abilities. In 2017 the Suicide Prevention Resource Center (SPRC), a federally supported resource centre devoted to advancing the implementation of the US National Strategy for Suicide Prevention, designated PST as a "program with evidence of effectiveness". It was deemed effective for addressing suicidal thoughts and behaviours, depression and depressive symptoms and self-concept. See https://www.sprc.org/resources-programs/problem-solving-therapy-pst.

The goal of problem-solving training is to improve clients' ability to cope with life stressors and engage in alternative solutions to suicidal behaviour when faced with problems. In an SFI we have had a dual task which is to help patients address and, where possible, resolve their problems, but an equal aim is to help patients feel more confident they can address problems effectively, which is important as suicidality is often a recurring problem for those who are vulnerable. This means that we facilitate, coach and foster flexibility rather than coming up with our own solutions and proposing those to our clients (Table 3.4).

The following steps are involved:

Table 3.4 Problem-solving

Step	*Task*	*Example*
Step One	Define the problem: What is the problem? Remember there are direct and indirect drivers, so the problem may include how the person perceives this as well as the actual triggering situation.	I can't get work and provide for my family. I feel a failure as a man, a father and a husband.
Step Two	Identify the causes of the problem: and the obstacles to solving it.	I don't feel confident in going for jobs and don't do well in interviews. I've given up on even looking for a job.
Step Three	Identify realistic and achievable goals to address the problem and meet your priorities and needs. This isn't always straightforward as the person may well come up with goals that are unrealistic or unworkable. I suggest brainstorming possible goals and then evaluating them for workability (Harris 2019).	Earn more money. Try and get a job.

(*Continued*)

Step	*Task*	*Example*
Step Four	Generate or brainstorm possible solutions. All ideas are welcome. Be inclusive; don't reject anything.	Learn interview skills. Apply for more jobs. Go to the job centre. Look for a job online every day. Be willing to try different jobs to get my confidence back. Help my brother-in-law on the building site when he needs people. Advertise to do odd jobs on my neighbourhood website.
Step Five	Evaluate the options and pros and cons. Select the solution(s) that are the closest fit with your values and goals and are most likely to be effective. "Do what works" (Harris 2019).	e.g. Go to the job centre.
Step Six	Troubleshoot the plan. How might it go wrong? What might get in the way? The client may have deficits in skills or motivation. Develop an action plan. This may include a role-play or writing a script of what to say to someone.	I'll bottle it on the day. Agree to coach your client through it or go with someone on the day. Role-play or write a script of what to say.
Step Seven	Implement the plan. You may want to positively reinforce new behaviours, and this is more effective close to the event.	Get your client text you after and cheerlead anything positive, beginning with going at all.
Step Eight	Evaluate the outcome and revise the plan if need be. Go back to previous steps if need be.	How did they do? Is there something they need more practice in.

Solutions that prove to be successful serve as corrective learning experiences that help us develop a more flexible approach to problem-solving and modify beliefs that their problems are unsolvable or unbearable. Enhanced problem-solving also has the potential to reduce "attentional fixation" (Wenzel & Jager-Hyman 2012).

3.7 Building positive experiences and a life worth living: working with needs, values and goals

Maslow's "hierarchy of needs" (Maslow 1943) has been hugely influential in the field of psychology and motivation. Maslow proposed that people are motivated to achieve certain needs and that some needs take precedence over others. When a need deficit has been "more or less" satisfied it will fade in salience, and we then focus on meeting the next set of needs that we have yet to satisfy. These then become our salient needs. Initially it was thought that individuals must satisfy lower-level deficit needs before progressing on to meet higher-level growth needs. Maslow later clarified that not everyone will move through the hierarchy in a unidirectional manner but may move back and forth between different needs. Maslow explained that *growth needs* stem more from a desire to grow as a person than a lack of something. *Growth needs* continue to be felt and may even become more salient once they have been engaged with. Maslow noted that the order of needs might vary based on external circumstances or individual differences. For example, he notes that for some individuals, the need for self-esteem is more important than the need for love. For an artist, the need for creative fulfilment may supersede even the most basic needs. Maslow (1987) also pointed out that most behaviour has multiple motivations and noted that "any behaviour tends to be determined by several or all of the basic needs simultaneously rather than by only one of them" (p. 71) (Figure 3.2).

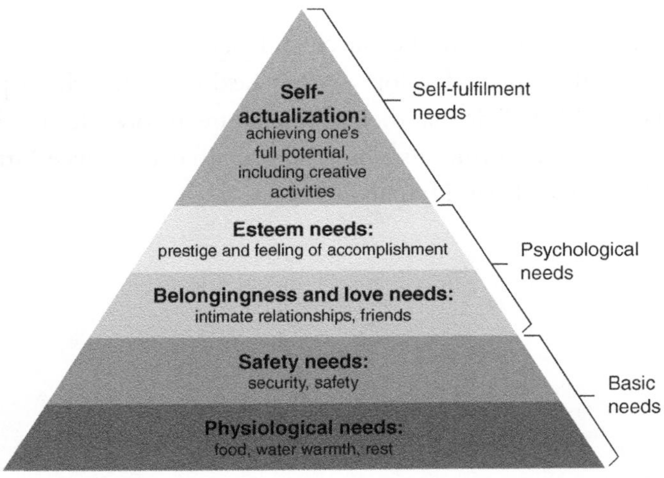

Figure 3.2 Maslow's hierarchy of needs (1943).

Maslow continued to refine his theory based on the concept of a hierarchy of needs over several decades.

In summary

- Human beings are motivated by a hierarchy of needs.
- Needs are organised in a hierarchy in which more basic needs must be more or less met (rather than all or none) prior to higher needs.
- The order of needs is not rigid but may be flexible, based on external circumstances or individual differences.
- Most behaviour is multi-motivated, that is, simultaneously determined by more than one basic need.

Needs are also central in the practice of non-violent communication (NVC) (Rosenberg 2001). NVC proposes that all behaviour stems from attempts to meet universal human needs. Further, it proposes that everything we do is in service of our needs. According to NVC, there are seven universal needs – for **connection, physical well-being, honesty, meaning, play, peace and autonomy**. NVC is based on the following assumptions:

- All human beings share the same needs.
- All actions are attempts to meet needs.
- Emotions tell us whether our needs are met or unmet.
- People resort to violence or behaviour harmful to others only when they cannot use more effective strategies to meet their needs.

The aim of NVC is to observe our feelings, identify our needs or values and make skilful requests.

Identifying needs and wants when working with people with mental health problems and/or suicidal thinking is important. Poor mental health is associated with social deprivation and real unmet needs. The concept of "unmet needs" is also central in a cognitive analytic therapy formulation (Ryle 1994).

For example, we all have a need for safety. People whose living situation is unsafe (such as those exposed to domestic violence) are highly likely to be anxious and distressed. However, they may have become habituated to their situation so disconnected from their need for safety and the cost of not having their need for safety for met. Domestic violence is associated with a raised risk of suicide. Addressing and prioritising the person's need for safety will be critical and an important aim of any SFI with someone currently experiencing domestic violence.

However, there are problems with the "needs" agenda and psychological approaches have shifted their emphasis in the third wave "revolution" within psychological therapies. *Third wave therapies* prioritise the holistic promotion of psychological and behavioural processes associated with health and well-being over the reduction or elimination of psychological and emotional symptoms. They target the process of thoughts rather than their content, using tools such as mindfulness and acceptance. Third wave therapies also place more emphasis on values (Harris 2009, 2019). Unmet needs can be validated but not necessarily filled. Reinforcing the sense that I will be happier or more fulfilled if I get more of something may be part of the problem rather than part of the solution. We can become "attached" to or fuse with our needs. Let me share one example which can illustrate the difference between connecting to values rather than needs. During the early months of COVID-19 lockdown we were all unable to touch each other than those in our immediate household. Touch is definitely a basic human need. What I noticed after three months was that what I missed more was sharing food with others. So perhaps that is more closely aligned to a value than need, the value of sharing and giving. Being connected to values and acting in line with values is also important to one's mental health. Rather than thinking needs and values are different, they are, of course, closely related; sharing food may be an important way of meeting a need for social connection and could meet that need more deeply than simply talking. See https://www.kindful.com.au/blog/2016/2/27/needs-and-values for an exploration of needs and values. In summary, I would suggest that high-priority needs for housing (shelter) and safety should be addressed with an SFI, but lower-priority needs may be better addressed by working with values.

Connecting to our values helps us to do what matters with clear intention, motivation and committed action. *Values* are like a compass that keep us heading in a desired direction and are distinct from *goals. Goals* are the specific ways you intend to carry out your *values*. A *goal* is something that we aim for and check off once we have accomplished it. Goals can be achieved, whereas values are desired qualities of behaviour: what a person finds to be important; who we want to be in the world; what sort of employee, manager, co-worker, friend or partner we want to be. In this moment now, I can be curious, but I can never achieve "curious". When we act in line with our values, we never reach our destination; there is always something more we can do. Values are qualities we choose freely. As soon as we start to feel we have to follow a value, it loses its vitality. It stops being a value and starts to be a rule.

Exploring values can be very helpful. When we understand our values, we can gain a better understanding of our goals and what we want from life, the type of person we want to be and how we want to behave. It helps to align our goals with our values, so the things we are trying to achieve are things that really matter to us, that are important and give us meaning. Clarifying someone's values is important and will help you set therapeutic goals that really matter to that person (Vyskocilova et al 2015). For example, there is considerable evidence that behavioural activation (BA) improves mood (Veale 2008), but increasing activity which is also in line with values will bring more meaning, purpose and motivation than just being more active. Veale gives the example of using BA with someone who identifies one of their key values is to be a good parent. We may then suggest a goal (such as spending a specified time each day playing, reading or talking with their child) in line with that value.

Zhang et al (2018) propose "individuals improve maintenance of long-term health behaviour change through committed acts in the service of chosen values, while acknowledging and accepting the existence of contrary thoughts, rules and emotions as part of themselves but not determinant of their behaviours". Zhang et al recommend researchers and practitioners design health behaviour change interventions in accordance with ACT (Hayes et al 1999; Harris 2009, 2019). ACT promotes wide accessibility of tools and resources to support this approach such as

https://thehappinesstrap.com/upimages/Long_Bull%27s_Eye_Worksheet.pdf.

Working with values includes:

1. Helping the client identify their own personal values.
2. Exploring how their current choices or actions are in line with their values or not.

3. Choosing goals consistent with values and setting goals from a place of being more connected to one's values.
4. Noticing how and when the client is acting in line with their values or not and reflecting on this with them.

See https://www.psychpoint.com/mental-health/worksheets/values-self-exploration/.

The aim of goal-setting is to build positive experiences (mastery and pleasure) and a life worth living. Goals may arise when we are co-writing someone's safety plan. Initially the safety plan should include actions which the person has a good chance of carrying out and will confer likely immediate benefits. However, each area covered in the safety plan (see p...) can also generate longer-term goals. Positive goal-setting (shaping new skilful behaviours) is more likely to motivate us and be effective than goals which aim to reduce unwanted behaviours (such as thinking about, planning, rehearsing or attempting suicide). It is widely held that goals in life generally and health care in particular should be "SMART", i.e. Specific, Measurable, Attainable, Relevant and Timely. However, with goals in mind (and SMART goals in particular), clinicians may push to specify a goal or to propose specific goals too quickly rather than support the client to articulate their own goals and reasons for change. Goals are much more likely to be followed through if the person identifies and articulates their own goal. Remember you want to elicit change talk.

Use open-ended questions such as *Take a moment to think about how things might be different.*

What's important to you here? How would you like to be? If it is a goal you have proposed (such as means reduction), ask if the person would be willing to do that.

See https://www.youtube.com/watch?v=mxJtBkH0JgI.

See Kennedy and Pearson (2020) for how to incorporate CBT with third wave approaches.

3.8 How to make and use a hope box

One way of challenging suicidal thoughts is to cultivate hope. The *hope box* is a collection of various items that can remind someone that life is meaningful and worth living. Discuss collaboratively with your client how they can get a box (or a bag, a large envelope or anything else that can hold objects) and fill it with reminders of the things that give them hope, or that have given them hope in the past. They may even want to decorate their hope box creatively. Items in a hope box may include:

- cards, notes or emails with special meaning.
- photos of special times and places in the past or desired destinations for the future, a vacation spot or an activity previously enjoyed.
- photos of loved ones.
- spiritual verses, prayers or objects.
- recordings of relaxing or uplifting music.
- letters or recordings from loved ones offering positive, caring messages.
- inspiring articles, affirmations, quotes or poems.
- jokes or stories that are uplifting or funny.
- lists of goals, dreams and aspirations.
- coping cards with skills or activities used to cope with stressful situations.
- anything else that reminds the person of RFL.
- their RFL list.

Other possibilities for their hope box:

- write a letter to themselves to remind them of RFL and ways they have coped with difficult times in the past.
- a statement of hope and recovery from suicidal thinking; see http//www.connectingwithpeople.org/DearDistressed.
- put a copy of their safety plan in the Hope Box; the safety plan lists things they can do to help, people they can call to talk to (with phone numbers) and services they can contact for help.

Discuss how they can keep the hope box nearby and use its contents whenever they feel distressed, depressed or suicidal. It may be necessary for some to practise using the hope box independently of whether they are distressed or not. This can help challenge negative thoughts and beliefs. By looking at the items in the hope box, they can learn to directly challenge distressing and negative thoughts by being reminded of previous successes, positive experiences and RFL.

Hope is like a muscle that works with practice, so we need to persevere before we can use it effectively. Clinicians need to:

- elicit willingness you may need to "fake it till you make it".
- support persistence.
- expect cynicism; "what's the point?" thoughts to arise.
- understand and use the principles of stimulus control and shaping (operant conditioning; see above).

3.9 Building mindfulness and mindfulness-based skills

Mindfulness is intentionally paying attention to the present moment, without judging it, pushing it away or holding on to it. It is an endeavour rather than an end goal to be achieved. It is a set of skills that can be learnt. This document outlines what mindfulness is and how it can help our mental health: https://www.mind.org.uk/media-a/2891/mindfulness-2018.pdf.

There is evidence that mindfulness can help with a wide range of conditions, including stress, anxiety, depression, addictive behaviours such as alcohol or substance misuse and gambling, and physical problems like hypertension, heart disease and chronic pain. With respect to mental health problems, a systematic review by Potes et al (2018) found mindfulness interventions led to clinical improvements in symptoms of psychosis and depression, cognition, mindfulness, psychosocial and vocational factors. Mindfulness was not taught in early CBT-SFIs, but it has been recommended to be included (Matthews 2013).

In people with a history of suicidal depression, recurrence of depressive features can reactivate suicidal thinking. Mindfulness-based cognitive therapy (MBCT) is aimed at helping patients "de-centre" from negative thinking and is recommended by NICE (2009) to prevent relapse in people who are currently well but have experienced three or more previous episodes of depression. Forkmann et al (2014) investigated the effects of MBCT on suicidal ideation in an RCT of 130 patients with residual features of depression. There was a significant reduction of suicidal ideation in the MBCT group but not in the waiting list control group. The authors conclude MBCT may reduce suicidal ideation in patients with residual features of depression and that this effect may be mediated in part by participants' enhanced capacity to distance themselves from worrying thoughts. Barnhofer et al (2015) found MBCT for those with a history of suicidal depression can help to weaken the association between depressive features and suicidal thinking, and thus reduce vulnerability for relapse to suicidal depression. Chesin et al (2015) adapted MBCT to enhance patients' awareness of suicide triggers and appropriate coping strategies (MBCT-S) and found MBCT-S significantly reduced suicidal ideation and depressive symptoms, but not hopelessness. MBCT-S was also acceptable and safe for participants. Chesin et al (2016a) conclude from this pilot study that MBCT-S may improve cognitive deficits specific to suicidal ideation and attempts in depressed patients.

Another study (Anastasiades et al 2017) found mindfulness moderated the mediated effect of depressive symptoms on perceived stress and suicidal ideation. Chesin et al (2016b) reviewed this limited evidence for mindfulness-based interventions (MBIs) for suicidal behaviour and conclude it supports targeting suicidal ideation with MBIs. They found additional studies show deficits that are associated with attempting suicide (namely attentional dyscontrol, problem-solving deficits and abnormal stress response) are improved by MBIs, which strengthens the rationale for using them with individuals at high risk of suicide.

Another important aim of mindfulness is the development of skilful means or being effective which has clear relevance to reducing suicidal states. Suicide is seen by an individual as their only solution for managing intolerable states, and mindfulness can help us tolerate difficult states and enable us to notice when we need to practice strategies for addressing problems. Mindfulness is a gateway skill to living skilfully or what is known in third wave practice as *skilful means*. However, teaching mindfulness to people who have suicidal thoughts and urges needs particular care and sensitivity. Practising mindfulness is not always pleasant. Mindfulness is not intended to make us feel better but more aware, so if one's mood is low and you have suicidal thoughts or urges, these may be felt more intensely.

Good practice point

Mindfulness can help reduce suicidal thinking and behaviour. However, it is not advisable to teach mindfulness within an SFI unless you are experienced at teaching mindfulness to people with mental health problems and tailoring it to their needs and vulnerabilities. It is also important that you are experienced in practising mindfulness yourself as you can then understand from direct experience how "opening" it can be and how "internal" practices may need to be balanced with activities or practices where you direct your attention outwards.

Teaching mindfulness

Linehan (1993, 2015a, b) breaks down mindfulness into "what" and "how" skills, which is a very useful teaching aid.

Mindfulness "what" skills are:

- Observe: Notice your environment and what is around you. And notice what is going inside you. What thoughts, feelings and sensations you are experiencing.
- Describe: Use words to describe your experience and what you can observe.
- Participate: Become one with whatever you are doing and enter the experience as fully as you can rather than avoiding, suppressing or blocking the present moment.

Mindfulness "how" skills are:

- Non-judgementally, acknowledging and then letting go of judgements or evaluations.
- One-mindfully, doing one thin at a time.
- Being effective. Focus on what works and being skilful.

Mindfulness is not relaxation and we're not trying to feel better or calmer but to be here now. Emphasise that mindfulness is a practical skill used to treat a variety of mental health problems and is no longer specific to any religious practice. "We are all in the same soup or boat". The aim is to be less caught up in the content of our thoughts; to "unhook" from them.

There are two key elements to practising mindfulness:

- the action of deliberately focusing our attention (like a mental muscle);
- accepting current experience (being in the moment).

Mindfulness is a practice, so we need to notice any thoughts about whether it is working or not working – to be aware of our expectations, assumptions and judgements about the practice and its outcome. We are trying to "unhook" from the expectation of what the current moment should deliver and to focus instead on experiencing it as it is. You can use a metaphor here such as "What happens if you keep watching a soufflé?"

Some people are not comfortable with the concept of mindfulness. There may be several reasons for this. The person may feel it conflicts with their religious faith or their previous introduction to mindfulness may not have gone well. Perhaps it has been described as a panacea leading to an inappropriate expectation that mindfulness will make them feel better. Or they simply feel they can't do it because their mind is busy and distracted. We may need to gently persevere with the practice before experiencing any benefit. If need be, mindfulness can simply be introduced as awareness or being in the moment, or elements of it tried without promoting it as a way of life.

Dunkley and Stanton (2014) provide excellent suggestions for how to teach mindfulness and recommend you:

- Model warmth, compassion acceptance and interest.
- Be open to questions.
- Use personal examples to indicate we're all in the same boat.
- Model curiosity about what our minds do.
- Avoid using a "therapist" voice; try to have a normal tone. Do not speak more slowly or softly as this suggests you are trying to induce preferred, i.e. relaxed states of mind.

Dunkley and Stanton suggest the following tips for teaching mindfulness:

- Start simple, vary practice and build on what the client finds helpful; prioritise those practices with the most day-to-day utility.
- Encourage exploration of mindfulness – YouTube, apps, books, etc.
- Link the practice to your agreed goals.
- Shape the three "As": Attention, Awareness and Acceptance; for example, inserting the phrase "I notice that" I am experiencing anxiety.
- Identify obstacles (our untrained "monkey" mind) and normalise these.
- Ask for feedback, using it as an opportunity to shape mindfulness.
- Vary practices. Mindfulness can be practised in a variety of positions and environments. Avoid creating special conditions, for example, always sitting in a chair or having one's eyes closed. Move towards your client integrating them into their daily life.
- Look for opportunities to generalise to everyday life. Invite clients to give suggestions for how they can and do apply mindfulness in

everyday life. Point out situations from your client's daily life when mindfulness could be helpful and notice and celebrate how and when your client has been mindful, highlighting new learning.

Clients may *struggle* to learn or practise mindfulness. They may not readily see its application to helping with their problems. The most effective response is to validate these difficulties. Using metaphors to obstacles to mindfulness can be helpful such as "thought traffic" or "monkey mind". If clients get distressed during mindfulness, use "grounding" with senses or physical practices, such as noticing the floor under our feet.

There are two elements to teaching a mindfulness practice – the chosen focus for attention and your verbal guidance. You don't want to speak constantly through an exercise but give your client time and space to apply your instruction independently. How much guidance you give will vary depending on the ability of the client and stage of their practice. If you ask your client to close their eyes, do keep yours open so you can observe and monitor how they are getting on (you may close them together initially to model the practice). With any mindfulness practice, one's thoughts spontaneously go to other matters, such as past memories, upsets or future planning. When that happens, we want to just gently steer our attention back to the task or object of mindfulness. One metaphor for mindfulness practice is steering a boat, which gets pulled by tides and winds. We want to stay at the helm, as calm as we can, gently steering the boat (our direction of travel is the art of focusing our attention). Normalise that our mind wanders and give instructions about how to respond when we notice that. Point out to your client in noticing it they are being mindful.

It is good practice to ask your client for feedback after a mindfulness practice in order to monitor your client's comprehension and skill level, identify any obstacles and problem-solve these. Dunkley and Stanton suggest you:

- adopt a light, interested tone;
- ask what the client noticed during practice;
- highlight when client is mindful;
- label types of internal experience;
- link practice to everyday life.

When teaching, we are practising a specific skill but we also want to draw from this some general learning about the mind – noticing our mind states means we are more than the content of our minds. We are not our thoughts. Everything is subject to change.

Introductory mindfulness practices:

Keep early practices short. Starting with sensory practices is usually the easiest way for people to learn such as:

- Observing and participating in tastes, smells, sounds, sight or touch is generally easier for people than practices such as mindfulness of thoughts.
- Mindfulness items you can use: stones, shells, conkers, feathers, pieces of fabric, buttons, leaves. Choose an object which is common and fairly neutral. Notice all its features – texture; colour, etc. Experience the sensation of touching the object. Consider the function of that object and what the object does for you.
- Focus your attention on your feet touching the ground. Focus your attention on your body touching the chair you sit in. Consider how you are connected to and supported by it.
- Mindful single or simple common activities such as making and drinking tea; washing up; bathing; stroking pets.

Mindfulness of the breath

This is the main meditation technique for training the mind to focus, decentring from thoughts and grounding. Mindfully count your breath or say silently to yourself "breathing in" as you breathe in and "breathing out" as you breathe out. Gently bring your attention back to your breath and body sensations. It can also be difficult, especially for patients with anxiety disorders who hold their breath or over-breathe. Simplifying it by adding the task of naming in and out breaths or counting breaths can be helpful. Include dialectics when teaching, i.e. we are not aiming to change the rate of breathing and it may well change.

Generalising mindfulness skills to daily life

Homework practices start with building on these, with the person practising them in their own home or other settings. You can also start to build practices which are more activity-based such as going for a walk or a jog (also building behavioural activation which can help improve mood), focusing on this experience and your immediate environment. Using mindfulness when in challenging emotional or suicidal states is the hardest practice of all and therefore the last application to address. If your client needs to develop more willingness and acceptance, mindful emotional exposure may be helpful (e.g. someone struggling with unresolved grief or anticipated grief). However, this may be difficult for someone to tolerate until they have a certain level of skill in mindfulness practice and feel familiar and comfortable with it.

Applying mindfulness to your client's individual needs and goals

Based on your formulation and understanding of your client skills, you may want to include practices such as emotional exposure or opening to painful emotions. The client will need to be "signed up" to acceptance as an agenda and have established capacity to use their safety plan. You will then need to explain the rationale for this. Avoidance may work in the short term, but then prevents us from building resilience.

Surfing urges and defusing from thoughts

Research studies demonstrate that suppressing a thought (Wegner et al 1987; Clark et al 1991; Wegner & Gold 1995) or sensation such as pain (Cioffi & Holloway 1993) tends ultimately to intensify it. For example, Wegner et al (1987) conducted experiments to assess the effects of thought suppression called the "white bear" experiments. In one experiment people were shown a film about white bears and then given a sorting task which required concentration. They were divided into two groups. The first group was instructed to suppress the white-bear thoughts. The second group was given no instruction to suppress these thoughts. Both groups were asked to hit a button every time they thought of white bears while doing the other task. The initial suppression group reported a significantly higher rate of "white bear" thoughts during this time.

There are a number of visual metaphors for the mind and thoughts within it, such as clouds in the sky or leaves on a stream or items on a carousel or conveyer belt. For example, you can introduce the image of a conveyor belt as a metaphor for the mind, and watch thoughts and feelings coming down the conveyor belt or carousel. Place thoughts as we catch them on the conveyor belt and let them fade as they move on. I often describe the aim of this practice as having more space around thoughts, to let them be just that; not to control or change our thoughts but for the thoughts to have less power over us. These are known in ACT as *defusion* exercises. Another mindfulness practice is to name types or categories of thoughts, such as "worry" thoughts, planning or analysing. This can also be helpful in defusing from their content and help us take them less personally. Validate and normalise how we all have unhelpful thoughts.

Explain that thoughts are not facts. This can be illustrated with an example of an emotionally charged thought alongside a comical thought. For example, we can have the thought "I'm worthless" and we can have the thought "I'm a purple cat"; both are thoughts which don't make them true. Use personal examples where you have had a thought, noticed it and let it go. The *tug-of-war* metaphor is helpful in explaining defusion and how we can let go of the struggle we can get into when we experience "charged" thoughts (thinking it and not wanting it). This metaphor suggests that if we insist on struggling with a thought, then the thought may continue to control us (Harris 2019). In ACT we describe dominant, pervasive or persistent thoughts (as suicidal ideation can be) as "sticky thoughts". When using ACT techniques with someone contemplating ending their life, it is important we don't trivialise their struggle, as could be done for example, if we said, "that's just a thought". The extent to which we are irreverent or challenging will depend on the strength of our working alliance with a client. If you have good working alliance, then humour and even irreverence can be helpful and release tension at times.

Mindfulness of challenging thought states is the most demanding or advanced application or practice and without considerable building of foundation skills, people can feel unable to do it. In a short SFI you are unlikely to have time to build that practice unless the client already practises mindfulness and understands the dialectical balance of awareness that is skilful when our mood is low. Although mindfulness isn't about being successful at anything (rather endeavouring to be mindful and accepting that one often isn't), it is important when working with people who have suicidal thoughts not to add experiences which may be demoralising for them. If and when the person has some faith in mindfulness and understands this ebb and flow of being more or less attentive, then mindfulness of thoughts can be introduced, but not initially with any aim to let go of suicidal thinking. Rather, one introduces the practice with other, more everyday thoughts. Again, I would only progress to more challenging thoughts if the person was confident in the practice and understood that mindfulness is not pushing thoughts away.

Discuss how your client responds to suicidal thoughts and urges. Often people try to suppress urges by distraction or "fighting them". With mindfulness, we endeavour to step aside and watch the cravings, impulses and urges. Ask your client whether there have been times they did not give in to an urge when it arose. Did the urge pass? The main message is that urges do not have to be acted upon. Invite your client to do a behavioural experiment such as deferring acting on an urge and exploring the outcome of that.

Exercise: Experiencing the changing nature and impermanence of urges

Start mindfulness of breathing. Wait for any sense of discomfort, e.g. restlessness, an itch. Note the desire to move and resist it. Notice thoughts that arise, e.g. "I wish this itch would go"… "It is driving me crazy"… Say to yourself, "this too will pass" – in a calm tone … "This too will pass". Gently bring your attention back to your breath and bodily sensations. Note the changing position, shape and quality of the discomfort over time. Be interested in feeling it as precisely as you can. Notice how the shape and intensity change with the cycle of the breath. Is it stronger during the in-breath or during the outbreath?

Exercise: Holding arms out in front of you and surfing the urge to put them down. Another practice is to sit completely still for five minutes, resisting any urges to move, blink or swallow.

Any of these mindfulness-based skills could be helpful in an SFI:

- Beginners mind;
- Wise Mind;
- STOP & TIP;
- Opposite-to-emotion action;
- Self-soothe;
- Surfing urges;
- Skilful occupation;
- Pros and cons;
- Checking the facts (Does my emotion or its intensity actually fit the facts? How warranted is it?);

- Build mastery or positive experiences;
- Interpersonal skills (if you are in relationship crisis);
- Reducing vulnerability (eating, sleeping, exercise; taking medication). *Sleep hygiene.*

Address sleep disturbance

People who die by suicide have higher rates of sleep disturbance, insomnia and hypersomnia as compared with matched controls (Bernert & Joiner 2007; Goldstein et al 2008), and this is over and above differences due to depression. Unlike other suicide risk factors, sleep complaints may be particularly amenable to treatment. So do assess your client's sleep pattern and address strategies that will help improve their sleep (see Linehan 2015b, p. 259), including, if need be, medication, especially in the context of depression or a mood disorder.

Note we want to coach clients to use a balance of acceptance and change skills. These are easily available in manuals and self-help websites such as www.getselfhelp.co.uk or https://dialecticalbehaviortherapy.com/. The DBT community have published a range of DBT skills workbooks. There is a general manual of all the DBT skills (Linehan 2015a, b; McKay et al 2019) and specific manuals for anger (Chapman & Gratz 2015), bulimic disorders (Astrachan-Fletcher & Maslar 2009) or bipolar disorder (van Dijk 2009).

DBT also places emphasis on practising willingness which may be helpful in an SFI. For example, when negotiating reducing access to means, we may ask someone if they would be willing to give up the means or willing to practise some emotional exposure (initially feeling worse by having less ready access to means), in the interest of their safety and survival. ACT, another mindfulness-based therapy (Hayes et al 1999; Harris 2009, 2019), emphasises developing flexibility and this is also helpful to attend to in an SFI. Lack of flexibility will most definitely contribute to people seeing suicide as a solution. In short, it can be helpful to invite people to intentionally practise either willingness or flexibility as part of their journey past suicidality.

Distress tolerance skills

Distress tolerance is the ability to tolerate and survive crisis situations without making things worse. Also, these skills teach us how to accept and fully enter into a life that may not be the life we hoped for or want. They include crisis survival skills to enable us to tolerate painful events, urges and emotions and reality acceptance skills to help us reduce suffering by acceptance. One of these skills is *self-sooth* which helps to calm us when we are feeling overwhelmed both physically and emotionally. They help to regulate our emotions. It is what parents do when they pat their child's back or rock them to sleep. People with states of acute mental distress by definition have not been able to effectively self-sooth, and it is worth spending some time exploring that. What have they tried? Does it ever work? If not, what might make it less or more effective? Did they give it sufficient time or participate fully? Activities which are most soothing affect as many senses as possible. You can make a self-soothe box like a hope box. You could include:

- something to smell, such as essential oil (peppermint or lavender or rose).
- something to touch. Stress balls are great for this; they're satisfying to touch, and easy to put force into and relieve some stress.
- something to look at a beautiful place for example (be careful not to evoke sadness and loss for happier times).
- something to hear and listen to – a particular CD or wind-up music box.
- perhaps even something to taste.

You also want a range of self-soothing activities depending on the circumstances. What is workable in a public place or at home will be different, when you're alone or in company.

Emotion regulation skills

When our emotions feel overwhelming, it's difficult to think clearly and address problems effectively. To bring down very high levels of emotion we want to:

1. Calm the body

   You can do this by putting your face in very cold water and/or slowing down your breathing. Activating the parasympathetic nervosa system and vagus nerve has been described as *putting your foot on the brakes* rather *than taking your foot off the accelerator* – i.e. it is more effective for slowing the car engine (or stress or threat response). There are a number of breathing practices which activate the parasympathetic nervosa system and vagus nerve; square (i.e. even) or rectangular (longer outbreaths) breathing, or soothing rhythm breathing or diaphragmatic breathing. See for example Dr Alan Watkins https://youtu.be/Q_fFattg8N0 or https://mi-psych.com.au/soothing-rhythm-breathing/. In DBT, patients are taught to STOP and TIP (Linehan 2015b, pp. 327, 329).

2. Calm the mind

   With simple mindfulness practices or counting

3. Block unhelpful action urges

   Ask yourself, what is the emotion urging you to do? and then do the opposite.

4. Address problems that need to be tackled (now or later)

   This is the spirit of being effective or doing what works. Is there a problem which needs tackling (when you are ready)? See Linehan (2015b, pp. 230, 231); see 3.6 problem-solving (page 157).

Emotional suppression plays an important mediating role in *both* suicidal ideation and suicide attempts, irrespective of levels of depressive symptoms (Kaplow et al 2014). Kaplow et al suggest effective suicide preventive interventions may need to include techniques to reduce emotional suppression in those who have been exposed to adverse life events. There may be particular emotional states linked to suicide drivers such as unresolved grief which indicate emotional exposure will be helpful to enable a client to learn they can tolerate that which their mind tells them is intolerable. This YouTube clip expresses this very simply as well as providing education about the naming of functions of emotions: https://youtu.be/SJOjpprbfeE.

Mindfulness of emotions

See https://cdn.gottman.com/wp-content/uploads/2018/10/Compressed6-Steps-to-Mindfully-deal-with-difficult-Emotions-Social.jpg.

3.10 Telephone coaching

If you have the training, experience, support and supervision, providing telephone coaching when people are contemplating suicide can be invaluable. However, a lone counsellor or therapist could be vulnerable doing this. Rather you would then want to consider other services your client could use at their most challenging times, notably Samaritans or the mental health service if they are open to that service.

Staff are generally anxious that clients will overuse or misuse telephone coaching, but this rarely happens. Many people have anxiety or shame, or believe they are undeserving or their needs are invalid, all of which tends to inhibit help-seeking. Telephone coaching aims to provide opportunities to change these patterns. Telephone calls may need to be shaped to increase or decrease; the great majority of patients under-use telephone coaching. Few patients find a middle way, either calling for minor reasons or calling too late (when drunk or standing on a bridge).

There are a number of reasons for maintaining contact with your client at unscheduled times if you are able to:

- Build therapeutic rapport and repair ruptures in the therapeutic alliance.
- Shape safety behaviours and provide in vivo coaching. Suicide rates fluctuate over time and providing coaching during a critical window can save lives.
- Positively reinforce behavioural change (e.g. "text me or give me a call when you have got rid of the tablets/moved them to the shed").
- If you are able to provide it, maintaining contact between scheduled sessions has multiple benefits.
- It demonstrates your genuine commitment to that individual and your desire to help them and support them when they most need it.
- You get to know the true nature of the difficult mind states your client can get in. You are much more likely to pitch expectations and coping strategies accurately when you are familiar with these states.
- Just being there then and listening increases human contact, connection and compassion, all of which are antidotes to suicidality.
- You can then give *in vivo* coaching (any parent, teacher or CBT therapist will understand the merits of coaching "in the moment").

Suicidal thoughts and urges tend to fluctuate and clients during scheduled sessions may be quite upbeat and may even minimise the severity of their suicidal risk, which can limit how much skills-coaching you can do at those times.
- As well as coaching and practising new coping behaviours you can provide on-the-spot positive reinforcement for these behaviours by cheerleading.

If a client phones to avert self-harm or suicide, assess risk and problem-solve. "What have you tried?" "What skills could you use right now?" Think of it as doing something akin to a *sports coach before a game,* i.e. keep the discussion relatively brief and focused and dealing with the immediate task at hand to avert suicide.

It may be helpful to establish and actively request willingness, explaining that you can't help someone who is unwilling to keep themselves safe. Although this sounds challenging in fact it is generally well received and demonstrates how focused and committed you are to helping the person stay alive. Using a metaphor can help clients remember how critical it is for them to contact you before acting on urges to attempt suicide, such as emphasising they need to contact you before "walking to the edge of the cliff". This is also a compassionate way of explaining that you want them to seek professional help before self-harming.

Obviously, this needs to be done with clear expectations and do agree some rules beforehand, planning for all contingencies. There a number of things that can go wrong for you or them. Think together about these:

- They call you in a desperate state and you can't answer.
- Clients asking you to call them back communicate their acute distress to you and then you can't get hold of them.
- Their phone runs out of charge or funding.
- They call too late for you to help, e.g. after an overdose.

I would discourage texts unless they are about a request for a call or very brief practical information, e.g. cancelling sessions. From experience, they have a higher chance of not arriving or being missed and also of people using them inappropriately. I would not provide coaching if someone has already self-harmed (in DBT the rule is within the last 24 hours), as the person has passed the window for skills-coaching and you do not want to provide positive reinforcement. At these times you courteously provide the minimum duty of care: *Do you need to go to A&E? Do you or I need to call an ambulance?* If you fear for their safety and they are unable to assure they can keep themselves safe, consider calling the police or involving someone else who may keep them safe. This requires a careful balance between keeping the client safe and supporting their independence. Most people in this situation have a legal capacity to make choices. (This would not be the case if the person was acutely psychotic.)

As stated in Part 1, positive risk taking is identifying the potential risks involved, and developing plans and actions that reflect the positive potentials and stated priorities of the service user. It involves using available resources and support to achieve the desired outcomes, and to minimise the potential harmful outcomes. It requires an agreement of the goals to be achieved, or a clear explanation of any differences of opinion regarding the goals or courses (Southern Health NHS Trust 2012). Positive risk taking is about individuals taking control of their lives and making choices – either positive or negative – and learning from the consequences of those choices – again positive or negative. In practice this requires a balance between the interests of the individual and societal pressures to control risk (Felton et al 2017).

Suggested guidelines for telephone coaching:

- 24-hr rule. No coaching after self-harm for 24 hrs.
- Agree times when the clinician or team are available.
- Agree the time frame in which a telephone call by the client will be responded to.
- Length of call should be 10–20 minutes.
- You may also want to agree the process, i.e. is the call prefaced with a text and, if so, set limits on purpose and length of texts.

Encourage clients wherever possible to take action to ensure their own safety. If they require medical attention, ask the person to seek assessment or treatment from a walk-in centre or ED. You may want to request the client tells you the outcome if you agree they will take some action. If you have serious doubts they will do this and believe they could be at risk, you may need to contact mental health crisis service or, if more urgent, the police. Depending on what you have agreed with your client, it may be appropriate to politely end the call (courteously) if the client:

- has already self-harmed (ensure they don't need medical help or encourage them to seek this if they do);
- is intoxicated or has taken illegal drugs;
- refuses to engage in problem-solving.

References

Ajdacic-Gross V, Weiss MG, Ring M, Hepp U, Bopp M, Gutzwiller F, Rössler W. Methods of suicide: International suicide patterns derived from the WHO mortality database. *Bull World Health Organ.* 2008;86(9):726–732. doi:10.2471/blt.07.043489

Anastasiades MH, Kapoor S, Wootten J, Lamis DA. Perceived stress, depressive symptoms, and suicidal ideation in undergraduate women with varying levels of mindfulness. *Arch Womens Ment Health.* 2017;20(1):129–138. doi:10.1007/s00737-016-0686-5

Astrachan-Fletcher E, Maslar M. *The dialectical behavior therapy skills workbook for bulimia: Using DBT to break the cycle and regain control of your life.* Oakland, CA: New Harbinger Press; 2009.

Bakhiyi CL, Calati R, Guillaume S, Courtet P. Do reasons for living protect against suicidal thoughts and behaviors? A systematic review of the literature. *J Psychiatr Res.* 2016;77:92–108. doi:10.1016/j.jpsychires.2016.02.019

Barnhofer T, Crane C, Brennan K, Duggan D, Crane RS, Eames C, Radford S, Silverton S, Fennell M, Williams JMG. Mindfulness-based cognitive therapy (MBCT) reduces the association between depressive symptoms and suicidal cognitions in patients with a history of suicidal depression. *J Consult Clin Psychol.* 2015;83(6):1013–1020. doi:10.1037/ccp0000027

Baumeister RF. Suicide as escape from self. *Psychol Rev.* 1990;97(1):90–113. doi:10.1037/0033-295x.97.1.90

Bernert RA, Joiner TE. Sleep disturbances and suicide risk: A review of the literature. *Neuropsychiatr Dis Treat.* 2007;3(6):735–743. doi:10.2147/ndt.s1248

Bowers L, Banda T, Nijman H. Suicide inside: A systematic review of inpatient suicides. *J Nerv Ment Dis.* 2010;198(5):315–328. doi:10.1097/NMD.0b013e3181da47e2

Britton PC, Patrick H, Wenzel A, Williams GC. Integrating motivational interviewing and self determination theory with cognitive behavioral therapy to prevent suicide. *Cogn Behav Pract.* 2011;18(1):16–27. doi:10.1016/j.cbpra.2009.06.004

Brown GK, Steer RA, Henriques GR, Beck AT. The internal struggle between the wish to die and the wish to live: A risk factor for suicide. *Am J Psychiatry.* 2005;162(10):1977–1979. doi:10.1176/appi.ajp.162.10.1977

Brüdern J, Stähli A, Gysin-Maillart A, Michel K, Reisch T, Jobes DA, Brodbeck J. Reasons for living and dying in suicide attempters: A two-year prospective study. *BMC Psychiatry.* 2018;18(1):234. doi:10.1186/s12888-018-1814-8

Chapman AL, Gratz KL. *The dialectical behavior therapy skills workbook for anger: Using DBT mindfulness and emotion regulation skills to manage anger.* Oakland, CA: New Harbinger Publications; 2015.

Chesin MS, Benjamin-Phillips CA, Keilp J, Fertuck EA, Brodsky BS, Stanley B. Improvements in executive attention, rumination, cognitive reactivity, and mindfulness among high-suicide risk patients participating in adjunct mindfulness-based cognitive therapy: Preliminary findings. *J Altern Complement Med.* 2016a;22(8):642–649. doi:10.1089/acm.2015.0351

Chesin M, Interian A, Kline A, Benjamin-Phillips C, Latorre M, Stanley B. Reviewing mindfulness-based interventions for suicidal behavior. *Arch Suicide Res.* 2016b;20(4):507–527. doi:10.1080/13811118.2016.1162244

Chesin MS, Sonmez CC, Benjamin-Phillips CA et al. Preliminary Effectiveness of Adjunct Mindfulness-Based Cognitive Therapy to Prevent Suicidal Behavior in Outpatients Who Are at Elevated Suicide Risk. *Mindfulness.* 2015;6:1345–1355. https://doi.org/10.1007/s12671-015-0405-8

Chowdhury AN, Banerjee S, Brahma A, Das S, Sarker P, Biswas MK, Sanyal D, Hazra A. A prospective study of suicidal behaviour in Sundarban Delta, West Bengal, India. *Natl Med J India.* 2010;23(4):201–205.

Cioffi D, Holloway J. Delayed costs of suppressed pain. *J Pers Soc Psychol.* 1993;64(2): 274–282. doi:10.1037//0022-3514.64.2.274

Clark DM, Ball S, Pape D. An experimental investigation of thought suppression. *Behav Res Ther.* 1991;29(3):253–257. doi:10.1016/0005-7967(91)90115-j

Cole-King A, Green G, Gas, L, Hines K, Platt S. Suicide mitigation: A compassionate approach to suicide prevention. *Adv Psychiatr Treat.* 2013:19.276–283. doi:10.1192/apt.bp.110.008763.

Crane C, Barnhofer T, Duggan DS, Eames C, Hepburn S Shah D, Williams JMG. Comfort from suicidal cognition in recurrently depressed patients. *J Affect Disord.* 2014;155(100):241–246. doi:10.1016/j.jad.2013.11.006

Cwik JC, Siegmann P, Willutzki U, Nyhuis P, Wolter M, Forkmann T, Glaesmer H, Teismann T. Brief reasons for living inventory: A psychometric investigation. *BMC Psychiatry.* 2017;17(1):358. doi:10.1186/s12888-017-1521-x

Daigle MS. Suicide prevention through means restriction: Assessing the risk of substitution. A critical review and synthesis. *Accid Anal Prev.* 2005;37(4):625–632. doi:10.1016/j.aap.2005.03.004

Department of Health and Social Care. *Preventing suicide in England: Fourth progress report of the cross-government outcomes strategy to save lives.* London: Department of Health and Social Care; 2019.

Dunkley C, Stanton M. *Teaching clients to use mindfulness skills.* New York: Routledge; 2014.

Felton A, Wright N, Stacey G. Therapeutic risk-taking: A justifiable choice. *B J Psych Advances.* 2017;23:81–88. doi:10.1192/apt.bp.115.015701

Fitzpatrick KK, Witte TK, Schmidt NB. Randomized controlled trial of a brief problem-orientation intervention for suicidal ideation. *Behavior Therapy.* 2005;36(4):323–333.

Forkmann T, Wichers M, Geschwind N, Peeters F, van Os J, Mainz V, Collip D. Effects of mindfulness-based cognitive therapy on self-reported suicidal ideation: Results from a randomised controlled trial in patients with residual depressive symptoms. *Compr Psychiatry.* 2014;55(8):1883–1890. doi:10.1016/j.comppsych.2014.08.043

Fruzzetti AE, Ruork A. Validation principles and practices in dialectical behavior therapy. In: Swales MA, editor. *The Oxford handbook of dialectical behaviour therapy.* Oxford University Press: Oxford; 2018. pp. 325-345.

Galfalvy H, Oquendo MA, Carballo JJ, Sher L, Grunebaum MF, Burke A, Mann JJ. Clinical predictors of suicidal acts after major depression in bipolar disorder: A prospective study. *Bipolar Disord.* 2006;8(5 Pt 2):586–595. doi:10.1111/j.1399-5618.2006.00340.x

Gibbs LM, Dombrovski AY, Morse J, Siegle GJ, Houck PR, Szanto K. When the solution is part of the problem: Problem solving in elderly suicide attempters. *Int J Geriatr Psychiatry.* 2009;24(12):1396–1404. doi:10.1002/gps.2276

Goldstein TR, Bridge JA, Brent DA. Sleep disturbance preceding completed suicide in adolescents. *J Consult Clin Psychol.* 2008;76(1):84–91. doi:10.1037/0022-006X.76.1.84

Harris KM, McLean JP, Sheffield J, Jobes D. The internal suicide debate hypothesis: Exploring the life versus death struggle. *Suicide Life Threat Behav.* 2010;40(2): 181–192. doi:10.1521/suli.2010.40.2.181

Harris R. *ACT made simple: An easy-to-read primer on acceptance and commitment therapy.* Oakland, CA: New Harbinger; 2009; reprinted 2019.

Hawton K. Restricting access to methods of suicide: Rationale and evaluation of this approach to suicide prevention. *Crisis.* 2007;28:4–9.

Hawton K. Studying survivors of nearly lethal suicide attempts: An important strategy in suicide research. *Suicide Life Threat Behav.* 2001;32(1 Suppl):76–84. doi:10.1521/suli.32.1.5.76.24215

Hawton K, Bergen H, Simkin S, Dodd S, Pocock P, Bernal W, Gunnell D, Kapur N. Long term effect of reduced pack sizes of paracetamol on poisoning deaths and liver transplant activity in England and Wales: Interrupted time series analyses. *BMJ.* 2013;346:f403. doi:10.1136/bmj.f403

Hayes SC, Strosahl KD, Wilson KG. *Acceptance and commitment therapy: An experiential approach to behavior change.* New York: Guilford Press; 1999.

Hettema J, Steele J, Miller WR. Motivational interviewing. *Annu Rev Clin Psychol.* 2005;1:91–111. doi:10.1146/annurev.clinpsy.1.102803.143833

Jobes D. *Managing suicidal risk: A collaborative approach.* New York: Guilford Press; 1st ed., 2006, 2nd ed., 2016.

Jobes DA, Mann RE. Reasons for living versus reasons for dying: Examining the internal debate of suicide. *Suicide Life Threat Behav.* 1999;29(2):97–104.

Joiner TE. *Why people die by suicide.* Cambridge, MA: Harvard University Press; 2005.

Kaplow JB, Gipson PY, Horwitz AG, Burch BN, King CA. Emotional suppression mediates the relation between adverse life events and adolescent suicide: Implications for prevention. *Prev Sci.* 2014;15(2):177–185. doi:10.1007/s11121-013-0367-9

Kennedy F, Pearson D. *Integrating CBT and third wave therapies (The CBT Distinctive Features Series).* London: Routledge; 2020.

Kleiman EM, Coppersmith DDL, Millner AJ, Franz PJ, Fox KR, Nock MK. Are suicidal thoughts reinforcing? A preliminary real-time monitoring study on the potential affect regulation function of suicidal thinking. *J Affect Disord.* 2018;232:122–126. doi:10.1016/j.jad.2018.02.033

Kovacs M, Beck AT. The wish to die and the wish to live in attempted suicides. *J Clin Psychol.* 1977;33(2):361–365. doi:10.1002/1097-4679(197704)

Linehan MM. *Cognitive-behavioral treatment of borderline personality disorder.* New York: Guilford Press; 1993.

Linehan MM, Goodstein JL, Nielsen SL, Chiles JA. Reasons for staying alive when you are thinking of killing yourself: The reasons for living inventory. *J Consult Clin Psychol.* 1983;51(2):276–286. doi:10.1037//0022-006x.51.2.276

Linehan MMa. *DBT skills training manual.* 2nd ed. New York: Guilford Press; 2015.

Linehan MMb. DBT *Skills training handouts and worksheets.* 2nd ed. New York: Guilford Press; 2015.

Mann JJ, Apter A, Bertolote J, Beautrais A, Currier D, Haas A, Hegerl U, Lonnqvist J, Malone K, Marusic A, Mehlum L, Patton G, Phillips M, Rutz W, Rihmer Z, Schmidtke A, Shaffer D, Silverman M, Takahashi Y, Varnik A, Wasserman D, Yip P, Hendin H. Suicide prevention strategies: A systematic review. *JAMA.* 2005;294(16): 2064–2074. doi:10.1001/jama.294.16.2064

Maslow AH. A theory of human motivation. *Psychological Review.* 1943;50(4):370–396.

Maslow AH. *Motivation and personality.* 3rd ed. New York: Harper & Row; 1987.

Matthews JD. Cognitive behavioral therapy approach for suicidal thinking and behaviors. In: Woolfolk R, Allen L, editors. *Depression. Mental disorders—Theoretical and empirical perspectives.* IntechOpen; 2013. Rijeka, Croatia pp 23-44

McKay M, Wood JC, Brantley J. *The dialectical behavior therapy skills workbook. Practical DBT exercises for learning mindfulness, interpersonal effectiveness, emotion regulation, and distress tolerance.* 2nd ed. Oakland, CA: New Harbinger Publications; 2019.

Miller M, Lippmann SJ, Azrael D, Hemenway D. Household firearm ownership and rates of suicide across the 50 United States. *J Trauma*. 2007;62(4):1029–1035. doi:10.1097/01.ta.0000198214.24056.40

Miller WR, Leckman AL, Delaney HD, Tinkcom M. Long-term follow-up of behavioral self-control training. *J Stud Alcohol*. 1992;53(3):249–261. doi:10.15288/jsa.1992.53.249

Miller WR, Rollnick S. *Motivational interviewing: Preparing people to change addictive behaviour*. London: Guilford Press; 1991.

Miller WR, Rollnick S. *Motivational interviewing: Preparing people for change*. 2nd ed. New York: Guilford Press; 2002.

Nezu AM, Nezu CM, Perri MG. *Problem-solving therapy for depression: Theory, research, and clinical guidelines*. Chichester: John Wiley & Sons; 1989.

NICE. Depression in adults: recognition and management. Clinical Guideline 90. NICE, 2009 (updated 2016). Available at: www.nice.org.uk/cg90

Nock MK. Self-injury. *Ann Rev Clin Psychol*. 2010;6:339–363. doi:10.1146/annurev.clinpsy.121208.131258

Pollock LR, Williams JM. Problem-solving in suicide attempters. *Psychol Med*. 2004;34(1):163–167. doi:10.1017/s0033291703008092

Potes A, Souza G, Nikolitch K, Penheiro R, Moussa Y, Jarvis GE, Looper K, Rej S. Mindfulness in severe and persistent mental illness: A systematic review. *Int J Psychiatry Clin Pract*. 2018;22(4):253–261. doi:10.1080/13651501.2018.1433857

Reinecke MA. Problem solving: A conceptual approach to suicidality and psychotherapy. In: Ellis TE, editor. *Cognition and suicide: Theory, research, and therapy*. Washington, DC: American Psychological Association; 2006. pp. 237–260.

Rosenberg M. *Nonviolent communication: A language of compassion*. Encinitas, CA: Puddledancer Press; 2001.

Ryle A. Persuasion or education? The role of reformulation in cognitive analytic therapy. *Int J Short-Term Psychother*. 1994;9:111–117.

Sarchiapone M, Mandelli L, Iosue M, Andrisano C, Roy A. Controlling access to suicide means. *Int J Environ Res Public Health*. 2011;8(12):4550–4562. doi:10.3390/ijerph8124550

Southern Health NHS Trust. *Positive Risk-Taking Practical ways of working with risk 'Whose risk is it anyway?'*. Southampton UK March 2012.

Stanley B, Brown G. *Safety plan treatment manual to reduce suicide risk: Veteran Version*. 2008. https://www.mentalhealth.va.gov/docs/va_safety_planning_manual.pdf

Stanley B, Brown GK. Safety planning intervention: A brief intervention to mitigate suicide risk. *Cognitive and Behavioral Practice*. 2012;19(2);256–264.

Stark CR, Riordan V, O'Connor R. A conceptual model of suicide in rural areas. *Rural Remote Health*. 2011;11(2):1622.

Sudak DM, Rajyalakshmi AK. Reducing suicide risk: The role of psychotherapy. *Psychiatric Times*. 2018;35(12):12–13.

Thomas K, Gunnell D. Suicide in England and Wales 1861–2007: A time-trends analysis. *Int J Epidemiol*. 2010;39(6):1464–1475. doi:10.1093/ije/dyq094

Townsend E, Hawton K, Altman DG, et al. The efficacy of problem-solving treatments after deliberate self-harm: Meta-analysis of randomized controlled trials with respect to depression, hopelessness and improvement in problems. *Psychol Med*. 2001;31(6):979–988. doi:10.1017/s0033291701004238

Van Dijk S. *The dialectical behavior therapy skills workbook for bipolar disorder: Using DBT to regain control of your emotions and your life*. Oakland, CA: New Harbinger Publications; 2009.

Veale D. Behavioural activation for depression. *Adv Psychiatr Treat*. 2008;14:29–36. doi:10.1192/apt.bp.107.004051

Vyskocilova J, Prasko J, Ociskova M, Sedlackova Z, Mozny P. Values and values work in cognitive behavioral therapy. *Activitas Nervosa Superior Rediviva*. 2015;57(1–2):40–48.

Wang YC, Hsieh LY, Wang MY, Chou CH, Huang MW, Ko HC. Coping card usage can further reduce suicide reattempt in suicide attempter case management within 3-month intervention. *Suicide Life Threat Behav.* 2016;46(1):106–120. doi:10.1111/sltb.12177

Wegner DM, Gold DB. Fanning old flames: Emotional and cognitive effects of suppressing thoughts of a past relationship. *J Pers Soc Psychol.* 1995;68(5):782–792. doi:10.1037//0022-3514.68.5.782

Wegner DM, Schneider DJ, Carter SR 3rd, White TL. Paradoxical effects of thought suppression. *J Pers Soc Psychol.* 1987;53(1):5–13. doi:10.1037//0022-3514.53.1.5

Wenzel A, Brown GK, Beck AT. *Cognitive therapy for suicidal patients: Scientific and clinical applications.* Washington, DC: APA Books; 2009.

Wenzel A, Jager-Hyman S. Cognitive therapy for suicidal patients: Current status. *Behav Ther.* 2012;35(7):121–130.

World Health Organization. *Preventing suicide: A global imperative.* 2014. Geneva

Zhang CQ, Leeming E, Smith P, Chung PK, Hagger MS, Hayes SC. Acceptance and commitment therapy for health behavior change: A contextually-driven approach. *Front Psychol.* 2018;8:2350. doi:10.3389/fpsyg.2017.02350

Zhang Y, Law CK, Yip PS. Psychological factors associated with the incidence and persistence of suicidal ideation. *J Affect Disord.* 2011;133(3):584–590. doi:10.1016/j.jad.2011.05.003

APPENDICES

- Example safety plan
- Example Standard Operating Procedure
- Mindfulness handout

Example safety plan*

Warning signs that things are difficult for me: Warning signs are changes in thoughts, moods or behaviours that suggest you may be heading towards a suicidal crisis. Knowing your warning signs can help you take action early.

My reasons to live

When you're having thoughts or feelings about suicide, it's easy to get caught up in the pain you're feeling and forget the positives in your life. Thinking about your reasons to live may help you change your focus until the suicidal thoughts pass.

Write down the things in your life, large and small, that are important to you and worth living for.

Make my environment safe

Creating a safer environment is important if you are having thoughts of suicide. This includes making it harder to act on urges or taking yourself out of unsafe situations. You can do some of these things right now, while others are plans for when you start to experience your warning signs.

Things I can do to help me cope/what have I done in the past that will help me now?
Things I can do to keep myself and others safe and reduce my distress

Things I can do by myself

Suicidal thoughts can make it hard to focus on anything else. Activities that distract you from them are an important strategy to keep you safe. List some activities to do by yourself.

Connect with people and places

Make a list of people you could spend time with or social places you could go. Trusted friends and family members can help you stay safe and feel better by providing practical support or just being there to listen. List supportive people you can talk to when feeling suicidal.

If you don't feel you can talk to friends or family about your suicidal feelings, you might find it helpful to speak with a trained counsellor or health practitioner:

Friends or family I can call?

Name	Number	Do they know I might call?	Am I going to give them a copy of this plan?

MY CONTACTS

Name

Phone

Alternative Contact

Professionals or agencies I can contact for support

Professional support is always available when things become too much.

List the names, numbers, and/or locations of mental health professionals, crisis teams and hospitals you can contact. In an emergency, always call 999.

The Samaritans 116 123

Crisis numbers

APPs

To support safety planning you may want to advise service users with an Android phone or an iPhone to download the Stay Alive suicide prevention app which has safety planning pages which include reasons for living, life box, how to stay safe right now, breathing and grounding techniques, etc.

http://prevent-suicide.org.uk/stay_alive_suicide_prevention_mobile_phone_application.html

For self- harm you can advise the DistrACT app: http://www.expertselfcare.com/health-apps/distract/

Hope app. Although the hope box is a helpful tool, it isn't always close at hand. To address these limitations, the Virtual Hope Box, a free smart phone application (Apple, Android), has been developed which allows someone to keep a virtual collection of their reasons for living close by at all times. The Virtual Hope Box has the same types of items (although in digital form) as the traditional hope box (photos, videos, music, messages from loved ones), plus tools for coping, relaxation, distraction and positive thinking.

The current version of the Virtual Hope Box app is organized into the following sections:

- "Remind Me" – Various media, including pictures, videos, music and recordings of personal significance, can be uploaded and kept here.
- "Distract Me" – Contains several games and puzzles for distraction from negative thoughts, such as Sudoku, word search and solitaire.
- "Inspire Me" – Several dozen inspirational quotes are pre-loaded and additional quotes may be added.
- "Relax Me" – Includes several guided exercises (with written scripts and accompanying audio commentary) for meditation, breathing and relaxation.
- "Coping Tools" – Two sections: (1) Coping Cards – Allows for creation of individualized coping cards which include an identified problem area, related negative emotions and symptoms and a specific positive coping skill; (2) Activity Planner – Schedule

specific enjoyable activities on a calendar, add invitees and text or email an invitation to them.

- "Support Contacts" – Create a customized list of key support persons or agencies along with their contact information.

The app also has an accompanying Clinician's Guide, which contains a detailed User's Guide with specific instructions for how to use each section of the app as part of a course of treatment. The Virtual Hope Box mobile app was the recipient of the 2014 Department of Defense Innovation Award. In a small initial study of the effectiveness of the Virtual Hope Box, 18 veterans deemed a high risk for suicidal thoughts were provided with the app in addition to their regular treatment regimen. Feedback about the app from both the veterans and their care providers was consistently positive. The veterans used the app frequently and found it to be helpful. Another app is called Hope Box. These apps are free.

* The service user should keep a copy of this plan, and, where possible, the carer and a copy should be stored on their notes.

Example Standard Operating Procedure

Outline of the intervention and who will deliver it

E.g. qualified staff with additional suicide-intervention training

Scope and definition

Risk assessment and allocation

When patients have been identified at significant risk of suicide and there are available staff trained and supervised a suicide-focused intervention should be considered even if the clinician is able to offer only a few sessions. Experience suggests just a few sessions can be extremely helpful and can identify appropriate actions for the patient or changes to the care plan. Allocation to a trained practitioner (band 6 or above) should be made wherever possible within the MDT or, alternatively, if that is not possible, a request could be made to the suicide intervention team.

A suicide intervention is indicated when the person:

- Has reported significant risk of suicide.
- Is able and willing to engage with the process.

If a patient has some suicidal ideation but not deemed at significant risk, then consider alternative recommendations to address their presenting problems, including other professional and voluntary services; debt advice; support for current or historical abuse, etc. Patients may be unsuitable if they are highly manic or psychotic or despite repeated goodwill attempts refuse to engage. If the person's mental state is so poor or suicidal intent so high that participation is prevented, then consider any action needed to keep the person safe and review commencement when they are able to participate.

If you are unsure of the level of risk (e.g. you suspect the patient is underreporting their risk) or their suicide risk fluctuates, then closely review this. Patients are discharged when their risk has reduced. If a patient declines either to participate or to take positive steps to maintain their safety, then consider referral to the Crisis Team or Mental Health Act (MHA) assessment as indicated.

A suicide-focused intervention

should be considered at any stage in treatment for any patient at risk of suicide. However, it is not a substitute for more intensive evidence-based therapies, notably DBT.

Capacity

This intervention is a voluntary process which cannot be done against a person's will and requires their consent for involvement. Efforts should always be made to try to establish consent and support a person's capacity to engage. This can involve extended time working with the person or working with other staff or family members. If someone does not or cannot engage, we should also document our efforts to engage them.

Working remotely

If need be, this intervention can be delivered by telephone or internet platforms.

If the practitioner delivering the intervention is off sick

For more than a week, the team manager should ensure the patient is reviewed. An interim plan to manage risk should be in place. Ideally the patient should be given a choice whether to wait or be re-allocated.

Delay in allocating a patient identified as appropriate

If a team identifies a patient as at significant risk of suicide and the patient is willing to work with someone to address this but there is delay in allocating them then a practitioner within the MDT should continue to support the patient with the following elements:

- reviewing their suicide risk as a primary focus at each contact;
- agreeing and reviewing a personalised safety plan.

Ending

Ideally the intervention should end when:

- the patient is managing suicidal thoughts and feelings and
- there has been no suicidal behaviour for the past three weeks.

If other interventions are indicated these may be planned within the service or outside, i.e. patients may or may not be discharged from the mental health service at that point, depending on their broader care plan. If risks remain high, then discuss in wider MDT and consider CRHT referral.

If patients have participated and become suicidal again

Suicidality is often episodic in nature. If the person resolved suicidality recently, and is suicidal again, review risk and revisit treatment goals. If someone has had an intervention that finished some months ago and becomes suicidal again, we can begin the initial assessment process and consider top-up or further intervention.

Mindfulness handout

What is mindfulness?

- "Mindfulness" is a word from the English language meaning **awareness.** It is a quality or state of mind that can be cultivated and promotes psychological well-being or robustness.
- Mindfulness is the practice of becoming fully aware of each moment and one's experience of that moment.
- The skills associated with mindfulness are psychological and behavioural versions of meditation practices from Eastern spiritual training. Whilst mindfulness is a part of many religious traditions, you can practise mindfulness regardless of your religious background.
- Mindfulness is now commonly used in the treatment of chronic physical pain and in stress management programmes and is increasingly being used in the treatment of emotional disorders.
- As with any skill, mindfulness needs to be practised regularly in order for you to fully appreciate its benefits.

Mindfulness skills

Practising mindfulness is done using a variety of core skills we can call **"what"** and **"how"** skills.

Mindfulness "what" skills

1. **Observing**

   "Just notice the experience"

   - Observing requires you to pay full attention to an event or emotion.
   - Observing is sensing and noticing without labelling or judging an experience.
   - Rather than leaving a situation or ending an experience if it becomes unpleasant, observing is staying with that feeling. It is allowing yourself to experience whatever is happening and being fully aware of the reality around you.

   Exercise:

   Imagine that your mind is the sky and thoughts, sensations and/or feelings are clouds. Watch your thoughts coming and going. Gently notice each cloud as it drifts by.

2. **Describing**
   - Describing is using words to represent what you have observed and acknowledging when a feeling or thought arises.
   - It is putting an experience into words and describing to yourself what is happening.
   - It is helpful to distinguish between objective reality and subjective evaluations or judgements when describing.

For example

You are in a situation that feels uncomfortable to you and you do not know what to do. Rather than thinking, "I can't do this" and believing this to be true, if you were accurately describing you would acknowledge, "A thought 'I can't do this' has come into my mind".

This act of describing can make the thought less powerful, as we stop treating thoughts as unquestioned truths but rather as things to observe.

Exercise

Sit quietly on your own and hold a pebble (it may help to close your eyes). Notice sensations such as the smoothness or coolness of the pebble. Silently describe what you are sensing. Notice any judgements you may make, e.g. whether it is pleasant or unpleasant.

3. **Participating**
   - Participating is entering into your experiences and letting yourself get involved in the moment rather than avoiding, suppressing or trying to escape from unpleasant feelings.
   - You may have felt able to do this in positive states of mind such as when you are dancing, playing or being creative.

For example

An example of the importance of participating can be seen when people experience bereavement. All of us experience loss at difficult times in our life, particularly loss of a loved one. There is evidence that shows those who allow themselves to grieve (and thus participate in the feeling of grief) recover more quickly from the bereavement than those who avoid or suppress grief.

Exercise

When you find yourself in a situation that is irritating or frustrating, e.g. stuck in a traffic jam or delayed on public transport, you may have urges to fight the situation or wish it would be different. Resisting how things are usually compounds the problem; instead, try to accept and willingly participate in the experience.

Mindfulness "how" skills

These skills have to do with *how* one observes, describes and participates.

4. **Non-judgemental stance**
   - Having a non-judgemental stance involves attending, describing or participating without judgement, focusing on the reality of how things are rather than views, opinions or evaluations.
   - Even when you find yourself judging, do not judge your judging!

For example

Judgement	Vs	Non-judgement
I am stupid		I do not understand this information
I am fat		I am not feeling happy with the way I look
I am pathetic		I am feeling upset by what my friend has said

Exercise

Have you noticed yourself making any judgements like this?
What would be non-judgemental alternative thoughts or viewpoints?

5. **Being one-mindful**
   - Essentially, this is focusing on only one thing at a time. When you are eating, eat. When you are planning, plan. Do each thing with all your attention, and, if actions or thoughts distract you, let go of them and go back to doing what you are doing.

For example

We are often not in one mind; you may be sitting in this session whilst at the same time worrying about something that is happening tomorrow or driving whilst thinking through what has happened at work. To practise one-mindfulness, next time you drive the car, concentrate only on driving. If you find your thoughts drifting, bring them back to focus on driving – but do not berate yourself for this! Being mindful takes practice.

Exercise
Next time you have a drink, make your drink mindfully. Sit or stand for a few minutes and give the experience of drinking 100% of your attention.

6. **Being effective**
   - This involves focusing on what works and what needs to be done in a situation, rather than what you think *should* be done or what is the right/wrong response.
   - Act as skilfully as you can, meeting the needs of the situation you are actually in, not how you wish it to be.
   - Let go of anger and vengeance that hurts you and doesn't work.

For example
You are trying to get a refund in a shop for some faulty goods and the assistant is being unhelpful. You are feeling cross and angry. As you are being effective, you choose not to behave in an angry way because you are focusing on your goals of getting your money back. You choose to be polite and calm as this is more likely to get the assistant on your side. This requires mindfulness of your emotions and awareness of your goals.

Exercise
Think of an occasion recently when you were irritated and frustrated and could have handled the situation more effectively. What choices could you have made that may have helped you achieve a better outcome? Visualise and rehearse yourself doing that.

Basic mindfulness practice

1. Sit comfortably, with your eyes closed and your spine reasonably straight.

2. Direct your attention to your breathing. Focus on the passage of air in and out of your nostrils or watch the movement of your chest as your lungs expand with air then exhale.
3. When thoughts, emotions, physical sensations or external sounds occur, simply notice them, allowing them to come and go without judging or getting involved with them.
4. When you notice that your attention has drifted off and become engaged in thoughts or emotions, simply bring it back to your breathing and continue. If you are very distracted, try saying "In" and "Out" as you breathe. You can also count in 1, out 2; in-1, out 2.

If you decide to practise mindfulness, you will need to do this every day for a minimum of five to ten minutes. It is helpful to begin your practice in a supportive environment, i.e. preferably quiet and alone and with the minimum chance of you being disturbed (mobile phone off!). To establish a regular habit, it is also helpful to do this at a particular time of day. It may be easier to link it to another routine behaviour, e.g. before or after a meal. However, it is important to be alert! We are not practising mindfulness of sleeping!

Adapted from Linehan (2015b)

INDEX

Note: **Bold** page numbers denote the main entries.

For Product Safety Concerns and Information please contact our EU representative GPSR@taylorandfrancis.com Taylor & Francis Verlag GmbH, Kaufingerstraße 24, 80331 München, Germany

Printed and bound by CPI Group (UK) Ltd, Croydon, CR0 4YY

08/06/2025

01896986-0006